by Hugh Cameron & Roger Voight

WILEY

Wiley Publishing, Inc.

MindManager® For Dummies®

Published by
Wiley Publishing, Inc.
111 River Street
Hoboken, NJ 07030-5774

For general information on our other products and services or to obtain technical support, please contact our Customer Care Department within the U.S. at 800-762-2974, outside the U.S. at 317-572-3993, or fax 317-572-4002.

Wiley also publishes its books in a variety of electronic formats. Some content that appears in print may not be available in electronic books.

Library of Congress Control Number: 2004101957

ISBN: 0-7645-5653-3

Manufactured in the United States of America

10 9 8 7 6 5 4 3 2 1

IB/SS/QT/QU/IN

WILEY

About the Authors

Hugh Cameron began his seemingly random career with a degree in clinical electrical engineering from Purdue University. In an attempt to satisfy his entrepreneurial urges, Hugh started Camtech, Inc., a clinical engineering company that soon extended its reach to incorporate a diverse group of projects — from impedance cardiography and patient data acquisition (in the healthcare world) to computerized evidence analysis workstations (for use in the law enforcement arena). After earning his MBA from Indiana Wesleyan University, Hugh took a consulting position with a Fortune 100 company where he organized and set up the company's national and international service groups. He also initiated and received a National Institutes of Health, Small Business Innovation Research grant.

Throughout his career, Hugh has played the role of instructor at every opportunity. He is certified as a Myers-Briggs trainer, Law Enforcement instructor, and Project Management Professional (PMP). Hugh applied his project management expertise and PMP certification to the role of technical editor on the recently published *PMP Certification For Dummies*. Currently, Hugh travels all over the world (well, to 40 countries, at least) to provide instruction in project management, leadership, systems integration, and requirements management to industry-leading companies such as BP, IBM, Hewlett-Packard, Abbott Laboratories, and Novartis.

Roger Voight, PhD, is a certified project manager with over 30 years of experience in software architecture, design, development and software project management, as well as training and business consulting in each of these areas. His experience includes many diverse industries such as travel, public accounting, wholesale and retail merchandising, medical, legal, insurance, education, and government. He has provided project management training and consulting on a world-wide basis to many of the Fortune 100 corporations such as IBM, AT&T, Nortel, Motorola, Eli Lilly, and Hewlett-Packard. With his experience as both an executive level manager as well as a business consultant, he understands very well the time pressures on managers and the desperate need for effective and pragmatic solutions to business problems.

He is a certified trainer for Microsoft Project and for Mindjet and has extensive experience customizing and integrating the Microsoft Office Suite for customer applications using VBA. He has developed numerous software-based tools which together facilitate the gathering of detailed and accurate user requirements and the development of reliable time and cost estimates in project management. Over the last 15 years he has developed many applications, some of which won national awards, based on the Pick operating system family of application development tools.

He has been a speaker at numerous national and regional meetings on effective tools for management of software projects and for software development. He was a contributing writer for more than a year to a national magazine devoted to the application development tool called Advanced Revelation and contributed to the recently published book, *PMP Certification For Dummies*.

Authors' Acknowledgments

Hugh Cameron: I want to thank our Acquisitions Editor Steve Hayes, Project Editor Andrea Boucher, and the other special person at Wiley Publishing for their help in making this book a reality.

Thanks also go out to Hobie, Don, and the others at Mindjet. Their continued cooperation as MindManager Pro came to life is greatly appreciated.

Nick, the technical editor, is much more than his title infers. His expertise with MindManager is fantastic. He helped us over hurdles and kept us honest.

My co-author, Roger Voight, made this book possible. His focus on completion and detail kept the book going. Thank you, Roger, for being a true friend.

Roger Voight: Many people have made it possible for me to contribute to this book. They certainly include all of those who have participated in my training classes over the years and have helped me to understand just how challenging it can be to learn to use a rich software package. Our project editor, Andrea Boucher, was unbelievably patient and helpful in getting me started in the right way and was always there with hints and help whenever asked. Dagmar Herzog provided early inspiration with her passion for MindManager and her writing about the software that was genuinely fun to read. My sisters read parts of some of the chapters, laughed at the right places, and encouraged me to press on. Nick Duffill of MindManuals contributed advice, help, and encouragement, as well as much of the material for Appendix C, with a generosity that was awe-inspiring.

None of this could have happened without my very good friend and co-author, Hugh Cameron, who first introduced me to MindManager and then to the possibilities of this book project. It has been a blast, good buddy, and I'm looking forward to whatever our next project might be.

Lastly, but really first and foremost, I must acknowledge my dear wife, Susan, who helped me find the courage to undertake this project, read many of the first drafts, and guided me in so many ways to finding my writer's voice. Sweetie, you have been my help — and soulmate for all of these years, and I love you!

Publisher's Acknowledgments

We're proud of this book; please send us your comments through our online registration form located at www.dummies.com/register.

Some of the people who helped bring this book to market include the following:

Acquisitions, Editorial, and Media Development

Project Editor: Andrea C. Boucher

Acquisitions Editor: Steve Hayes

Technical Editor: Nick Duffill

Editorial Manager: Carol Sheehan

Media Development Manager: Laura VanWinkle

Media Development Supervisor: Richard Graves

Editorial Assistant: Amanda Foxworth

Cartoons: Rich Tennant (www.the5thwave.com)

Production

Project Coordinator: Courtney MacIntyre

Layout and Graphics: Joyce Haughey, LeAndra Hosier, Michael Kruzil, Jacque Schneider, Julie Trippetti

Proofreaders: Carl William Pierce

Indexer: TECHBOOKS Production Services

Special Help
Andrea Dahl

Publishing and Editorial for Technology Dummies

　　Richard Swadley, Vice President and Executive Group Publisher

　　Andy Cummings, Vice President and Publisher

　　Mary C. Corder, Editorial Director

Publishing for Consumer Dummies

　　Diane Graves Steele, Vice President and Publisher

　　Joyce Pepple, Acquisitions Director

Composition Services

　　Gerry Fahey, Vice President of Production Services

　　Debbie Stailey, Director of Composition Services

Contents at a Glance

Table of Contents

Introduction

· ·

Welcome to *MindManager For Dummies*, your portal to levels of productivity and creativity that you have only dreamt about! You've heard of thinking outside of the box? MindManager doesn't even know where the box is. Open this book to any page and you will find ideas and examples that will open your mind and stimulate you to see new solutions in your world. This is a down-to-earth, practical book based on real ways to use the program. We remain astounded at the richness of MindManager: even as we were writing the last sentences in this book we continued to discover new ideas, new connections, and new possibilities.

We discovered MindManager by word of mouth. Most of the 300,000 plus users did, too. You can't walk into the local computer store and pick up a box with MindManager marketing hype. Go to www.minjet.com where a free download of MindManager Pro awaits you. The download is a fully functioning program that gives you a full three weeks to explore every facet of the software. You are not going to be bombarded with Mindjet extras and advertising. You'll get an e-mail thanking you for downloading the program and one inviting you to purchase and register the program. The program and this book get you going at warp speed.

You are going to find that the number of uses for MindManager grows each day you use the program. Imagine sitting in a large room. Innumerable things you have to solve, organize, or communicate surround you. There are doors on the opposite side of the room marked Web Interface, Document Publishing, Professional Presentations, and Task Tools, but they are all locked. A computer screen rises in front of you. MindManager is running. External information links are active. You look at each problem and solve it. One of the previously locked doors opens, easily, effortlessly. You take the tasks and organize them. Another door springs open. You structure and data mine seemingly unrelated bits of information. Now all the doors are open. You link stakeholder needs to activities. The mountain of tasks disappears, handled brilliantly. The sun shines, the birds sing, and work has become joyful and fulfilling.

MindManager is fun to use. You are going to see that simplicity and fun can bring big benefits. Enjoy yourself, and use the program in ways unimagined. Share your discovery with others.

About This Book

Take a look at the table of contents. The folks at Wiley Publishing look at the table of contents like a businessperson looks at a business plan. You should be able to see the flow of the book. Find a few chapters that stimulate your interest and dive in. Don't expect to read this book straight through. We didn't write it with that in mind. Pick the book up and put it down as the need arises.

Strategically placed throughout the book in the margin are cool little icons. Browse through and see what jewels you can find. Power users of MindManager may want to start your discovery by specifically seeking out the icons.

The stories used in this book are designed to stimulate your thinking. We use MindManager for a multitude of activities in our real world. Benefit from our experiences and make the solutions yours.

We hope you appreciate our humor. Good things happen when you laugh and smile.

We created this book using MindManager, in case you were wondering.

How to Use This Book

Get started with the first three chapters. You are going to find the book's overview and a few key definitions and basics. MindManager Pro Version 5.0 is significantly different than past versions of MindManager. You may want to start at the beginning even if you are a power user.

We don't assume you have MindManager running in front of you. The examples should be clear enough without the program. Mark interesting places in the book and try the examples when you are in front of your computer.

You can also approach this book from your current use of Windows software. Microsoft PowerPoint, Outlook, Word, and Project each have separate chapters. Check out these chapters if you use these products. You'll see how MindManager works together with some of your favorite programs.

Dig in and get both halves of your brain working.

Who Are You?

We made some assumptions about you as we wrote this book. You may be anywhere in the world. MindManager is an international program. You're adept at using your computer and aren't afraid to press the buttons. You know your way around some of the Microsoft programs like Outlook, PowerPoint, Project, and Word. You may not have ever heard of MindManager, but the name is pretty cool, and who doesn't want to get a little better at mind-managing? You could be a power user. There are a bunch of folks currently using MindManager. You might be a project manager, a banker, a lawyer, a pilot, an administrator, an artist, a police officer, an engineer, a student, or a software developer. We know people using MindManager in these professions and many more.

We wrote the book as though we were talking to you. We are excited to be working with you and we sincerely appreciate you taking the time to work with us.

How This Book Is Organized

We used MindManager extensively as we wrote this book. We'll use some examples of MindManager's simple brilliance to explain how this book is organized. There are five parts to the book.

Part 1

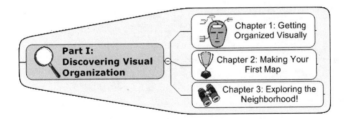

In the first part you learn about visual organization and the basics of MindManager. You set up the screen interface the way you want and get comfortable moving around in the program.

Part II

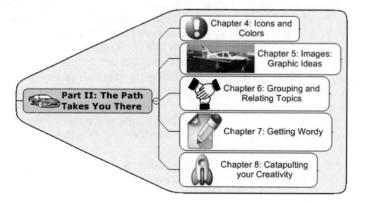

In the second part you explore how to add depth to your MindManager map. Icons, images, and borders are just a few of the additions. The foundation is now set.

Part III

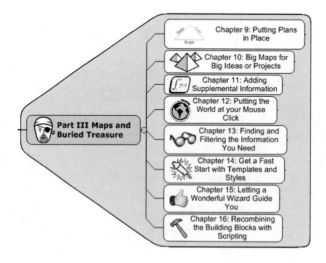

Part III explores the depth of the MindManager program. The examples show you new possibilities. You are putting the building blocks of the program together and creating solutions.

Part IV

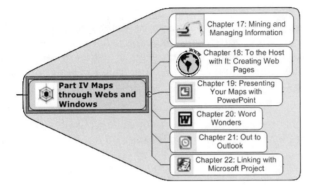

Part IV links MindManager to the outside world. The Microsoft suite of Word, Outlook, PowerPoint, and Project takes center stage. Web pages structured in powerful templates make a MindManager map quite impressive on the Internet. You'll learn ways to make your map communicate to others.

Part V

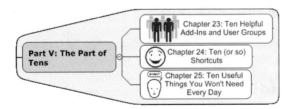

Part V, titled The Part of Tens, is a collection of informative chapters and reference guides. Mostly they are lists of extra stuff that didn't seem to fit anywhere else in the book.

Icons Used in This Book

 The information provided is used by a fraction of the people reading the book. A description like the *techno framer jammer is linked to the sky sourced plasti-magnet* might be fair game. Skip these if you don't want your brain to explode. Should you decide to read them, you get in-depth information found at the substructure of program operation.

 Don't go there. This is not a wet paint sign. Something is lurking in the corner that is going to bite you if you do this. Save the program, batten the hatches, mayday, mayday, mayday! Information preceded by this symbol describes some action that, if performed, causes the program to crash or some other computer disaster.

 A tip is a tidbit of knowledge that can usually make your life easier. Grab the tips out of the book as you go. We promise they do not pop up as you turn the page.

Be Careful is a bit less than a warning but you should still take notice. The information presented gives you a heads up about a nasty surprise if you aren't careful.

 You may need the information now or later, but you *are* going to need it. You could cut it out and use it as a bookmark, but something equally important on the other side of the page would go with it. Go back to this icon if something just doesn't seem to work right.

 You see this icon when we reference another chapter or another book entirely that you might want to check out — one that provides additional details on the topic at hand.

Feedback, Please

The MindManager community is very strong and active. We would love to hear from you. Please e-mail us at MMFD@Projecttools.com.

Part I
Discovering Visual Organization

The 5th Wave   By Rich Tennant

"Okay — let's try brainstorming again, only this time with a little less storm."

In this part . . .

You just had an idea! It was a solution to your latest dilemma at work. Quickly now, get to your keyboard at once. You must share your ideas with MindManager. MindManager guides you in a new way to organize and visually *experience* your ideas. Dive into the chapters in this part to discover the basics of exploring MindManager. The building blocks, such as creating a basic MindManager map, are right here at your fingertips.

One more thing while you're here — don't visit the local computer store to get MindManager Pro. Over 300,000 folks have found www.Mindjet.com. Go directly to this Web site to download a free, fully functioning copy of MindManager Pro. You have 21 days to investigate this truly remarkable program!

Chapter 1

Getting Organized — Visually

In This Chapter

▶ Beginning to get organized

▶ Seeing the depths of MindManager

▶ Dealing with complexity

▶ Linking to the outside

▶ Sharing with other programs

▶ Managing perceptions

*G*etting organized. Who has time? Project managers and just about every-body in business are under constant pressure to get their jobs done with fewer resources, less time, and less money. Organizations are flatter. The boss is not as close to the work being performed. Cross-functional teams are all the rage. Presentations and communication are more important up, down, and across the organization. Information haystacks are getting bigger and the needle is becoming more elusive. Efficiency is needed to sort through the information. You need a solution.

Imagine that your team completes a brainstorming session. You now have a map that shows how their ideas link together and identifies the next action steps. The elements of your map link to your calendar and to your project planning tool. Peer review and external information are added. Now the map is a dynamic picture. You look at the picture and see activity status with just one glance. The map is translated and sent to stakeholders. Stakeholders get a personal presentation with information specific to their needs. The dream continues with the thought that you need only one software program to make all this happen. You wake up and find that such a program does exist — MindManager X5 Pro. Throughout the book, I refer to this version of the pro-gram simply as MindManager.

MindManager is a unique software product. The MindManager map is the visual interface. The structure of the map is designed to integrate icons, graphics, and other visual elements with text material. The layout of the map presents your information visually. A MindManager map would be a wonder-ful tool, even if it stopped there — but it doesn't.

The map you can create is dynamic. Links can be formed between news services, search engines, and third party vendors to feed information into a MindManager map. Does it stop there? No! The MindManager map is shared and reviewed between colleagues. Comments are captured and added to the informational content of the map.

MindManager integrates with other programs such as Microsoft Outlook and Microsoft Project. The MindManager map takes presentation, exporting, and printing of the map to a new industry standard. Use an internal presentation mode to walk through the entire map in an interactive format. Microsoft PowerPoint presentations are a button click away. Complete Web sites composed of MindManager Web pages are as easy as choosing a design and saying go.

Visit www.Mindjet.com to get a fully functional, 21-day, free trial version of MindManager X5 Pro.

MindManager: An Organized Beginning

MindManager starts with simplicity. The user interface is understandable and uses a style similar to Windows. Plan on expending only a minimal amount of effort getting your first map started. The simplicity of construction is deceptive. You may have more difficulty getting your arms around the full power and uses of the program. Microsoft Excel is similar in this way. You can create a spreadsheet quite easily and be proud of your work. Humility arrives when someone shows you just how far you can actually take the Excel program.

Visual organization

MindManager is described as a *visual organization tool*. Visual organization describes the way information is displayed. Granted, an outline is visual and may be organized, but it is not the same. Try this experiment: Walk down a corridor of cubicles, taking just a second to look at each cube. Which ones strike you as being organized? You may see hobbies, school achievements, and family photos. The person's sense of humor may be obviously displayed. You gather information about a person by taking a mental snapshot of the cubicle habitat. Imagine a written cubicle description that includes an inventory of everything found and the location of each item. The mental snapshot would convey information the fastest. Our brain/eye coordination is incredibly quick when it comes to processing information. The inventory more fully describes the details of each item. Which one is best — fast conveyance of information, or a detailed description of the information? Choose the best answer — all of the above.

MindManager combines the speed of visual delivery with informative textual details. Figure 1-1 shows one of the tutorial MindManager maps found in the program.

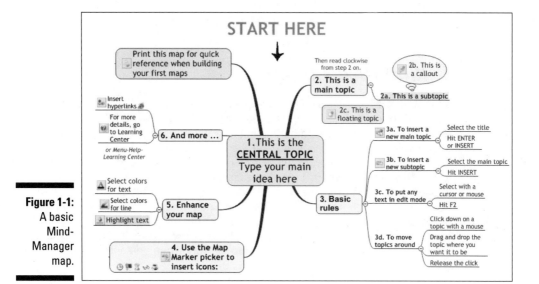

Figure 1-1:
A basic
Mind-
Manager
map.

You can use MindManager's visual organization in many different ways. I want to begin by describing an excellent starting point for your road to discovery.

Recording your brainstorms

Ideas come from many places, and one of the most common places is the brainstorming session. You assemble your team and each team member begins to contribute ideas. You use the Brainstorm mode in MindManager to capture all the ideas, and a MindManager map is then created. The generated ideas become MindManager topics. Refer to Figure 1-1. The topics are grouped together and new topics are added as headings. A productive brainstorming session can generate hundreds of ideas and, therefore, topics. MindManager makes it easy for the team to organize, reorganize, and re-reorganize the topics. Text and graphic notes can be added to each topic for further clarification.

Analyzing problems

The big picture is easy to see with a MindManager map. The details are not locked in a linear list or outline. All the elements of a problem are visible in the map, and external sources of information, such as a Google search, can be included in the map contents as well. The result is an excellent high-level view of a problem. Links between the problem issues can be identified using symbols, icons, graphics, and colors. You continue to add topics as you investigate, work through, and solve the problem. The finished map delivers a complete perspective of the problem and solution.

Taking meeting notes

MindManager includes several suggested templates, which can easily be modified to meet your needs. The template shown in Figure 1-2 is a meeting template. A MindManager meeting map is a planning, note taking, and action follow-up tool. You set the agenda in the map and then send it to team members for review. Review comments are added to the map, and notes are taken in MindManager. Links to Outlook are created after the meeting to schedule individual tasks. A presentation of key meeting items is made and sent to the boss. MindManager makes all of this easy. The template is filled out in minutes, using the template wizard. Did I mention that MindManager has more wizards than *Lord of the Rings*? You can even make your own wizards. The wizards hide among the templates, and they appear only when you activate one.

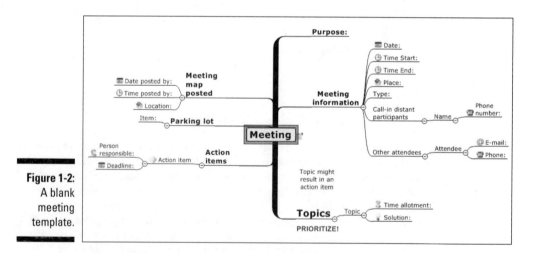

Figure 1-2:
A blank
meeting
template.

Setting up project tasks

A great many MindManager users are project managers. MindManager is ideal for such a tormenting activity. Work breakdown structures are a standard topic layout found in MindManager. Work breakdown structure tasks are a project manager's building blocks. You enter task information into a topic using the *task info* menu. The previous examples identified team brainstorming and meetings. Either activity can result in work to be assigned and accomplished. The MindManager map shows percent complete and priority as an icon attached to the topic. The task information can be sent to Microsoft Project and/or Outlook. However, it's not necessary to have either of these programs to make MindManager a useful project management tool.

Chain Linking

MindManager lets you visually connect your ideas. MindManager can link a map to a map, a map to the Web, a map to other programs, or a map to documents. The links are discussed in the following sections.

Linking map to map

Maps can get quite large if you pack all of your information into just one map. Links are used between maps like transporter beams are used on *Star Trek*. Click on the link symbol and you are whisked to a different map. The map-to-map links are useful in breaking down a topic into more detail. If you have a high level of detail, you may need another map. Individual topics can each contain a link. For example, I am currently working on a large device development project and I have 27 map-to-map links.

Linking to the URL world

A MindManager topic may need clarification or additional information, or it may be a gateway to somewhere else. URLs are the vehicle, and any topic in a MindManager map can connect to the Internet. The amount of information contained in a MindManager map grows exponentially with the addition of Internet URLs.

Linking to other programs

A MindManager topic can initiate the start of another software program. The program can run in the foreground and look like a part of the map. When I test different parts of a software product, I use this feature and have the various modules structured as topics. Each topic activates a specific module, which ensures that I am accessing all the modules as I perform the testing.

Linking to documents

The key to a good map is having the right information available. Sometimes, text notes associated with a topic are the way to go; other times, a link to a specific document works better. Almost any format works, as long as you have the necessary programs on your computer.

You have been developing your map up to this point. The basics of topics, icons, graphics, links, and so on have been added, but the potential for your map is far from realized. Now you can bring in topics from the outside.

Information Inclusion

MindManager is an information vacuum. New Web technology has expanded the number of ways you can get information. MindManager handles both the acquisition of the information and the organization of the information. Information quickly gets added to a MindManager map using news feeds and search tools.

News feeds

How much information is easily available? A bunch. The question then becomes how to organize all the information sources that are out there. Once again, MindManager has a solution. I have a map that includes news feeds from around the world from different news and information organizations. I organize them by purpose, so I have all my healthcare topics in one part of the map, and I have my technology, world, and aviation news in another part of the map. I continually refresh the news feeds and get headlines from each type of source. Sample news feed services are provided in MindManager. Figure 1-3 shows sample news feeds included in MindManager.

Searching

A MindManager map may contain a section on a competitor. A search feed is added to search the Internet for competitive product information. The topic immediately preceding the location of the search feed gives the search criteria. You refresh the search feed to obtain the latest information. A Google feed is provided with MindManager, though you have to sign up with the Google service to make the feed work properly. However, the price is definitely right — free. Figure 1-4 shows an example of how a search criteria is set up. The Google search would look for "B-2 Bomber Oxygen Generation O-system." The search result may be a knock on the door from the FBI wanting to know why you are looking for classified information.

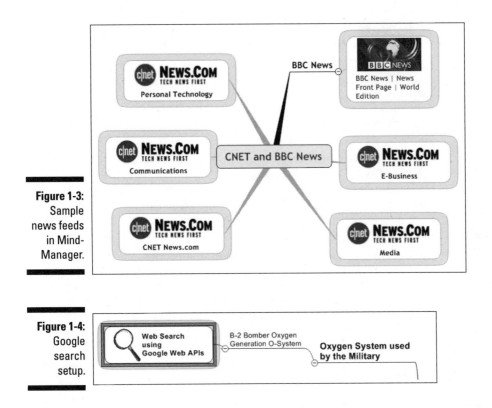

Figure 1-3:
Sample
news feeds
in Mind-
Manager.

Figure 1-4:
Google
search
setup.

Building on the Strengths of Other Programs

MindManager does not pretend to be the ultimate program. It knows its own limitations and lives by the old credo "if you can't beat 'em, join 'em." For tricky tasks that are beyond its own capabilities, MindManager interfaces with Outlook and Microsoft Project.

Microsoft Outlook

The MindManager to Outlook link is very strong. Appointments, contacts, notes, and task information are exported, imported, and synchronized between programs. The number of uses for this tool are staggering. Here are just a few of them:

✔ **Keep track of travel information.** Link Outlook calendar dates and tasks to MindManger topics that identify the reason for travel.

✔ **Create a map with all your monthly bills.** Attach the credit card company URLs to the topic. Use Outlook's task list as a reminder of when to pay each bill. After a bill is paid, Outlook updates MindManager and generates the next month's due date for MindManager — all of which happens automatically. One glance at the MindManager map, and you know the status of all your bills.

✔ **Tie a map to an Outlook calendar.** Your team has tasks to perform and deadlines have been established. You make a map directly from your team meeting map to identify each person and the expected completion dates. The team uses Outlook, so the tasks are in each person's calendar. Each day, you refresh your map to see whether tasks are being accomplished as expected.

✔ **Connect to a contact list.** You have developed a MindManager map as an emergency contact list. The map has different groupings depending on the type of emergency. A master list of all personnel is kept up to date in an Outlook contact list that you link to, so you simply refresh the MindManager map and the necessary contact information is there.

Microsoft Project or other MPX project tools

MindManager is a great tool for determining what tasks need to be completed in order to have a successful project, but it has no tools for actually developing a schedule and determining the start and finish dates for those tasks based on task dependencies, external constraint dates and resource availability. You must use project management scheduling software for this purpose.

With MindManager, you can export your map directly to Microsoft Project, the most widely used scheduling and project management software on the market today. You can also create a Microsoft Project Exchange (MPX) file from your MindManager map. This file can be read by all the other popular scheduling software packages, so you can use whichever package is standard at your company or is simply your personal preference.

You can also import project files (either directly from Microsoft Project or via an MPX file from other applications) back into MindManager along with schedule dates and resource information in order to create status reports or prepare for meetings. MindManager also includes itself in the Send To . . . options on the Project File menu so that you can create a map from a subset of project tasks directly from Project itself. This feature is particularly useful if you want to report on only currently active tasks.

Presenting MindManager Map Information to Others

The MindManager program presents map information in three ways. The first is an internal presentation mode. The second exports the map information in outline form to a Microsoft Word document. The third uses map information to create a Microsoft PowerPoint presentation.

MindManager presentation mode

You can project the MindManager map on a screen with the MindManager tool screen present. You must do all the opening, closing, and moving around on the map, which is rather cumbersome. MindManager presentation mode makes it easy. The map is interactive. When you click on different topics in the map, MindManager moves to those topics and opens all the subtopics. The previous topic closes automatically. Links are active and operational. You can enter topics, icons, and other map elements while in this mode, which works well when you are working with your team.

Export to Microsoft Word

You may want to change the format of MindManger from the visual organization style to a linear outline. When MindManager exports map information to Microsoft Word, an outline is created based upon the level of the topic. You can specify export characteristics that structure the export using Microsoft heading characteristics. The outline contains topic information and any associated text. A MindManager map can also import from Word to make a visual organization representation from a linear outline.

PowerPoint presentations

I like to make PowerPoint presentations from MindManager maps. You can specify PowerPoint styles and other output preferences. How easy is it to make a presentation? Very easy. Click the PowerPoint icon, and that's it! Your MindManager map is transformed into a professional-looking presentation. The export-to-PowerPoint feature is an excellent choice any time you want to present all or a portion of your map information to someone else.

Chapter 2

Making Your First Map

A few years ago, I got very excited about martial arts and decided to enroll in an introductory course. I had visions of myself quickly being able to toss people around, block punches with blinding speed, and say wise and fundamental truths like that guy in the "Kung Fu" television series. Reality actually turned out to be rather depressing. I spent many lessons just learning what to look for when I face an opponent, where to grab my practice partner, and how to fall down and get back up again. It was only later, after noticing that I was the one that was doing most of the flying through the air, that I understood just how important those early lessons really were.

In this chapter, I help you recognize what to look for when you work with MindManager: how you grab the right tool for the task at hand; how to add, change, and delete paths; and how to "get back up again" if you make a mistake or run into trouble.

I describe skills in this chapter that are necessary in order to explore almost every other technique described in this book. Like my martial arts skills (or whatever word would better describe my pathetic efforts), you cannot learn these skills just by reading about them. Fire up your computer and try out these things yourself!

Switching on MindManager

The first time you start MindManager, you see the Welcome to MindManager dialog box, shown in Figure 2-1. Well, actually, you will see this welcome screen *every* time you start MindManager until you click the check box *Don't show this screen again*.

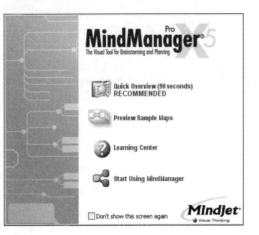

Figure 2-1:
Mind-
Manager
greets you
with this
screen
when you
start the
application.

This welcome screen gives you choices for previewing bits of MindManager's functionality, sample maps, and ways to find help. You can also make all these choices from the MindManager menus, but this dialog box provides a good path to get you started on the right foot.

Here is a brief description of your choices in the Welcome to MindManager dialog box:

- **Quick Overview:** This multimedia presentation shows many key features of MindManager, and it really does take only 90 seconds to view. Watching the Quick Overview show gives you a sense of the rich functionality of MindManager.

- **Preview Sample Maps:** This is also a multimedia presentation. It displays several different styles of maps and things that maps can be used for. If you want to actually work with any of these maps, you can open them in MindManager by clicking the Library tab and selecting the map from the Map Gallery section.

- **Learning Center:** Selecting this option launches MindManager and displays a help map that summarizes some important keystrokes and capabilities of the product. On the right side of the screen, you see a list of a wide range of help topics. In the section "Creating your first map," later in this chapter, I show you how to create a map from a template via the Learning Center.

If you want to explore some of the Learning Center topics right away, just click the topic of interest. You hide the Learning Center by clicking the Learning tab. Click the Learning tab again to restore the Learning Center display.

- **Start Using MindManager:** This option loads a blank document and then waits for your input. Because starting with a blank map may be a bit intimidating, I recommend starting with a skeleton map that can help with understanding map creation basics.

Scoping Out the Workspace

My father loved creating things and putting things together, and one of his many gifts to me was this same passion. When he was teaching me these skills as a young boy, however, I was always frustrated at his insistence that I must first organize and count all the parts to whatever I was assembling, as well as lay out all the tools that I would need. "A good craftsman always knows where his tools are and the materials he has to work with," he would say repeatedly. Being a bit stubborn, it took me many years of having to do work over before I understood that his guidance actually saved me time.

In this section, I tell you about the tool compartments in the MindManager toolbox: the panes, the menus, and the toolbars. In the remaining sections of this chapter, I explore some of the tools themselves.

Finding your home on the pane

Most of the work you do in MindManager (creating, editing, and outputting maps) takes place in three panes:

- ✔ **The Map pane:** This is the left side of your workspace (called a *frame*) where MindManager draws your maps. You use this pane to do much of your work as you create and refine your maps.

- ✔ **The Topic Notes pane:** This is the middle frame in your workspace where you can associate topic notes with any topic in your map and can include formatting, tables, and graphics.

    If you have started your map but don't see the Topic Notes pane, the pane's view status may be set to invisible. In this case, press F11 or click on the Topic Notes Toggle button on the Insert Toolbar to make the Topic Notes pane visible again.

- ✔ **The Task pane:** This is the right frame in your workspace where MindManager gives you single-click access to many additional tools as well as help topics. Select the Task pane page you want to display by clicking its tab at the far right-hand side of the workspace. If the Task pane is not visible, clicking one of the Task pane tabs will make it appear.

You can change the relative size of these panes by pointing your cursor to the edge of the pane (your cursor will change, as shown in Figure 2-2) and dragging the boundary to the left or the right. Both the Topic Notes pane and the Task pane have small X's at their upper right-hand corners. Click the X to close that pane entirely.

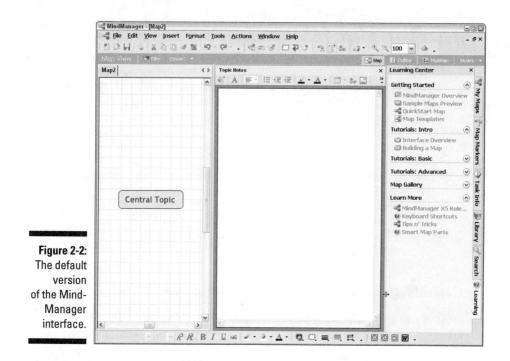

Figure 2-2:
The default
version
of the Mind-
Manager
interface.

It is also possible to completely hide the Topic Notes pane or the Task pane by dragging their left boundaries completely to the right-hand side of the workspace. If you have done this, the F11 key (for Topic Notes pane) or clicking a Task pane tab (for the Task pane) will not appear to have any effect at all. If MindManager "thinks" it is displaying these panes, however, the mouse cursor will change when you point to the right-hand edge of your workspace (as shown in Figure 2-2), and you can drag the edge of the pane to the left to make it visible again.

You can also restore them by selecting Tools⇨Options⇨Save and then clicking the Reset button. This also resets any menu or toolbar customizations that you may have made.

Gliding through the menus

The Menu Bar is the top menu line, and it functions like any normal Windows menu. You already know many of the menu selection items from other applications. You can also access many of the menu selection items through buttons on the various toolbars. I discuss the details of the various menu functions throughout this book.

These are the additional function groups that you will find on the main menu selections that are unique to MindManager:

- ✔ **File:** The Pack and Go wizard compresses your map and any other documents that are hyperlinked on your map into a zip folder, ready for e-mailing. See Chapter 17 for details.

- ✔ **View:** Determines the map display options (outline or multimap) and function modes (brainstorming, reviewing, and presentation). See Chapter 3 for details.

- ✔ **Format:** Specifies details for exporting a map to PowerPoint or to an MPX file. See Chapter 22 for details.

- ✔ **Tools:** Provides access to the template and style organizer (Chapter 14), wizards (Chapter 15), and macro scripts (Chapter 16).

- ✔ **Actions:** Exports tasks to Outlook and synchronizes topic display and exported Outlook tasks. See Chapter 21 for details.

MindManager displays the keyboard shortcuts associated with many menu items right next to the description of the function.

MindManager also has numerous *context menus* that are displayed when you right-click something in your workspace (a topic, something in your Notes pane or Task pane, or even the background of your map). They are called context menus because they display just those menu commands (from the menu bar) that are most likely to be used on the thing you just clicked. Because you must almost always select an item (by clicking it) before you can execute any menu item anyway, right-clicking the item and then selecting the desired command from the context menu will normally save you a great deal of time building your map. This is the approach recommended throughout this book.

Toolin' around the toolbars

The toolbars allow you to accomplish with one mouse click what might require two, three, or even four mouse clicks if you use only the Menu Bar. Some people love toolbars and others hardly ever use them. I tell you how you can customize each toolbar, reposition it, or even hide it in Chapter 3.

History was one of my least favorite subjects in school because my teachers always insisted that I memorize long lists of dates and names but never seemed to talk much about why they were important. I was so fortunate to have a teacher in my senior year of high school who was passionate about history and talked about the things that he found to be exciting. You will be happy to know that I haven't forgotten that early pain, though, so I will *not* now describe every button on every toolbar! There are a few, however, that I'm really excited about:

✔ **The Standard toolbar:** This toolbar is initially installed just below the menu bar at the top left-hand side of the workspace (see Figure 2-3).

• **Format Painter:** You've spent a lot of time getting the font, size, color, and background of a topic to look just the way you want, and you now want to change another topic to look exactly the same way. With your perfectly formatted topic selected, click this button (your cursor changes to a paint brush), and then click the topic you want to change. It's as easy as that!

If you want to apply the formatting to several topics, hold down the Control key as you click each one. Release the Control key before you click the last topic so MindManager will turn off the Format Painter.

• **Clear Formats:** This is the button for you when you have gotten too enthusiastic with the Format Painter! Click the topic you didn't mean to paint, and then click this button. Everything will be reset to the defaults. This also works if you just don't like your formatting experiment and want to reset everything.

Figure 2-3:
The
Standard
toolbar.

✔ **The Insert toolbar:** This toolbar is initially installed on the same line as the Standard toolbar and to the right of it (see Figure 2-4).

• **Level of Detail:** Select a topic on your map, and then click this button. All subtopics belonging to this topic will be hidden and the little minus sign at the end of the topic line (called the *control strip*) changes to a plus sign. Click the button again and all levels of subtopics are again displayed. You can also click the tiny down arrow to the right of the button and select how many levels of subtopics you want displayed. This is very useful when you want to hide most of the detail on your map so that you can focus just on one or two topics.

• **Zoom:** Click the magnifying glass with a plus sign to enlarge your map slightly (12.5 percent per click), or click the magnifying glass with a minus sign to shrink your map. You can also click the down arrow on the combo box and directly select the percentage of enlargement or compression that you want.

- **Map Overview:** Click this button to open a small window in the upper right-hand corner of your workspace that will display your entire map with a smaller rectangle showing the portion of your map that is currently visible in the Map pane. You can drag this small rectangle around to automatically shift the part of your map that is currently displayed. See Chapter 10 for more details.

Figure 2-4:
The Insert
toolbar.

✔ **The Format toolbar:** This toolbar is initially installed at the bottom left-hand corner of your workspace (see Figure 2-5).

TIP

If you find this to be a strange place for a toolbar, you can reposition it wherever you like. See Chapter 3 for details on how to do this. Note also that, unlike the button order used on the Office products, the Line Color button is to the left of the Background Color button. I tell you in Chapter 3 how you can use the Customize command to reorder these buttons if you like.

- **Shape:** Click this button to display a submenu of all the shapes (rectangle, oval, hexagon, and so on) that you may want to use in your map for the object you have selected. If shapes can't be used for the selected object, all the items in the submenu will be grayed out.

TIP

Every button on the Format toolbar that has a small black triangle on it has an associated submenu. If you click one button on the toolbar, you can point your cursor to any other button and its associated submenu will be automatically displayed.

- **Boundary:** Click this button and select the type of boundary you want to draw around the topic you have selected. The boundary will also enclose all associated subtopics that are displayed. See Chapter 6 for details and ideas about using boundaries.

Figure 2-5:
The Format
toolbar.

| Trebuchet MS | 12 |

The Topic Notes pane also has its own toolbars. I talk about these in Chapter 7.

Objects and things

MindManager can display many different things on a map. In this sense, even the background of the map is a "thing." Programmers don't like to talk about "things" (it doesn't sound complicated enough, I guess), so they call them *objects* instead. I'll use this term from now on when I want a simple term to refer to many different things that may appear on a map.

Look at Figure 2-6. Notice that items 1 and 2 (including 2a, 2b, and 2c) are all different types of *Topics*. (Topics are simply objects where I can type a small amount of text to capture a key idea, a task to be performed, some kind of instruction, or some other similar thing.) Main topics (#2 on the map) and callouts (#2b) are different in some important ways, but they also have many important things in common. So, when I want to talk about the differences, I'll say specifically what type of topic I'm referring to. However, when I want to talk about the things that are common to all topics, I'll talk about *Topic Objects*.

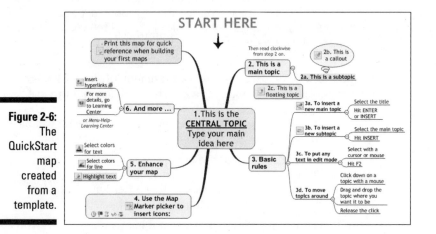

Figure 2-6:
The QuickStart map created from a template.

One thing that can be particularly confusing when I am talking about Topic Objects is that a given topic can be both a topic *and* a subtopic, depending upon whether I want to talk about that topic's children or its parent (see Figure 2-7). The siblings are, at the same time, topics with respect to the next lower level of topics and subtopics, with respect to the next higher topic level. There will be a few times in this book where I will need to say something about three levels of topics all at one time, so I'll need to talk about sub-subtopics, as shown in Figure 2-7. Theoretically, I could even go to four levels . . . nah, I think I would get totally lost if I tried that.

I explore objects in much more detail in Chapter 16.

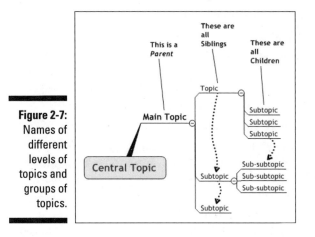

Figure 2-7:
Names of
different
levels of
topics and
groups of
topics.

Creating Your First Map

Creating maps is what MindManager is all about, but creating a useful map can take some effort and creative energy. You want to use maps that are already started, called *templates*, whenever possible. In this section, I tell you how to use an existing template to give you a head start on creating the map that you need. In Chapter 14, I discuss how to make maps you have created into templates. Finally, in Chapter 15, I explain how you can write wizards that will guide others in using the templates you have created!

Create your first map by opening your MindManager program and following these steps:

1. **Click the Learning tab at the bottom right-hand edge of the Task pane.**

   The Learning Center page opens in the Task pane.

2. **In the "Getting Started" section, select QuickStart Map.**

   This should be the third choice from the top of the list. The template opens as a sample map in the Map pane of your workspace, as shown in Figure 2-6. This is a map to use for practicing your basic MindManager skills. You can start over with this practice map as often as you like, so don't be afraid to experiment! Look through the topics on the map, reading in a clockwise direction. This will orient you to the names of the various things that may appear on a map and some of the basic keystrokes that you can use to build your map.

3. **Click anywhere on the Central Topic.**

   MindManager draws a blue rectangle around the central topic. This is how MindManager tells you that an object on the map has been selected.

4. **Type a new title for this map and then press Enter.**

   You are just discovering how to change text in a map, so it really doesn't matter what title you give it — "My First Map" or even "adshka!$" will do just fine.

   Your typing replaces the text that was there, and MindManager resizes the central topic so that it is just large enough to contain your text.

5. **Click the words "Start here" and then press Delete.**

   MindManager first draws the blue selection rectangle around the words and the down arrow, and then it deletes both the words and the image from the map. MindManager then draws the blue selection rectangle around the central topic again.

   The object you just deleted is an example of something called a *floating topic* because it isn't attached to anything else on the map. You can also use this technique to highlight an important part of your map. I tell you how to add a floating topic in Chapter 6.

6. **Press the Enter key.**

   MindManager draws another thick line from the central topic to a blue rectangle containing no text.

7. **Type a few words to represent your new main topic and press Enter.**

   It doesn't matter what you type — "This is my main topic" is as good as anything else. The blue rectangle expands to surround the text that you typed.

8. **Click twice just to the left of the letter "a" on the first line of topic 2.**

   MindManager displays the blue selection rectangle on the first click, and then it displays a flashing vertical line just before the letter "a." You are now in *insert mode*, and anything you type will appear at the point of the vertical line without deleting any of the existing text.

   You can select part or all the text by clicking and holding the mouse button down as you drag across the text. Your typing will then replace the highlighted text.

9. **Type MindManager's and then delete the "a."**

   Topic 2 now reads "2. This is MindManager's main topic" and it remains selected.

10. **Click the topic with the yellow-green background that begins "Print this map . . . "**

    MindManager draws the blue selection rectangle around the topic.

11. **Press Insert.**

    MindManager creates a subtopic and shows it as selected.

12. **Type in any text for the subtopic.**

    MindManager replaces the word "subtopic" with your typing. You have now created a subtopic.

13. **Click the Library tab on the Task pane, and then click Icons.**

    MindManager displays all the icons in its library in the lower half of the pane.

14. **Click the red check mark in the library display.**

    MindManager adds a small red check mark to the left of your new subtopic.

15. **Right-click the check mark in the subtopic and select Remove.**

    MindManager deletes the check mark from the subtopic.

16. **Click Images⇨Landmarks in the top half of the Library pane, and then click the picture that you would most like to visit on your next vacation.**

    The image appears to the left of your subtopic.

Go ahead and play with this map as much as you like. When you are finished, just close it and click the No button when MindManager asks you if you want to save your map. Of course, if you have done something wonderful, do save it (but you will have to give it a different name since this particular map is a read-only map)! Then grab a soda and c'mon back for the next part.

Exploring on Your Own

My father was an avid fisherman but had no patience at all with fishing from a lake or a boat. His passion was to quietly sneak up on a small eddy in a stream under a rock or bank overhang and lay his fly softly on the water, just advertising, "Here's breakfast." For him, actually catching a trout was almost incidental and quite unimportant.

I started fishing with him when I was four years old, listening carefully to his advice and then practicing a short ways up or downstream. However, the real moment of triumph came when I was 11 and, for the first time, went out to explore a tiny creek entirely alone and brought back my own trout. I assure you, this particular fish was far from incidental!

Guides, in the form of templates, are wonderful tools and can save you an enormous amount of time getting to the result you need. However, the time quickly comes when you need to leave your guide behind and discover new vistas on your own. To do this, you need the map-making fundamental tools that I describe in these last sections.

Setting up a document

The first step in creating your map is to set up your central topic to look like you want it to look. You do this using the following steps:

1. **Start MindManager and open the Task pane to the Library Page.**

   Refer to the section "Finding your home on the pane," earlier in this chapter, if you need help doing this.

2. **Click the New (standard) button on the Standard toolbar.**

   MindManager opens the new file with a Central Topic.

3. **Click the central topic, type in the title you want for your map, and press Enter.**

   Your map title replaces the words "Central Topic." The central topic remains selected.

4. **Click the plus sign next to Shapes in the upper part of the Library Task pane page and select one of the shape categories.**

   You see many choices for the shape and color of the Title block displayed in the lower half of the Task pane.

5. **Point your mouse to any format that you like and drag it on top of the central topic, then release the mouse button.**

   As you drag the shape near the central topic, MindManager displays a red shadow and connecting line indicating that it will attach the shape as a main topic if you release the mouse button at that point (see Figure 2-8). When you drag the shape on top of the central topic, the red shadow and connecting line disappear and the red box changes to green (see Figure 2-9). After you release the mouse button, the central topic acquires the shape and color you selected.

You can change the color, font, and size of the text in the central topic after applying the shape, but you can no longer change the background or line color of the shape. See Chapter 14 for details about creating your own custom shapes.

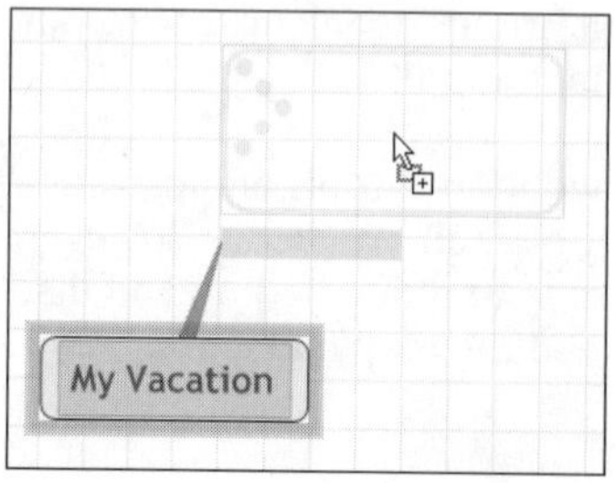

Figure 2-8:
A shape about to be connected as a main topic.

My Vacation

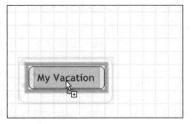

Figure 2-9:
The central topic shape is about to be changed.

Adding topics

Now the creative work begins! Whatever the purpose of your map is, you want to identify the highest-level items that break down your purpose into smaller segments. Here are some ideas to get you started:

- ✔ What are the main ideas you want to capture?
- ✔ What are the main tasks you want to accomplish?
- ✔ What are the main organizational themes you want to represent?
- ✔ What are the main agenda items you want to cover?

Don't worry if some of your ideas seem to be less "high-level" than other ones. The next section explains how to move topics to other places in your map. What is important right now is just to capture your ideas.

You can see the start of my map in Figure 2-10. I have entered all my first level items (or at least all that I can think of at the moment) and have changed the appearance of the central topic to something I like better. MindManager, however, has displayed my topics in a rather random way. No problem — I'll take care of this in a moment.

If you need help adding and changing main topics, refer to the section "Creating Your First Map," earlier in this chapter.

Eventually, you will run out of main ideas and find that you have one too many main topics. This really isn't a problem; after you add one branch too many, you can either click the Undo button or simply press the Delete key.

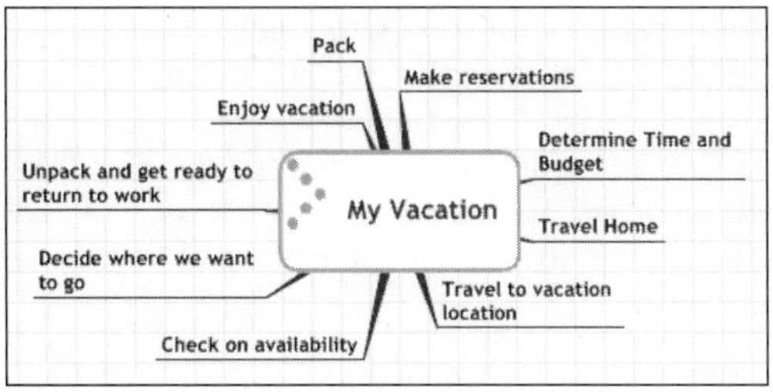

Figure 2-10:
Vacation map after entering all the first level items.

Pack

Make reservations

Enjoy vacation

Determine Time and Budget

Unpack and get ready to return to work

My Vacation

Travel Home

Decide where we want to go

Travel to vacation location

Check on availability

Now choose one of your main topics and identify as many of the sub-ideas that belong to that main topic as you can. In the case of the "My Vacation" map, shown in Figure 2-10, I asked myself what steps I needed in order to "decide where we want to go" and came up with the following list:

✔ Conduct "interest and wishes" meeting with family members. (Very important if I don't want to spend my vacation listening to whining and complaining about "Why did we haaave to come heeeere anyway?")

✔ Collect travel brochures.

✔ Estimate vacation costs.

✔ Choose three best prospects for further analysis.

Look at each of your other main topics and repeat this process of identifying the sub-ideas that belong to each main topic. You can also look at one or more subtopics and break each of them down into sub-subtopics. On the other hand, if you get bored after doing two or three, it's okay to stop. After all, the goal is only to practice adding topics!

The process I am describing is called *brainstorming,* and MindManager has a special mode to support this kind of creative work. I tell you all about this in Chapter 8.

To add a subtopic, follow these steps:

1. **Click the topic to which you want to attach a subtopic.**

   The topic is selected (MindManager draws a blue rectangle around the topic).

2. **Press the Insert key.**

   MindManager attaches a new subtopic to the selected topic, inserts the text "Subtopic," and places the text in edit mode.

3. **Type in the text you want and press Enter.**

   You have successfully created a new subtopic.

Selecting a topic and then pressing Enter always adds a new topic at the same level as the selected topic. Pressing Insert always adds a subtopic to the selected topic.

An alternative method to create a subtopic is to select the desired topic and then click the Insert Subtopic button on the Insert toolbar.

If the text you add to a topic exceeds 30 to 40 characters, MindManager automatically breaks the text into two or more lines. This may still leave a topic title that is longer than you want. To adjust the length of the topic text manually, follow these steps:

1. **Click the topic that you want to adjust.**

   The desired topic text is selected.

2. **Move your cursor to the left or right edge of the blue selection rectangle.**

   The cursor changes to a horizontal line with arrows pointing in both directions, and the edge of the blue selection rectangle turns red.

3. **Hold down the left mouse button and drag the margin to the left (or right) until you are satisfied with the text length, then release the mouse button.**

   MindManager automatically folds the text to fit in the specified length.

You can also force line breaks by selecting the text, going into edit mode, and then holding down the Control key and pressing Enter at the desired point in the text.

Rearranging topics

At this point, your map is probably beginning to look a bit busy, and the order and location of some of the topics may not be to your liking. In addition, MindManager assumes (for export purposes) that the correct sequence of topics begins at the upper right-hand quadrant and proceeds clockwise. Finally, you may have lower-order items as main topics and important topics as subtopics.

In this section, I tell you how you can rearrange your topics to make your map more accurate. To do this, follow these steps:

1. **Click the topic to be moved, hold down the mouse button, and drag the entire topic to the desired location.**

   MindManager will indicate the attachment point (when you release the mouse button) with a red shadow line (see Figure 2-11).

Figure 2-11:
Making a topic into a subtopic of another topic.

2. **Release the mouse button when you reach the desired location.**

   Voilá! You have successfully made the adjustment.

Rearranging subtopics is done in the same manner.

You will find this process to be quite simple with a few minutes of practice. Try moving some of your topics around, and don't worry if a topic ends up in the wrong place the first time. Just grab it again with the mouse and try again. You may even want to add some icons or images. (Refer back to the section "Creating Your First Map" if you need to.) Save your map when you are finished.

Remember, the blue rectangle shows you what you are moving, the red rectangle shows you the topic it will be attached to, and the red shadow box shows you the attachment position relative to its siblings. (See Figure 2-12.)

Figure 2-12:
Moving the "Check on Availability" subtopic ahead of the "Pack" subtopic.

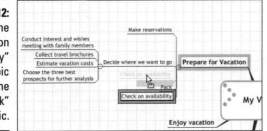

Adding text notes to a topic

You often want to save more information with your map than you want to display in the map graphic. For example, "Check project and administrative workloads during summer months" is a real mouthful, and the graphical space it takes up may be unacceptable with a large and complex map. The Topic Notes pane is the answer to this problem.

Topic Notes always remain associated with the topic even if you later attach the topic to a different place in your map. You can display or hide the notes with a single mouse-click depending on your needs.

To add Topic Notes, follow these steps:

1. **Click on the topic or subtopic to which you want to add Topic Notes.**

    MindManager displays any previously entered Topic Notes in the Topic Notes pane or displays a blank pane (with the text of the topic at the top) otherwise. (Press F11 to display the Topic Notes pane if necessary.)

2. **Click anywhere in the Topic Notes pane and begin entering your notes.**

    You can also enter tables and graphical objects using the buttons on the Topic Notes toolbar. I tell you about this in Chapter 7.

You can do a lot of formatting of text in Topic Notes, but it is not a full-featured word processor. For example, there is no ability to set and clear tabs, set up paragraphs with automatic numbering, or change the format of bulleted lists. Any required formatting other than simple paragraphs requires the use of tables, and the available table management tools are not as robust as those in Word.

Managing your maps

As you begin to create maps for different purposes, you may find that it becomes increasingly challenging to find the particular map that you are looking for. The My Maps tab of the Task pane is of great value in organizing your maps (see Figure 2-13).

The top box in this pane is the *Collections* box where you keep shortcuts to maps that you have stored in various folders along with other types of documents that are all related to some particular project or endeavor. MindManager always creates a *My Projects* collection folder for you here. Right-click My Projects, select Rename, and type in a more meaningful name if you **want**. MindManager will automatically create a new My Projects collection folder the next time you start the program.

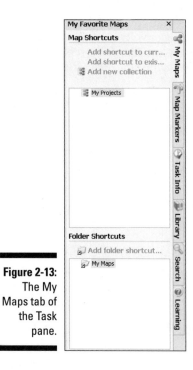

Figure 2-13:
The My Maps tab of the Task pane.

You can also create a new collection by clicking Add new collection and then typing the name you want.

If you have a map currently displayed and you want to create a pointer to this map in your collection, click the collection where the pointer is to be stored and then click *Add shortcut to current map*. If the map is not loaded in MindManager, follow these steps:

1. **Click the collection where the pointer is to be stored and then click *Add shortcut to existing map*.**

   MindManager will open the Select Map Files dialog box.

2. **Navigate to the desired map and click OK.**

   MindManager will display the name of the selected map under the collection name. You can now load this map simply by clicking its shortcut.

Use the bottom box (Folder Shortcuts) to automatically create shortcuts to all maps in a particular folder. The default My Maps folder points to the *My Maps* directory in your *My Documents*. There is no way to change the path once a folder shortcut has been created, so if you want to use a different directory, you must click Add folder shortcut — and navigate to the directory you want. After you click OK, MindManager will display the names of any maps contained in the directory you chose.

If you added a map to a directory with a shortcut, it will not be displayed until you close and restart MindManager. (MindManager will automatically update the folder shortcuts each time you start the application.) To force an immediate update of the display, right-click the folder name and select Refresh.

Chapter 3

Exploring the Neighborhood

Moving into a new home is always exciting, but it can also be challenging. Everything you own has disappeared into cardboard boxes, and the carefully written labels never seem to mention the particular thing you are desperate to find on your first morning, like the coffee pot, coffee, and spoons. Boxes are everywhere, the furniture is not really organized the way you want, and you aren't really sure if this thing you are holding in your hand should go in a drawer in the dining room or a closet upstairs. It's altogether a bit frustrating.

Finding your way around a new software application is a bit like that as well. You remember seeing something mentioned somewhere that you really want to do right now, but you just can't seem to find it again. You know there has to be a way to print out your map in a particular format, but the exact steps remain elusive.

This book is your guide to all the whats and hows of using MindManager, but even here there are several hundred pages and the labels we've put on our boxes (well, chapters) may not guide you to exactly what *you* are looking for. In this chapter, then, I try to distill the essential elements of using MindManager into a couple dozen pages with lots of references to the rest of the book for more details. Welcome to the neighborhood!

Moving In

Just where things should go in the kitchen seems to be a constant source of conversation between me and my wife. Part of the problem is that I'm well over six feet tall while she is closer to five feet. I'm perfectly happy with the rice being on the top shelf. Unfortunately, this often results in having three or four packages there since it is totally out of her sight and she therefore assumes she needs to buy more. Knowing where things are and putting the most important things where you can easily get at them is necessary before you can really cook efficiently.

In a similar manner, you may find that MindManager has put some things that you like to use all the time "on the top shelf." In this section, I tell you how you can move things around and put them where *you* want them as well as specifying how you want MindManager to do certain things, such as automatically opening a new document when you start MindManager or selecting a particular directory when you save a file.

Making yourself at home

MindManager displays only the most frequently used menu commands when you first click an item on the menu bar. If you want to see all the menu commands, you must click on the small chevron at the bottom of the menu display. MindManager keeps track of which menu commands you have recently used and updates the frequently used list. I find this a bit confusing and like to see the same (complete) menu list each time I select a menu item. I change this by selecting Tools⇨Customize from the menu bar, clicking Options, and changing *Personalized Menus* to *Always show full menu* (see Figure 3-1).

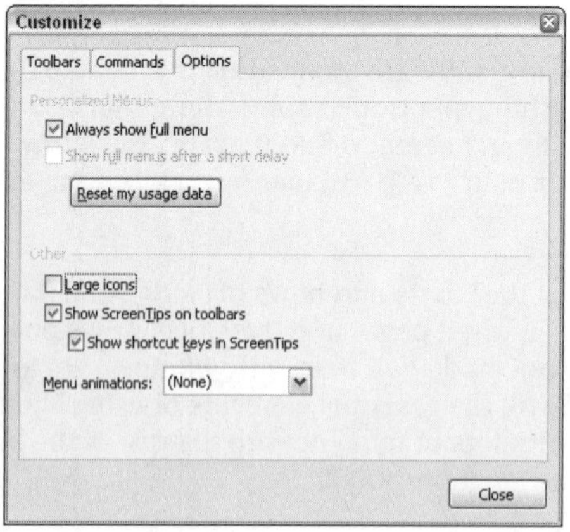

Figure 3-1:
The Options tab of the Customize dialog box.

Most of the default characteristics of MindManager are defined by opening the Options dialog box (Tools⇨Options). There are several pages in this dialog box that you select by clicking the page name in the list box on the left-hand side. Even if you make no other changes to any settings, do click

User Information and complete the fields for your name and your e-mail address, because this information is automatically included on map printouts (see Figure 3-2).

If you want MindManager to always suggest a specific directory when you save a new map, specify that directory on the Save page (see Figure 3-3). Clicking *Always create a backup copy* ensures that you can recover from accidentally overwriting a good map.

If you have other language dictionaries installed on your computer and want to create a map using a different language, you can define that, along with autocorrect and spell check options, on the Spelling page.

Rearranging the furniture

You may not like the default arrangement of the toolbars, or you may want to reorganize the icons on one or more toolbars to better suit your working style.

If you want to move a toolbar to a different location, follow these steps:

1. **Point your mouse to the "wrinkled" edge of the toolbar (shown by crossed arrows in Figure 3-4) that you want to move (at the left-hand side or the top). Press and hold the left mouse button.**

   The mouse cursor changes to crossed arrows.

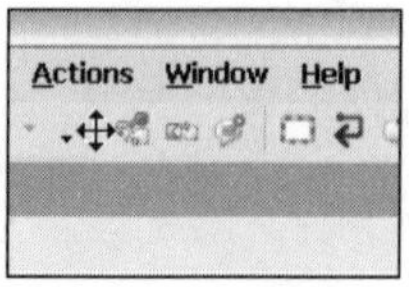

Figure 3-4:
The arrow points to the "handle" of the Insert toolbar.

2. **Press and hold the left mouse button and drag the toolbar to its desired new location.**

   The toolbar will change its shape and position to indicate its new appearance. If you drop the toolbar near the window edge, it will automatically be one icon wide, as shown in Figure 3-5. If you drop the toolbar away from the edge of the MindManager workspace, it will become a *floating* toolbar (see Figure 3-6).

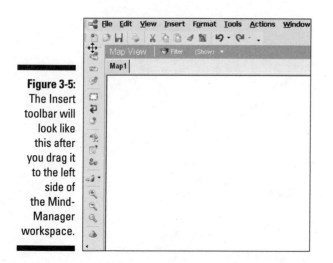

Figure 3-5:
The Insert toolbar will look like this after you drag it to the left side of the Mind-Manager workspace.

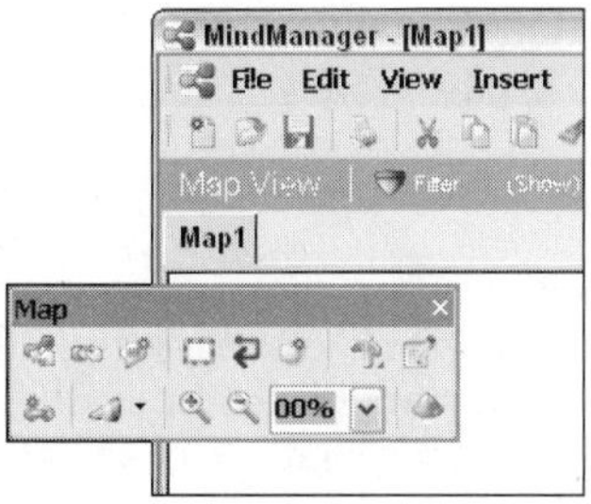

Figure 3-6:
The Insert
toolbar
dropped as
a floating
toolbar.

3. **If you have a floating toolbar, adjust the number of rows of icons by pointing your mouse to the right-hand edge of the toolbar, pressing and holding the left mouse button, and dragging it to the left.**

   The toolbar will adjust its height and width (see Figure 3-7).

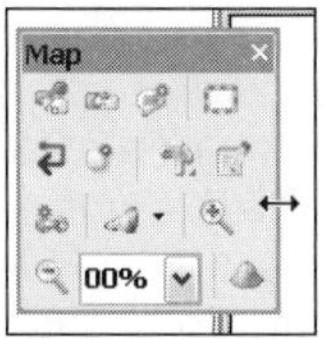

Figure 3-7:
Adjusted
height/width
ratio of the
Insert
toolbar.

Day to Day Living

My maps start out small, but they have a way of growing and growing until they become difficult both to work with and to use in working with others. Often I want to work with more than one map at the same time, and having to flip from one to another can become inefficient and tedious. The standard Map view may not always serve your needs, so MindManager offers two other very useful alternatives.

Your map, your way

In this section, I tell you about a few tips and tricks that greatly facilitate working with multiple maps and with large maps.

Zooming

To magnify or shrink your map display, click the plus or minus buttons on the Insert toolbar. Each click will enlarge or shrink your map by 12.5 percent. The drop-down combo box will allow you to choose larger or smaller percentage changes with a single click. One of your choices will enlarge or shrink the map so that it is fully visible in your workspace.

Focusing and centering

If you want to focus on just one topic in your map, click the topic and then press the F3 key. All other topics will be collapsed to their respective main topics and your selected topic will be fully expanded to show all of its subtopics. Any callouts with their own subtopics that are associated with any topic, however, will not be expanded.

If you want to collapse all topics down to their respective main topics and center the map in your workspace, press Ctrl-F3.

If you want to center any subtopic in the middle of your workspace without expanding or collapsing any subtopics, click the desired topic and then press Alt-F3.

Showing or hiding map elements

You will often want to include information on your maps that you may not necessarily want to show to others when you use your map (for example, during a presentation or when you are exporting to Word). Figure 3-8 shows the map that I am using to write this chapter. I have included a lot of notes to myself as callouts and floating topics that I will not want to include in the Word document that I will create from this map. Selecting View⇨Show/Hide from the menu bar brings up a submenu where I can selectively hide different map elements by clicking on the map element category. Each circled number in Figure 3-8 corresponds to hiding the corresponding element listed below:

1. The *control strip* (where hyperlinks and the notes icons appear).

2. All task information (in this case, the estimated time to write this section).

3. All callouts.

4. All floating topics and relationships.

I can redisplay any hidden element by returning to the Show/Hide submenu and clicking the element category that I want to show.

MindManager offers many additional tools for hiding and showing map elements. See Chapter 13 for more details.

Arranging and splitting the screen

If your map is large, you may want to work on one part of the map while viewing a different section. You accomplish this by selecting Window from the menu bar and then choosing either Split Map Horizontally or Split Map Vertically. This will create two different windows for your map, each of which can be scrolled horizontally and vertically independently of each other.

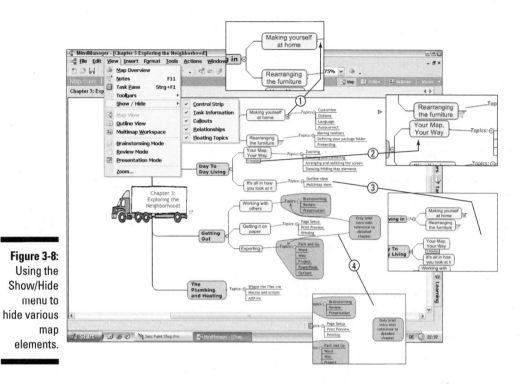

Figure 3-8:
Using the
Show/Hide
menu to
hide various
map
elements.

If you want to work with two or more different maps at the same time, select
Window⊃Arrange from the menu bar. The Arrange Windows dialog box will
appear (see Figure 3-9). Hold down the Ctrl key while you click on the maps
that you want to work with simultaneously. As soon as you have selected two
or more maps, the Tile and Cascade buttons will become active. Tile horizontally will divide your workspace into horizontal strips and display each of
your selected maps. Tile vertically will create vertical strips to display your
maps, while Cascade will stack the maps one on top of the other with just the
title bars of each visible.

To return to single map view, simply click the Maximize button on the
window of the map you want to work with. The Notes pane will display the
notes associated with whichever topic you have selected in any of the windows. Remember that you can gain more space to view your maps by hiding
the Notes pane (press F11).

It's all in how you look at it

The map view is a very useful and informative way to present information
and the relationship between topics. Because images and spatial relationships can be part of a map, this mode supports creativity by involving both
sides of the brain.

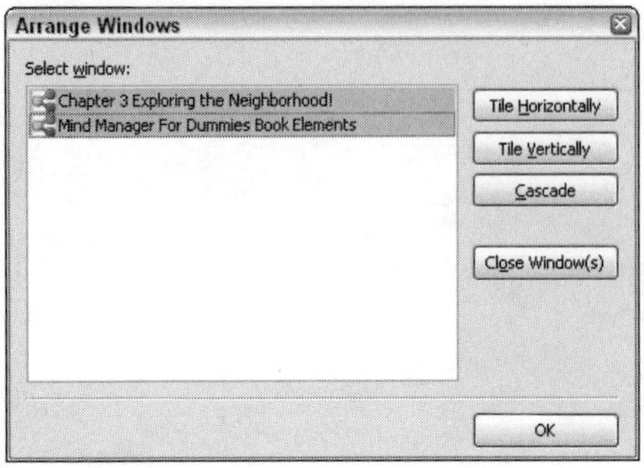

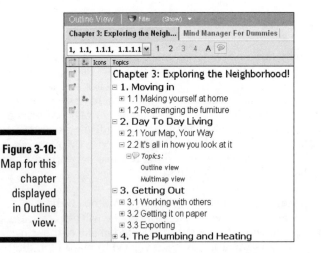

Figure 3-9:
The Arrange
Windows
dialog box.

Nevertheless, there are times when a more traditional presentation of information is required. Click Outline on the View Bar to transform your map into a traditional outline format (see Figure 3-10). In this mode, the notes can still be viewed for each topic by clicking on that topic with the Notes pane open. Any hyperlinks defined for a topic are represented by the hyperlink icon in column 2 and are active in this view (meaning that you can jump to the hyperlink topic by clicking the icon). Any other icons associated with the topic are shown in column 3.

Figure 3-10:
Map for this
chapter
displayed
in Outline
view.

You can define the numbering scheme for your outline using the drop-down combo box (see Figure 3-11), and you can restrict the display to only higher-level topics by clicking on the map detail level numbers. Clicking the callout icon will show or hide all map callouts in the outline. You can display or hide detail levels by clicking on the plus or minus symbol next to the topic description.

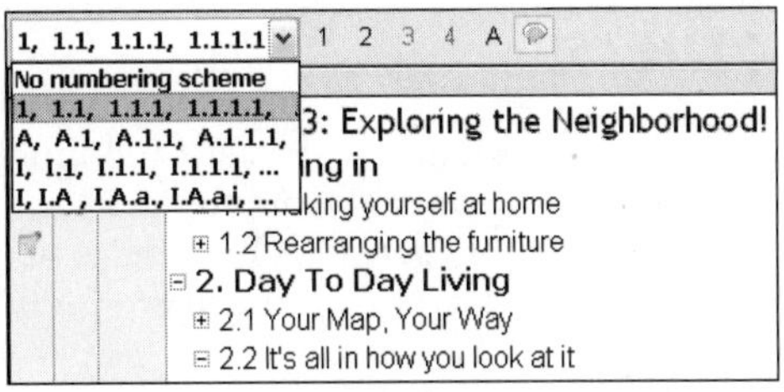

Figure 3-11:
Outline view
numbering
scheme
drop-down
combo box.

| 1, 1.1, 1.1.1, 1.1.1.1 ▾ | 1 2 3 4 A |
| No numbering scheme |
1, 1.1, 1.1.1, 1.1.1.1,	3: Exploring the Neighborhood!
A, A.1, A.1.1, A.1.1.1,	ng in
I, I.1, I.1.1, I.1.1.1, ...	king yourself at home
I, I.A , I.A.a., I.A.a.i, ...	⊞ 1.2 Rearranging the furniture
	⊟ **2. Day To Day Living**
	⊞ 2.1 Your Map, Your Way
	⊟ 2.2 It's all in how you look at it

Click the Print button to print your entire outline or selected topics.
MindManager displays the Outline Print dialog box (see Figure 3-12) where
you can specify exactly what is to be included on the printout. The result is
very similar to what you can expect from exporting to Word, except that no
file is actually created.

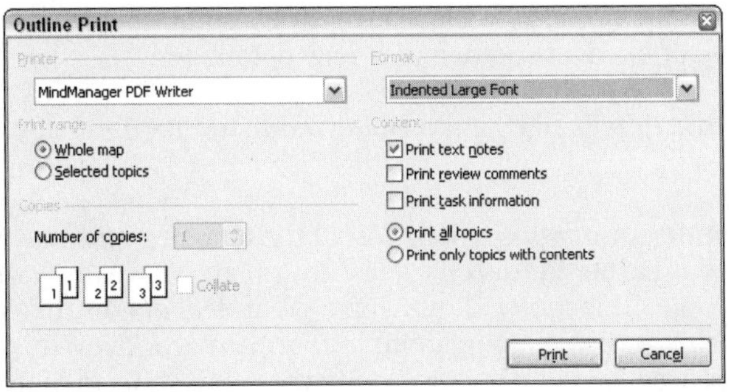

Figure 3-12:
The Outline
Print dialog
box.

Multimap view allows you to work with thumbnail sketches of all the maps
linked to one another by topic hyperlinks. I cover all the details about creating the links in Chapter 12. In Chapter 14, I talk about applying styles so as to
have the same colors, fonts, and shapes on all linked maps. Finally, I cover
tips and tricks in working with linked maps in Chapter 10.

Getting Out

I work a lot with MindManager just on my own. I find that it is a marvelous
tool for capturing bits and pieces of what I want to do even when I am not
really clear what I want my final result to look like. The time comes, however,
when I need to communicate with others or to involve others in the creative
process. In this section, I introduce many of the tools that MindManager provides to support effective and creative collaboration.

Working with others

There are three key points where I particularly want help and input from my colleagues: when I am starting a map, while I am working on it, and after I have finished. Well, unfortunately, I seldom get this much help, but it is really great that MindManager provides a special mode to facilitate group work at each of these points in the process.

You choose the mode you want by clicking Mode at the far right of the View bar and selecting one of the following options:

- ✔ **Brainstorming:** To bring others into the creative process of figuring out what topics should be on the map.

- ✔ **Presentation:** To involve others in the review of what you have done and to add more detail as is appropriate.

- ✔ **Review:** To allow others to make structured comments about your completed map at both a general and a very detailed level.

I talk about all the details of Brainstorming mode in Chapter 8 and Review mode in Chapter 11.

Presentation mode automatically handles all the focusing and centering tasks that I talked about earlier in this chapter ("Your Map, Your Way") when you simply click a topic. This mode allows you a great deal of control over how much of your map is visible at any point in time. Any work you do on the map, however, is captured just as if you had done the same steps in Map view.

Figure 3-13 shows the map for this chapter as MindManager displays it when I choose Presentation mode. All topics are collapsed so that only the main topics are visible, the size of the map is adjusted so that it fully uses the available workspace, and the map is centered. I can switch from one open map to another in presentation mode by clicking the Maps button on the Presentation mode toolbar and choosing the map I want.

I can control which elements are visible on my map with the Show/Hide button (see Figure 3-14). MindManager hides all of its workspace toolbars in Presentation mode by default, but you can show them again by selecting Toolbars from the Show/Hide menu. MindManager also fades all other topics when you click your topic of interest. You can turn off this behavior by selecting Transparent Fade Out. All the other choices function in the same way, as illustrated in Figure 3-8.

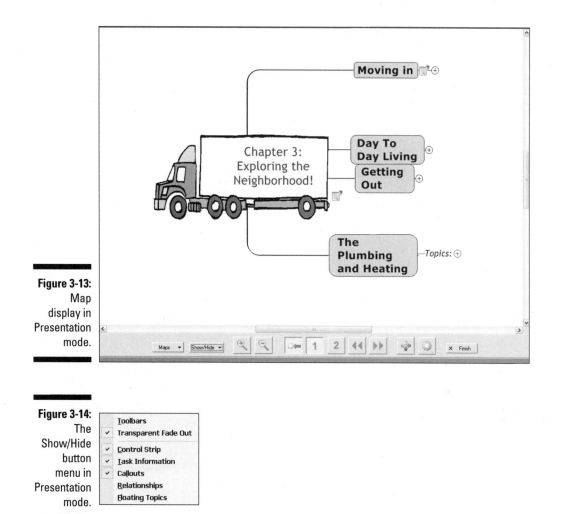

Figure 3-13:
Map
display in
Presentation
mode.

Figure 3-14:
The
Show/Hide
button
menu in
Presentation
mode.

You can use the double arrows to automatically navigate through your map in a clockwise direction (the 1 and the 2 buttons refer to how many levels of topics are displayed at any one time) but you can also click any topic of interest to open and display its subtopics (see Figure 3-15). Any ideas, suggestions, and input for your map from your colleagues can be entered directly in this mode using either the context menu (right-click on a topic) or the regular MindManager menu bar or toolbars. This is just a super mode for group work.

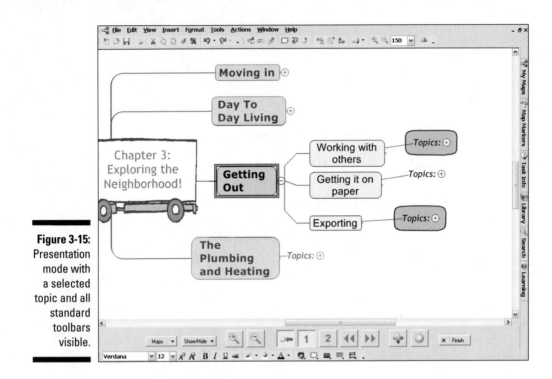

Figure 3-15:
Presentation
mode with
a selected
topic and all
standard
toolbars
visible.

Getting it on paper

It's a paperless world (so I'm told), but I still find I need to get my maps on paper from time to time. Getting exactly what I want on the paper can sometimes be a challenge. MindManager has three menu options on the File menu to help meet this challenge:

- ✔ Page Setup
- ✔ Print Preview
- ✔ Print

You will recognize the Page Setup options because they are very similar to those found in all the Microsoft Office applications. With Print Preview, you can see your page exactly as it will be produced. You can also access this mode from the Print dialog box. The Print Preview toolbar provides a way to enlarge or shrink the display, to display one or two pages at a time, and to scroll from one page to the next (see Figure 3-16).

The Print Map dialog box (see Figure 3-17) has all the usual things you would expect but also one that you may not expect: a very powerful scaling tool. Select Half Page if you want to reduce the size of your map printout to leave room for text or other images on your page, or select any of the other choices to *enlarge* your image so that you can create poster-sized (billboard-sized?) maps up to 4 feet by 8 feet. MindManager automatically calculates the necessary overlap margins so that the pages can be taped or pasted together to create a seamless-appearing map. With a very large map and a lot of subtopics several layers deep, this may be the only way you can produce a legible printout!

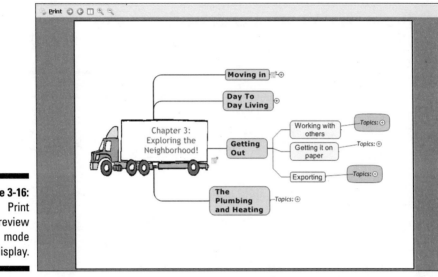

Figure 3-16:
Print
Preview
mode
display.

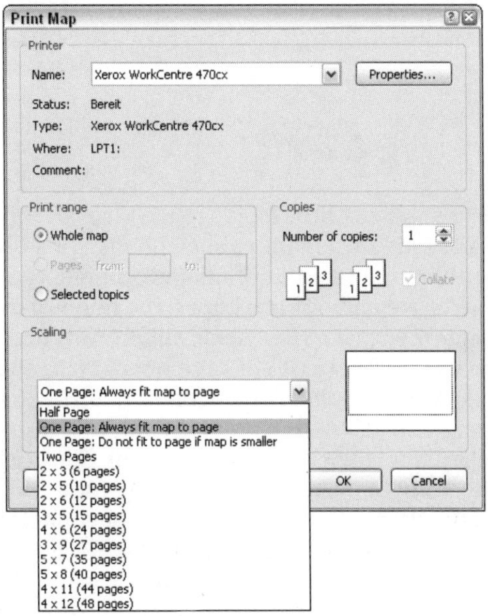

Figure 3-17:
The Print
Map dialog
box showing
the scaling
factor
options.

Exporting

MindManager is a fabulous tool for creative thinking and organization of ideas. With its group interaction tools and multimode view options, it can be a complete and self-contained application. MindManager goes a step further, however, and provides many export capabilities that allow you to use the product of your creative work in many other applications as well.

I devote Part IV entirely to a thorough exploration of these exciting MindManager interfaces, but Table 3-1 provides a quick sneak preview:

Table 3-1	MindManager Application Interfaces
Chapter	*Topic*
17	Gathering your map and all its linked files into a compressed directory, ready to send to a colleague.
18	Transforming your map into Web pages.
19	Creating a PowerPoint presentation from your map.
20	Creating a Word document from your map.
21	Linking task topics to Outlook and maintaining their status from either your map or Outlook.
22	Creating a Project file from your map or importing a Project file with actual data into a new map.

The Plumbing and Heating

When I was in my twenties (don't ask how long ago that was), I took great pride in being able to do all of my own maintenance on my car. I bought timing lights, books, and other equipment; did my own tune-ups; and performed all but the most major repairs. Today, I open the hood of my car and scarcely recognize anything. Yep, that's the engine right there, and here is the radiator, and then — well, mostly I just shut the hood again and plan on calling for roadside assistance if anything goes wrong.

I do know, however, that there are a few things I need to be responsible for to minimize the chances of needing to make that call — make sure that there is enough oil and water, that the various plastic reservoirs have their liquid contents somewhere between two lines, and that the tires have the right pressure.

Similarly, a few "oil and water checks" in MindManager may be useful to know about. The most important, perhaps, is where your files are located. By default, MindManager places all of your maps in your *My Documents* folder. You can change this, either to a subdirectory in *My Documents* or to some other location on your drive (see "Making Yourself at Home" and Figure 3-3, earlier in this chapter). If you haven't changed your default map directory and you need to find a map when you are not running MindManager, look in *My Documents*.

MindManager creates a separate copy of all its templates, styles, map markers, and other such things for each user on your computer. You probably won't have any need to access these files outside of MindManager. However, you might decide that you really want to directly use one of the icons or images in your Word document or PowerPoint document. If so, you will find them all in this directory:

```
Documents and Settings\User\Local Settings\Application Data\
            Mindjet\MindManager\5\Library
```

Remember to substitute the logon ID you use on your computer for "User."

MindManager can be extended to perform many additional functions either through scripting (see Chapter 16 for a brief introduction) or through the creation of special applications called *add-ins* (which are totally beyond the scope of this book). There are a number of advantages to add-ins, and Mindjet (the creator of MindManager) has used this approach for several of the import and export functions. Other add-ins will undoubtedly be available from other developers by the time you are reading this. You can see the add-ins that are currently functioning on your computer by selecting Tools⇨Add-Ins . . . from the menu bar (see Figure 3-18). A green check mark means the add-in is working.

Figure 3-18:
The Add-Ins
dialog box.

If some import or export function does not seem to be working, look here to see if the green check mark is present.

Part II
The Path Takes You There

In this part . . .

Remember the mythical Land of Oz? The road to Oz was paved with magical yellow brick. In this part, you find out how to take a basic black-top MindManager map and turn it into gold. Your ideas and logic expand beyond words to seek visual representation. MindManager shakes your mind to find new ways to communicate your thought processes.

We're off!

Chapter 4

Icons and Colors

· ·

In This Chapter

▶ Speaking plainly with icononic symbology

▶ Adding, changing, and rearranging icons

▶ Adding colors to the text, topics, and titles through toolbars

· ·

*I*n this chapter, you are going to delve into MindManager's corners and crevasses. Icons are lurking and waiting for you to use them. Icons enhance meaning, but the sender and receiver must understand the icon's intent. Not everyone sees the same thing. You have to choose icons carefully; the presence of an icon says, "I mean something here, so pay attention."

Colors have a similar impact. Please follow the bright red stripe to the Emergency Room. After the Emergency Room, follow the money-green stripe to the cashier. Don't cross the double-yellow line when passing in a car. You get the idea. Colors help to guide and inform.

In this chapter, you use icons and colors to add information and depth to your MindManager map. Refer to Chapter 2 to reinforce how to make a basic map with topics.

Up ahead, an iconic stoplight, and it's green. Let's go!

Inserting Icons

I recently received the notification that I am getting older. The notice was cleverly disguised in the form of an invitation to my high school reunion. The invitation was typical. It described many of the details of the reunion and was coated in frivolity masking its dastardly underlying message.

The reunion facts have been altered slightly to be used as an example. Figure 4-1 shows the reunion letter in a basic boring MindManager map. I would be more inclined to go if the map grabbed my interest. I am going to show you how to insert icons to add depth and meaning to your maps.

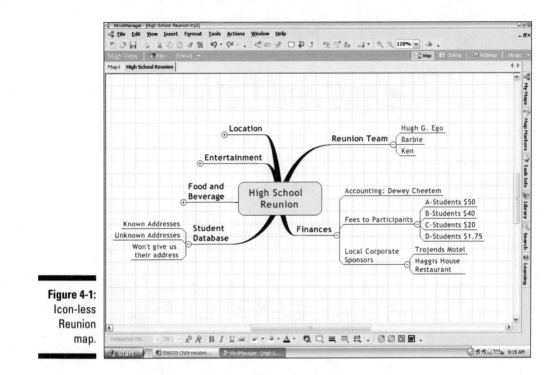

Figure 4-1:
Icon-less
Reunion
map.

MindManager contains a default list of icons. Choosing an icon from this list is our starting place. After this is mastered, I describe a way to personalize your icon use.

Icons in the Map Marker menu

The default list of icons is strategically, but somewhat strangely, placed in the menu titled Map Markers. Map Markers, shown in Figure 4-1, is on the right in a vertical menu list. The Map Markers menu is shown in Figure 4-2.

Click the plus sign next to Smileys, Arrows, Flags, and Single Icons to expand the menu. The default icons are shown in Figure 4-3. The plus sign indicates that submenus can be found underneath. The minus sign indicates that all submenus are showing. Click the minus sign to close the submenus.

The Task Priorities and Task Complete menu items, shown at the top of the list in Figure 4-2, are covered in Chapters 8 and 9, respectively. Priorities and tasks completion icons can be automatically inserted by other parts of the MindManager program.

Figure 4-2:
Map
Markers
menu.

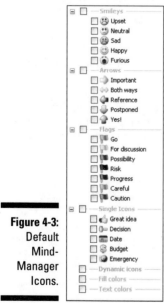

Figure 4-3:
Default
Mind-
Manager
Icons.

Time to insert an icon.

1. **Select a topic. I selected the topic titled Ken (refer to Figure 4-1).**

   Ken is one of the reunion team members. He is the chairman of the committee and makes the final decisions. An icon is needed that conveys this responsibility. Look through the icon list shown in Figure 4-3. Search, search, ah ha!

2. **Click the gavel found under Single Icons.**

   The gavel now appears left of the actual topic. In this case, left of the name Ken. Refer to Figure 4-4. Placing the cursor over the gavel gives the name of the icon itself, which is Decision.

3. **Select each of the A, B, C, and D student topics.**

   To select all the topics, click the first topic, and then Ctrl+click the last one — this gets 'em all for you in one easy step.

   All students are going to be charged something. Which icon infers money? Search, search, ah ha!

4. **Click the dollar sign icon.**

   The dollar sign is placed next to each of the selected topics. But wait, there is a problem. Did you notice the name of the dollar sign icon? Budget is not the right name for the icon. The name should be something like bucks, moola, dinero, revenue, extortion. How about *contribution*?

5. **Right-click the name Budget (next to the dollar sign icon).**

6. **Select Rename from the pop-up menu that appears.**

7. **Type Contribution as the new name.**

   The new name appears. Placing the cursor over the icon in the map now gives the name as Contribution.

I have added another couple of default icons to the map. Barbie is the keeper of the schedule, so I added the calendar icon to her name. I renamed the icon from Date to Schedule Keeper. Hugh gets the happy smiley icon because he is the marketing/sales person, and he is always happy. The results to this point are shown in Figure 4-4.

To remove an icon, select the topic with the icon and then click the same icon found in the Map Marker list.

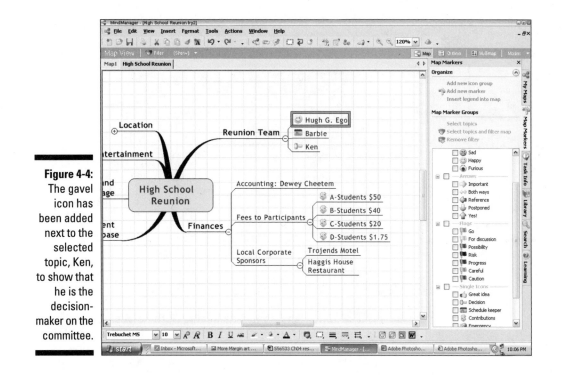

Figure 4-4:
The gavel icon has been added next to the selected topic, Ken, to show that he is the decision-maker on the committee.

Switch to another Map Marker set

MindManager tries to read your mind. Icon sets based upon common uses are included in the program. The way to change the default, however, is not intuitive. Follow me to the changing box.

Select Format⇨Map Markers⇨Assign from Template Organizer.

The Select New Marker List for Current Map dialog box appears, as shown in Figure 4-5. Icons appropriate for various activities are displayed. Click the various choices to bring up each icon set.

I have just run through the typical way to use icons. This method is the quick and easy way to add icons. There is another way, coming up next. Get your SUV dirty. Set the gears to imagination. Throttle to creativity.

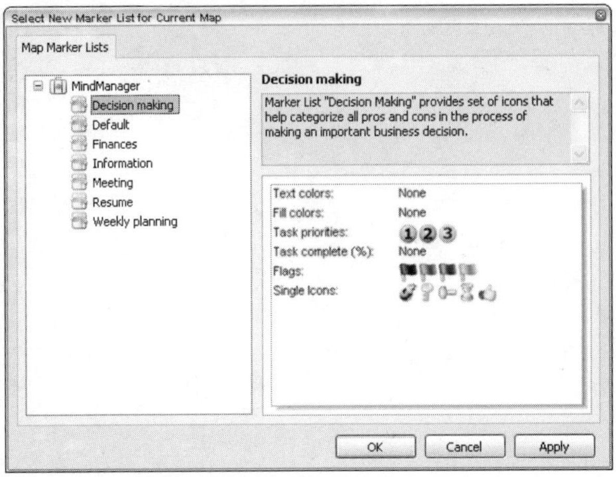

Figure 4-5:
The Select
New
Marker
List for
Current Map
dialog box.

Brains up

Getting the most out of MindManager means having both halves of your brain engaged. Left-brain, right-brain theory says the right brain is artistic, and the left brain is logical. I may have simplified the theory a bit. The map appears quite logical but would not stimulate much left brain reaction. How does the left brain get charged up?

Use emotions, reactions, and senses to stimulate your left brain. Let's employ this for the Reunion map. Remember Hugh G. Ego. What was he like in high school? Loudmouth? That fits. How about Ken? Nerdy, but fair? That fits, too. Barbie? I didn't actually know her but I used to dream that I did.

Choose an icon with these thoughts in mind by selecting Insert⇨Map Markers⇨More Icons. The Library appears. Figure 4-6 shows the Library and some of the available icons.

You can also bring up the library by selecting the Library menu tab in the vertical menu on the right side of the screen.

So to get back to Hugh, Ken, and Barbie, what icon fits a loudmouth? A megaphone! Nerdy, but fair? A weights and measures balance! Now for Barbie. Stop and Go light? No, not appropriate. How about an old fashioned thumbs-up?

The result of the additions, plus a few more, is shown in Figure 4-7.

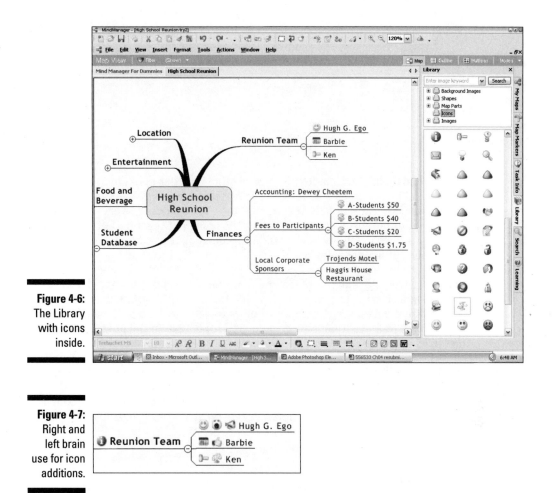

You aren't done yet, though. The next step is to name the icons. The icons that you pull from the Library are nameless. Let's go back to the Map Marker menu now. Click on the Map Marker menu tab. The icons added from the Library are placed into the Dynamic Icon list. (Refer to Figure 4-2 to see the Map Marker menu.) Change the names of the icons the way we did above by right-clicking the icon, selecting Rename, and then typing in the new name. I changed a couple of them and Figure 4-8 shows the results. I suppose the name of the thumbs-up symbol should be changed, too. I'll name it Great Idea. After you change the icon name, it jumps into the Single Icon list.

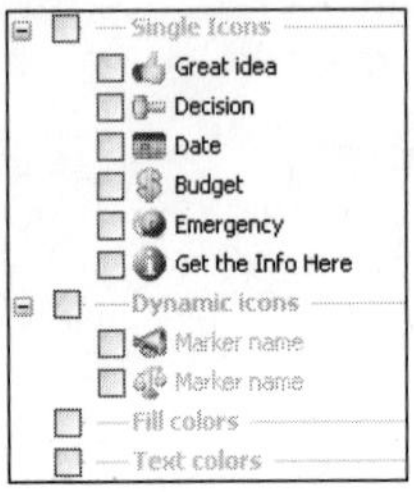

Figure 4-8:
Dynamic
Icons with
new names.

The added icons have made the original MindManager map much more interesting and informative. Just look at the two maps side-by-side. Cut Figure 4-8
out of this book and hold it next to Figure 4-1 (just kidding). Very different.
Placing your cursor over the icon gives the name of the icon. Had I received
the map shown in Figure 4-8, I would have been distracted long enough to
forget the subliminal aging message.

Icons increase the amount of information that can quickly be transferred by a
MindManager map. The story of this chapter is not yet complete, however.
Colors are the next step. Add some colors to go from drab to dynamic. Colors
are applied to lines, topic background, and topic text. In the next section, you
get involved with all three.

Clicking the icon in the Map Marker menu will remove icons from selected
topics in the MindManager map. You may not be able to see the selected
topic with the icon because it is scrolled out of view. A good habit is to click
on a vacant part of the map before clicking on any icons. Clicking a vacant
part of the map deselects topics.

Color Inside the Lines

MindManager offers a ton of places to add color. I like to start with lines. Line
color has a tendency to grab the eye. The Reunion map from Figure 4-9 is still
fresh, but the lines need sprucing up.

The Line Color tool is the easiest way to change line color — imagine that! The
Line Color tool is at the bottom of the screen, as shown in Figure 4-9. The
buttons are shown here in the margin. The Line Color tool is the tool on the
far left.

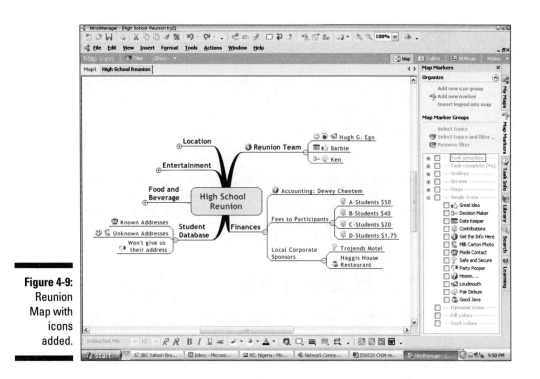

Figure 4-9:
Reunion
Map with
icons
added.

Use the tool by first selecting a topic. Select a level 1 topic if you want to make the topic and all subtopic lines the same color. (Level 1 topics are the first topics from the center of the map and are also called Main Topics.) Figure 4-9 shows Reunion Team, Finances, and Student Database as some of the Level 1 or Main Topics. Refer to Chapter 2 for the basics of adding topics. The Reunion map from Figure 4-9 needs some line color now.

1. **Select a topic.**

2. **Click the drop-down arrow on the Line Color tool.**

   The Line Color dialog box appears, as shown in Figure 4-10.

3. **Click the color you desire.**

4. **Close the pop-up color chart.**

You may have many lines to color. In that case, leave the Line Color pop-up color chart open. Then you can select other topics and choose and change line color in the entire map, pronto.

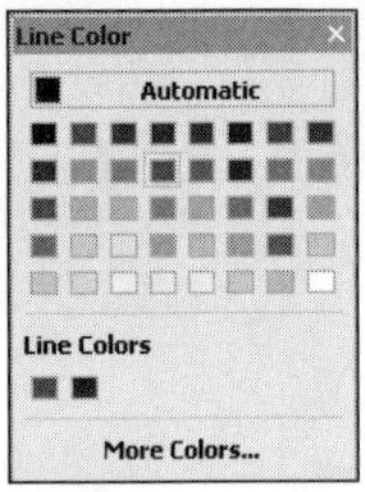

Figure 4-10:
Line Color
choices.

The line color can't be named, nor does it show up in the Map Marker menu. MindManager did not read my mind on this one — it would've been nice to be able to give the line color a meaning. But, names *can* be assigned to Text and Fill colors, which makes me a little happier.

Color the Text and Give It a Name

The Text Color tool is the right-hand tool shown in the margin art. Give text a color the same way you add color to a line. Select a topic and then choose a new color from the pop-up Font color chart. The new color is added to the text. Quite simple, actually, but there is a twist. The new text color is added to the Map Marker menu under the title Text Colors, and you can assign it a name by following these steps:

1. **Open the Map Markers menu by clicking on the Map Marker tab.**

   The new text colors are shown.

2. **Right-click Marker Name, which is located next to the *A*.**

   Note that the letter A is shown in the color of the new text color.

3. **Select Rename.**

4. **Type the new name for the color.**

I have added some text color to the Reunion Map. Figure 4-11 shows the Entertainment topics and the renamed titles. The Text Color names are found in the Map Marker section. (Take a look again at Figure 4-9 for the Map Marker section.) The Text Colors selection is located at the bottom of the menu list.

The text color gives more information about the topic. In this case, the topic's text color is linked to a location. The Older Than Dirt Band text is blue and the band is playing in the Bald Room. The Who Remembers text is red and the band is playing on the Center Stage. Hee Haw's performance is a pea green and is playing in the Basement.

Figure 4-11:
Text colors
and their
names.

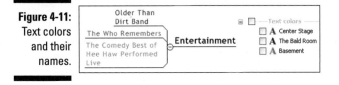

So far the lines have color, and the text has color. What more of the rainbow can we throw at a MindManager Map? In the next section you are going to fill in the background of topics with color.

Topical Application of Color

The default for a topic is no shape and no color. The text just sits on top of the line. I like to change the shape and background color of topics, which makes the visual impact on the map much stronger. The background color of a topic is called the *fill color.* In the Map Marker section you create a name for the new fill color.

I am going to walk you through adding and naming a fill color.

1. **Select a topic on the MindManager map that you want to receive the new fill color.**

2. **Select Format⇨Topic Shape and Color.**

3. **The Format Topic Shape and Color dialog box shown in Figure 4-12 appears.**

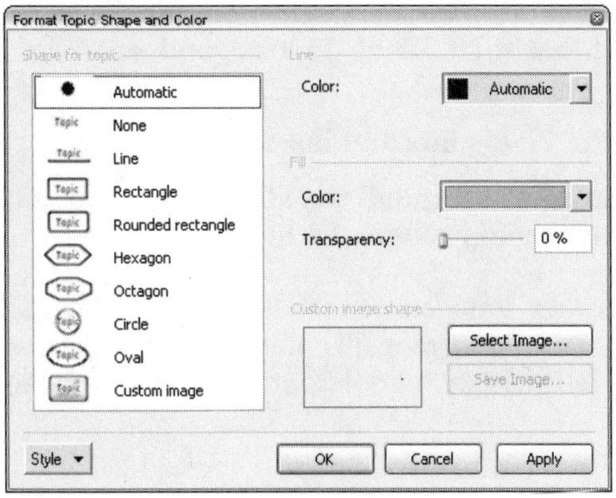

Figure 4-12:
Add a fill
color and
change
a topic
shape, too.

Format Topic Shape and Color	
Shape for topic	Line
● Automatic	Color: Automatic
Topic None	
Topic Line	Fill
Topic Rectangle	Color:
Topic Rounded rectangle	Transparency: 0 %
Topic Hexagon	
Topic Octagon	Custom image shape
Topic Circle	
Topic Oval	Select Image...
Topic Custom image	Save Image...
Style ▾	OK Cancel Apply

4. **In the Fill Color section, click the drop-down arrow, and our friend the Color chart, shown in Figure 4-10, appears.**

5. **Choose a color.**

6. **Slide the transparency bar to 50 percent.**

   You can change the fill color other ways, but the transparency bar is available only in this dialog box. The transparency bar changes how transparent the fill color is to the text color. The higher the percentage of transparency, the easier it is for text, regardless of text color, to show through. I start with 50 percent because most text colors show through. Color coordination perfectionists beware, changing the transparency percentage alters the fill color slightly. The changes don't show up in the color box; they show up only in the MindManager map itself.

   The background color, topic color, and topic text color must work together. The Fill color acts as a buffer between the background color and the text color. The contrast characteristics between the various colors can make the text difficult to see. The order of the overlay is background color first, then topic fill color, and finally the text color.

   Fill colors require a bit more care to use. You have to be concerned about the text color. Use the wrong fill color, and *kaboom* — the text is gone. Each time you adjust a color's transparency, MindManager thinks you are assigning a different color. The Map Markers may have the same shade of green but different transparencies. Stick with one level of transparency for consistency. I use 50 percent when I change from the default of 0 percent.

7. **While you're here, go to the Shape for Topic section and select a topic shape by clicking it.**

8. **Click Apply.**

   You may have to move the dialog box to see the topic you selected. The new fill color should be visible. Change the color or the transparency settings if it doesn't look right. When it looks good, continue with the next step.

9. **Click OK to close the dialog box and insert the fill color.**

10. **Open the Map Markers and expand the Fill Color menu item. Right-click the marker name and rename the fill color.**

The fill color can add another dimension to the information that is contained in the MindManager map. I can add a green fill color to the topics Entertainment and Food and Beverage in the High School Reunion map and name the fill color *Additional Cost*.

Figure 4-13 shows the explosion of information that is now found in the High School Reunion MindManager map.

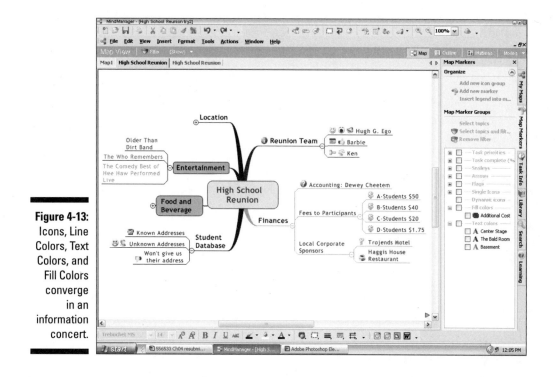

Figure 4-13:
Icons, Line
Colors, Text
Colors, and
Fill Colors
converge
in an
information
concert.

Chapter 5

Images: Graphic Ideas

In This Chapter

▶ Storing images in the library

▶ Adding images to all topic types

▶ Changing the size of an image

▶ Including images as a background

▶ Adding keywords to images

▶ Using images to enhance a map

*I*mages add life to a MindManager map and stimulate our brains. Advertising would be a bit dull with just text. Your mind seeks out the stimulus of images.

While I was teaching in Germany, a student handed me a circular outline of all the topics presented in class. Every topic introduced in class became a branch in the outline. The student's handwriting was incredibly small but completely legible. I could see the message of the class as a thread weaving through the outline. The document was clear and completely detailed but contained only text.

Years later, a student was taking notes using a laptop computer. The same circular outlining technique was being employed — but with a big difference. The student used images and icons to open up the meaning of the map. The same type of information found in the text-based circular outline became a story with depth. The software she was using? MindManager, of course!

MindManager opens the door for you to add images to your map. Any type of MindManager topic can accept an image. Topics are the elements of the map that contain textual ideas and images. The images are the enhancer or the storyteller. The background of the map can even be made of images. Create backgrounds made of very tiny stacks of money. Your boss may get the message.

In this chapter, you add images to the library and then to a MindManager map.

Opening the Door of the Library

Come with me to the library. I am going to show you the images collected by MindManager's curators. You probably have photographs or works of clip art in your own collection. Would you like to add to the library's selections? Excellent. Off you go to the check-in window to add your images to the library stacks.

The following steps show you how to check your images into the library:

1. Click the Library tab located in the vertical menu on the right side of the MindManager window.

Have patience, because the window may take a couple of seconds to open. Don't be surprised if you double-click because you think that the first click didn't work. The program has to gather everything together before opening the menu. Figure 5-1 shows the open Library window. You may have to open the Images menu to see all the image files.

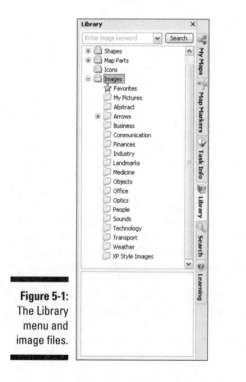

Figure 5-1:
The Library menu and image files.

2. Right-click the My Pictures image file.

The pop-up menu shown in Figure 5-2 appears.

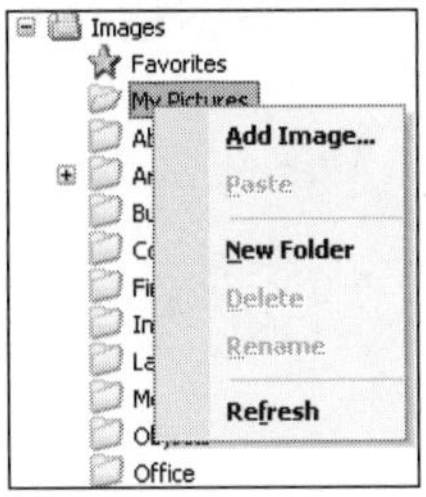

Figure 5-2:
The Add
Image pop-
up menu.

3. **Click Add Image.**

   The file search screen appears. Move through your files until you find a
   picture or clip art that you want to add. Figure 5-3 shows the Select Image
   dialog box that you use to search through your files.

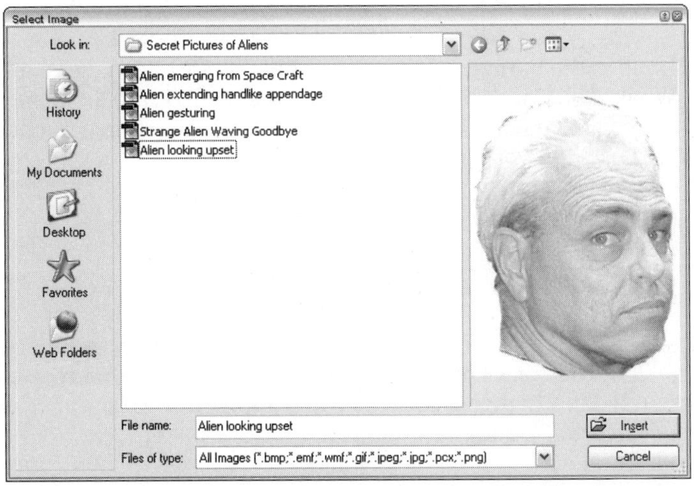

Figure 5-3:
The Select
Image
dialog box.

MindManager accepts graphic files with the following extensions: .bmp,
.emf, .wmf, .gif, .jpeg, .jpg, .pcx, and .png. Figure 5-3 identifies the acceptable files in the *Files of type* drop-down list box. Most graphic files are
covered by these extensions. My photographs are stored in a .tif format.
The .tif format is not on the MindManager list. As a result, my pictures
can't be added to the library. I convert photographs to another image
format — usually .jpg — before I add them to the library.

Pictures have to be pretty small to look good in MindManager. The
thumbnail size picture is a good indicator. If you don't think the picture
looks right as a thumbnail, it won't look good in the map. Simple and
small works best.

4. **Click Insert to add your special picture or clip art to the library and prepare it to be added to the map.**

   The My Pictures folder now contains the new picture, as shown in Figure 5-4.

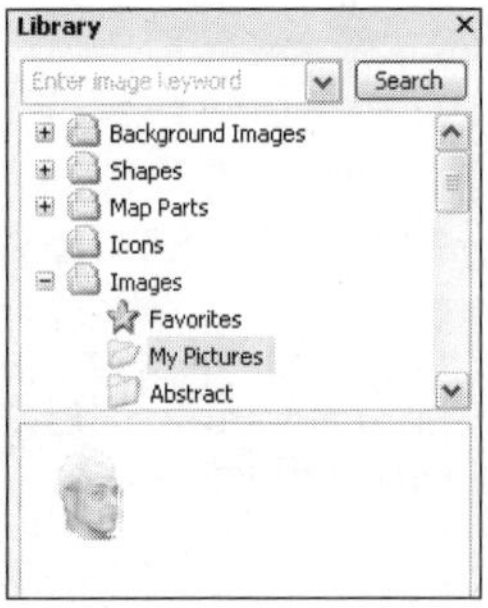

Figure 5-4:
The My Pictures folder contains the added picture.

Take a look at the various images in the library. MindManager contains quite a few. What MindManager calls an image is more like clip art than a picture. Now that you have made a donation to the library, it is time to check out an image and use it in your MindManager map.

Installing Images into a Map

You can add images to almost any element of a MindManager map. Refer to Chapter 2 for the basics of how to add topics to a map. One type of topic is not discussed in Chapter 2: An image taken from the library and placed on the map can also be a topic.

The method for adding an image is the same for all topics. The following steps show you how to add an image to each topic type:

1. **Select the central topic of the map, and press Insert.**

   A main topic appears.

2. **Select the new main topic and press Insert again.**

   So far, you have created a map with a main topic extending off of the central topic and a subtopic attached to the main topic. The next step is to add a floating topic and a callout topic.

3. **Click on the Insert Floating Topic toolbar button. Refer to the margin art. Place the topic on the map by clicking at the preferred location.**

4. **Insert a callout topic by first selecting any of the topics in the map. Click the Insert Callout Topic toolbar button.**

Refer to the margin art. The callout topic is attached to the topic you selected.

5. **Open the Library menu. Expand the Images folder and open one of the image categories. Click and drag an image from the library onto the map.**

Notice that the red tractor beam grabs the image if you get it close to another topic. By the way, you didn't miss the Insert Image Topic button on the toolbar. It isn't there.

Pressing the Shift key while you drag the image onto the map can turn off the red tractor beam.

A good habit is to always click a vacant area of the map prior to performing Step 5. This action deselects all topics. I have unintentionally placed many images into a map by not following this habit. It seems to be human nature to click on the library image when you find one you like. If you do and a topic is selected somewhere in the map, the image is transported directly to the selected topic. You may not even realize this has happened. The selected image may not be visible on the screen. Everything looks fine until you look around the map and see an image that doesn't belong. Where did that come from? Follow my suggestion, and you can click on images in the library all you want and nothing happens.

MindManager provides another way to add an image topic that is worth mentioning. You can use the following method in place of Step 5: Click on the map. Make sure a topic is not selected. Open the Insert menu. Select Image⇨From File. (Refer to Figure 5-5.) A small symbol appears on the map. Refer to the margin art. Click on the map where you want to insert the image. The Select Image dialog box appears. (Refer to Figure 5-3.) Select an image and click Insert. The image is placed into the map. Use this technique for images you only use once and don't want to add to the library.

You could also have selected Image⇨From Library. Making this selection does not add an image to the map. It opens the library. Should you make the From Library selection, you are back to the original Step 5. Seems like a circle, doesn't it?

The image is inserted into the map. MindManager treats the image like a topic. I refer to it as an image topic. Add text to the image topic by selecting the image and typing. Typing in text does not replace the image. You may have been frustrated at trying to change the text in a topic. You erase all the text if you start typing just after selecting the topic. Not so with an image topic. One caveat is that you can have only one image. Trying to add a second image replaces the first image.

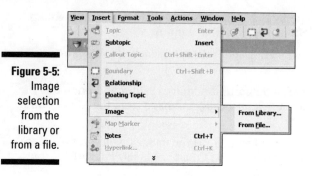

Figure 5-5:
Image
selection
from the
library or
from a file.

All the inserting of the last few steps results in the MindManager map shown in Figure 5-6. I added a picture of the triple constraints of a project. The triple constraints show how cost, time, and scope are connected in a project. Change one of the constraints, and one of the others is going to change.

An image topic does not export well. Exporting to a Web page may distort the image. Sending the map to Word leaves the image behind. Exporting to PowerPoint is okay, though. The image is processed correctly.

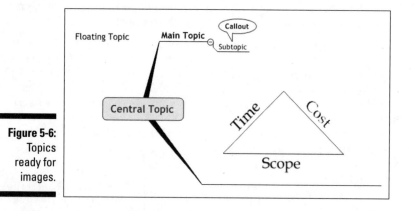

Figure 5-6:
Topics
ready for
images.

6. **Select Floating Topic in the map. Place your cursor over an image in the library, but don't click yet.**

   The image that you click on is immediately placed into the topic. Got the right one? Click. The image is transported directly to the selected topic. Repeat this step for the central topic, main topic, subtopic, and callout. The process works the same for all.

7. To change the size of an image, select the topic and click on the image.

Eight small adjustment handles appear around the image. Figure 5-7 shows that the topic is selected (as indicated by the blue box) and that the image is selected (as indicated by the appearance of the movement boxes or handles). Put the cursor over one of the handles, and little arrows appear. Click and drag the image to the size you want. Use the corner handles to ensure that the image continues to look the same as you change the size.

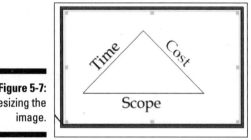

Figure 5-7:
Resizing the
image.

You can easily remove an image. Select the topic and click on the image. The eight sizing handles appear. Press delete, and the image is removed from the map.

You have now added images to every type of topic in the MindManager map. Images find a home in other areas of the MindManager program, too. The next stop on the image express is the map background.

Subliminal Background Images

Background images aren't really intended to be subliminal. A pattern of dollar bills quietly laced throughout the map background may get the ball rolling on your next raise. Let me know if it works.

The background images are found in the library. They are secretly hidden in a file called — surprise! — Background Images. Open the library and select the background image files. Open one of the files. I personally am not a botanical background kind of guy. I shoot straight for the geometric. Figure 5-8 shows the available selections.

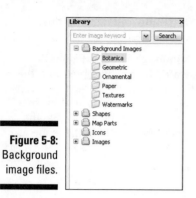

Click on any of the selections, and the background images are shown below the file list. I wear bifocals, and I can't see the background image. They are very tiny and faint. The following steps show you how to see, choose, and get rid of a background image:

1. **Starting with a blank map, click on Geometric.**

   The various geometric background images appear.

2. **Click on any of the patterns.**

   The map background changes. The options are much easier to see when they cover the map. Try the tartan background image on the map. Interesting, isn't it?

   I could be mean at this point. Now that the tartan background is installed, how do you get rid of it? Sure, you can just click on another background image, but that would just change the background to the new image. What about right-clicking on the image in the library? There is a delete selection, but don't choose it. You would just delete the image from the library. In some cases, that may be a good idea.

3. **Select Format⇨Background from the menu bar.**

   The Background dialog box appears, as shown in Figure 5-9.

4. **Adjust the transparency of the image by sliding the transparency bar.**

    The higher the number, the more transparent the background image is. More transparent means the image is lighter and does not stand out as much. A more transparent background image is desirable if the background image is distracting when looking at the MindManager map. The Color selection box refers to the background color of the map. Leave the background color set to none or white when using a background image.

5. **Click Remove Image to delete the background image.**

I have a confession. I don't like background images. I remove the default background image every time I start a map. Changing the default background image is probably covered somewhere in this book. I better go look it up.

Background images are not treated the same as other images. The more images you add to the library, the more choices you have to sift through every time you want one. MindManager has a search feature that lets you use keywords to find just the right graphic. However, you can't use keywords to search through background images.

Background images are also removed by clicking on the *Remove Background Image* link found in the background images library section. The link is at the bottom of the images in light blue. You may miss it if you aren't looking for it.

Searching Images by Keyword

The keyword search for images is a useful tool. All the images supplied in MindManager have at least two or three keywords associated with the image. I use the feature whenever I am going to add images to a map. I start by thinking of a word that describes the idea that I have. In the next section, I describe the emergency response process of the Civil Air Patrol. The emergency response is fast. I enter the word *fast* into the keyword search. Thirty-four images in some way depict the idea of fast. I also look for words that describe a specific item. I need an image of an airport. The word *airport* goes in the search box, and three images are shown. Figure 5-10 shows the search box and the response.

Figure 5-10:
A keyword image search.

A bug exists in the MindManager program. When you have finished a search, do *not* right-click on the image and delete it. The image is not deleted from the search file that is created. Instead, the image is deleted from the *original image file*. After you delete the file, you can't search on anything else, and the program crashes.

You can add keywords to any image. Open an image file and display the images. Right-click on the image. Choose Select➪Edit Keywords. The current keywords for the image are displayed. You can add, change, or remove keywords. The name of the image file is also included in the search. Descriptive file names help locate images. The name of the file is not added to the keywords.

Looking at Images in a Different Way

I am going to show you how to use images in a different way. Start looking for the edges of the containment structure. You are going to visit the external facets of paradigmatic life. In short, to use a worn out business cliché, I am going to take you outside of the box using MindManager.

Most business presentations use text information as the focus. Images are added to highlight or enhance the text material. How many times have you started with the images and then created the text to enhance the story told by the images?

The most common way to build a MindManager map is to add topics that contain text. The images are added after the map is complete. I am going to turn the tables a bit. I am going to show you how to use images to create a story that describes a process. The text is added later. This reverse method can be quite useful. The old adage that a picture is worth a thousand words is true. The key is to get the right images to tell the story. Remember the old days of reading comic books? Comic book artists knew how to use images to make a story come alive.

I am going to build a story that describes the emergency response process of the Civil Air Patrol (CAP). I can choose almost any process activity. The story may help a new member understand one of the CAP missions. The story could also assist mission planners in operating the process and organizing an emergency response.

The story begins when an aircraft has an unfortunate meeting with the ground — a crash. Takeoff did not equal landing. Every aircraft carries an Emergency Locator Transmitter. The beacon is turned on by a severe jolt — and a crash constitutes a severe jolt. The search for the right images begins by looking in the library.

The following steps show you how to use MindManager to demonstrate a process using images. Refer to prior sections of this chapter for a review of how to add images to a map:

1. **Think of your process as a series of images.**

   The CAP process begins with someone in distress. What is a symbol or image that indicates distress? The emergency can happen at any time. Satellites pick up the emergency beacon and transmit the location information to earth. The information is transferred from Air Force Rescue Coordination Center at Langley Air Force Base to the CAP squadron that is closest to the emergency location. What images can depict these events?

2. **Create a blank map and begin to search the library using keywords.**

   I used the following keywords: danger, satellite, weather, night, day, communication, worry, concern, thinking, mobile, aircraft, plane, airport, fast, plan, and a bunch more. Most of the words produced results.

3. **Place images that seem to fit over to one side. Press the Shift key as you click and drag the image.**

   The Shift key turns off the tractor beam. Figure 5-11 shows images that I selected from my searching. The SOS is the only one that was not in the library.

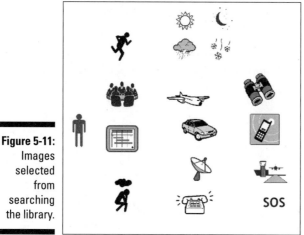

Figure 5-11: Images selected from searching the library.

4. **Arrange the images according to the order found in the process. Use topic and subtopic arrangements where appropriate.**

   I am going to put the images in a circular pattern. A circle is not a normal MindManager map style. I have to turn off the tractor beam as I move images around the map. You may want to choose a more normal map arrangement. I am not going to be able to export the features of my map unless I connect the central topic to the map items. I have also added a couple of arrow images to show the direction of the flow. Figure 5-12 shows the result of the arrangement.

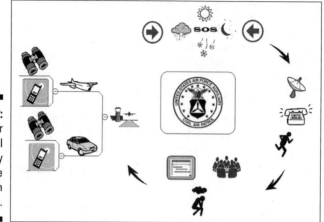

Figure 5-12: The Civil Air Patrol emergency response process in images.

5. Now add the text.

I added basic text to the map. Figure 5-13 shows the map with text. The map can contain much more information. The entire CAP search-and-rescue process is not shown. I would add links to regulations, telephone call lists, personnel data, planning requirements, and other processes to make the map complete and useful. In Figure 5-13, the images show the process, and the text gives the details of each step.

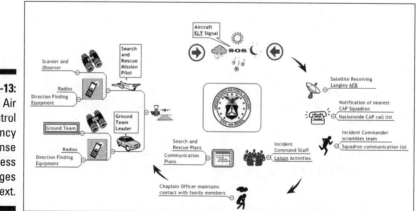

Figure 5-13: The Civil Air Patrol emergency response process in images with text.

Chapter 6

Grouping and Relating Topics

. . . .

In This Chapter

▶ Drawing attention to topics

▶ Adding interest to your topic groups with colors

▶ Showing relationships between topics

▶ Making fancy pointers with callouts

. . . .

*I*f I am in a meeting with no access to my computer and MindManager (deep, despairing sigh) and I want to lead a discussion about a topic, I begin with a blank sheet of paper on a flip-chart (or a clean white board) and begin writing. When I need to illustrate something, I draw a picture or diagram near the topic. I use lines and arrows to relate topics together and draw circles (that's being generous — I couldn't draw anything other than an ugly, wiggly line if my life depended on it) around things that I want to group together.

When I'm finished, the white board or flip-chart may be a total mess and utterly undecipherable to anyone who might now walk into the room, but it doesn't matter because my audience participated in the process and knows how I got to the end result.

Unfortunately, this isn't enough. I almost always need to communicate the results to others who were not present. What is more, I need to document the results so that we all have something to refer to in a couple of weeks when conversations start sounding like, "But we agreed . . ." and "That's not what we decided!"

Fortunately, with the meeting over, I can now retrieve my laptop and MindManager (are you seeing Linus with his blanket here?) and get these meeting minutes organized in a map. If my map is going to capture the flavor of the discussion, however, I need to be able to segregate, relate, and group topics on my MindManager map in the same way that I did it on the flip-chart or whiteboard. In this chapter, I tell you how.

Corralling Topics with Borders

Figure 6-1 shows a completed map of a project status meeting. Even though many of the topics are hidden, the map is still fairly complex and the fact that the project manager is facing some serious problems is not immediately apparent. (This time, I made sure I had MindManager available at the *start* of the meeting!)

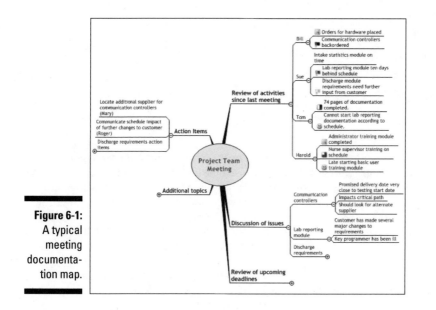

Figure 6-1:
A typical meeting documentation map.

Bill has reported a problem with the delivery schedule of some critical hardware, while Sue has indicated that the programming of one of the software modules is seriously behind schedule. I want to emphasize that there are two distinct problems here and to visually tie the problem identification (under the topic "Review of activities since last meeting") with its associated discussion and resulting action item.

I begin by drawing a border around either a single topic or a related group of topics, which I explain here:

1. **Right-click the topic you want to emphasize. Choose Insert Object⇨ Boundary.**

MindManager confirms your selection (see Figure 6-1). If the topic has subtopics, MindManager automatically selects the subtopics as well.

MindManager confirms your mouse click on a map object containing text or an image (a *topic*) by drawing a blue border around it. If it is not the object you intended, just adjust your mouse pointer and click again.

2. Right-click the border and choose Format Boundary . . .

The dialog box shown in Figure 6-2 appears.

If you don't see a Format Boundary option, it probably means that MindManager did not recognize that you were pointing at the border (MindManager isn't particularly smart). Adjust your mouse pointer just a little bit and right-click again.

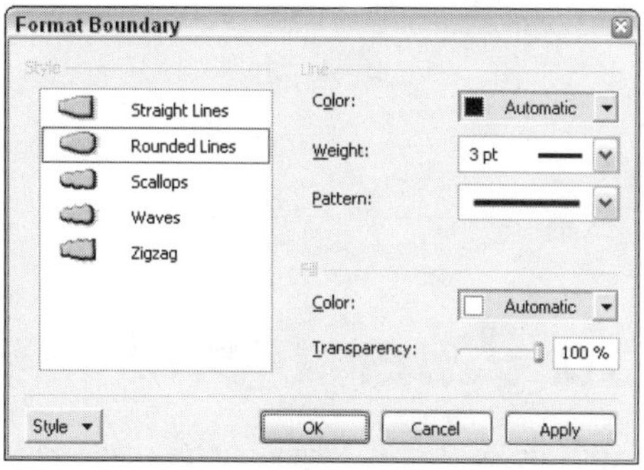

Figure 6-2:
Adjust the
appearance
of your
boundary
using this
dialog box.

3. Choose the characteristics and fill color you want for your border, and then click OK.

MindManager redraws your border according to your specifications.

I've used different border styles in Figure 6-3 to distinguish the two key problems in my meeting report because I want to print this map and my printer cannot print colors. If I were planning to send this map in an e-mail, I would probably use colors rather than border styles, because this is even more distinctive.

If I wanted to include some additional text inside the border area to further describe this grouping, I would add something called *floating text*. I tell you about this in Chapter 7.

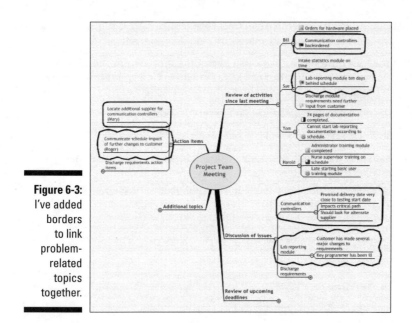

Figure 6-3:
I've added
borders
to link
problem-
related
topics
together.

Pointing the Way to Other Topics

Anyone who looks at my map now probably looks at the enclosed topics first. Because the word "controller" appears in each group enclosed in a curved box, people quickly understand that these topics are related. I want the user, however, to also know that the schedule problems of both Tom and Harold are actually related to Sue's problem, rather than being completely different issues. I do this by showing a pointer between Sue's lab reporting problem and the late starts on tasks reported by Tom and Harold.

Creating and adjusting a pointer

MindManager calls pointers "relationships" to emphasize that there is some kind of logical association between two topics. The problem is, this makes it rather difficult to know whether I am talking about the nature of the relationship itself or about its representation on a map. I've solved the problem in this book by using the word "pointer" for the graphical representation. Just remember, though, that if you are checking out the MindManager help file you need to look for the keyword "relationship".

1. **Click the Insert Relationship button on the Insert toolbar.**

   MindManager adds the insert relationship icon above and to the right of the mouse arrow. The red circle with the slash through it means that the cursor is not currently pointing to a valid topic that can be the start of the relationship (the *originating* topic).

2. **Point the cursor to the desired originating topic.**

   The red circle with the slash through it is replaced by a small plus sign, and MindManager displays a tan border around the topic.

3. **Click the topic.**

   You have now defined the originating topic. The cursor plus sign is replaced by the red circle with a slash through it, telling you that you cannot relate a topic to itself. If you move the cursor away from the topic, MindManager displays a dotted line between the cursor and the originating topic.

4. **Point the cursor to the destination topic.**

   MindManager draws a tan border around the topic and the red circle with a slash is replaced by a plus sign. The dotted line that was following your cursor now acquires an arrow that points to the destination topic rather than to the cursor.

5. **Click the destination topic.**

   MindManager returns the cursor display to its normal form and displays and selects the completed relationship arrow.

   MindManager tells you that you have selected a pointer by displaying red dots at the origin and destination of the pointer, and it attaches *adjustment handles* (short blue lines ending with small yellow lozenges) to these red dots. If you change your mind about the originating or destination topic, drag the red dot at the start of the pointer to a different originating topic or drag the red dot at the end of the pointer to a different destination topic. If you don't want the relationship at all, right-click the pointer and select Delete Relationship.

6. **Click and drag the small yellow lozenges until the shape and location of the pointer suits you.**

Adding words to the pointer

The pointer may be all that you need to help your reader recognize an important relationship. Sometimes, however, you may not be sure that your boss is astute enough to see the obvious, and one or two explanatory words may add a little insurance. Add a comment to your pointer this way:

1. **Right-click the desired pointer.**

   MindManager confirms the selection of the pointer.

2. **Select Insert Callout.**

   A small oval appears approximately at the midpoint of the pointer with the word "Callout."

3. **Type the words you want.**

   MindManager replaces the word "callout" with the words you type.

   If you want to change the text that you previously attached to a pointer, right-click the text (*not* the pointer!) and select Edit Text.

4. **Drag the callout to the desired position on the pointer.**

   Look at the final appearance of the pointers on my meeting map in Figure 6-4.

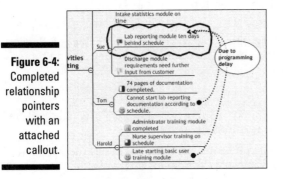

Figure 6-4: Completed relationship pointers with an attached callout.

Making fancy pointers

If you have a lot of pointers in your map, they can become more confusing than helpful. You can change the color and style of your pointers so that they can be more easily distinguished by following these steps:

1. **Right-click the pointer you want to change.**

   The adjustment handles appear on the selected pointer.

2. **Select Format Relationship.**

   The dialog box shown in Figure 6-5 appears.

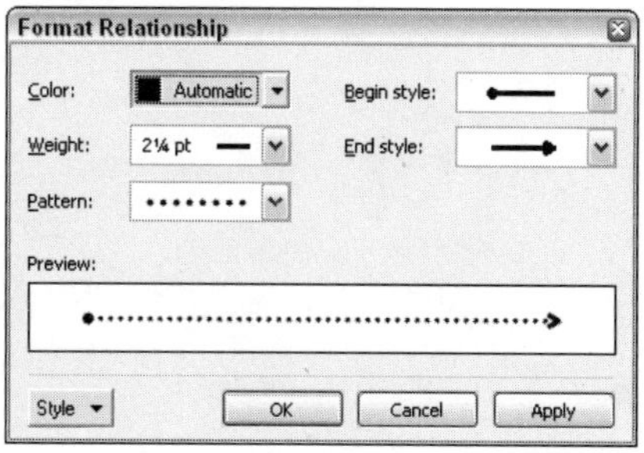

Figure 6-5:
The Format
Relationship
dialog box
lets you
customize
the
appearance
of your
pointers.

Format Relationship	⊠
Color:	■ Automatic ▼	Begin style:	●─── ▼
Weight:	2¼ pt ── ▼	End style:	───➤ ▼
Pattern:	••••••• ▼		

Preview:

●••••••••••••••••••••••••••••••••••➤

Style ▼   [OK]   [Cancel]   [Apply]

3. **Adjust the parameters until the pointer appears in the preview box as you would like it to appear; then click OK.**

   MindManager redraws the pointer on your map to conform to your specifications.

Pointers are not limited just to topics. They can originate or terminate in any MindManager object such as callouts and floating text. I tell you more about this in the next chapter.

Chapter 7

Getting Wordy

I wasn't particularly well organized in college. My English professor always told me on Monday the theme of the weekly paper that had to be turned in on Friday, but it was invariably Thursday night (sometimes distressingly late on Thursday night) that I would finally sit down to begin writing.

The blank sheet of paper in the typewriter was always so intimidating that I would just start typing topic sentences. Soon, the ideas were so jumbled that I would rip the page out of the typewriter and start drawing arrows here and there and scribbling brief notes around the edges. Somehow this became a makeshift outline of my paper (it was always too late to spend enough time to properly finish it before I began typing my "final" draft). Invariably, half way through, I would realize I had left something out or that there was really a much better way to organize after all. Rarely, I would be dissatisfied enough to trash the draft I was working on and start over; usually I would convince myself that it was good enough and that a little more sleep was more important.

It's a brand new writing world with MindManager. I can freely generate ideas in Brainstorming mode (see Chapter 8) and then organize those ideas into topics and subtopics (see Chapter 2). In this chapter, I tell you how to attach explanatory notes to each topic and begin the actual writing of the text that corresponds to those topics. If you change your mind about the organization, you just move the topic to its new place on the map, and the notes and text move right along with it. When you are satisfied, a couple of mouse clicks export everything to Word (I tell you more about this in Chapter 18), where you can do any last bit of necessary polishing.

When I use the word *topic* (or sometimes *subtopic* or *fixed topic*), I am refer-ring to a text object that is part of a topic tree. A *callout topic* is a comment that is attached to a topic, while a *floating topic* is a comment that is not attached to any topic. If you are interested in the reasons why the new ver-sion of MindManager has caused these naming difficulties, see "Objects and Things" in Chapter 2.

When the Topic Just Doesn't Say It All

I spend a lot of time trying to find just the right words for a topic so that the subject it refers to will be as clear as possible. Given that I usually don't want to put more than five or six words on the topic line, this is sometimes a chal-lenge. I solve this problem by using *callout topics* that are attached to a topic to provide additional space for notations. To create a callout, follow these steps:

1. **Right-click the topic to which you want to attach a callout and select Insert Object⇨Callout.**

   MindManager confirms the selection of the topic and attaches a callout object containing the word "Callout."

2. **Type the words you want to appear in the callout.**

   Your typing replaces the word "Callout."

3. **Right-click the callout and select Shape and Color . . .**

   MindManager displays the dialog box shown in Figure 7-1.

If MindManager objects to the spelling of one or more words in your callout (indicated by a wavy red underline), be sure you right-click the callout shape itself rather than the text. If you right-click the text, you will get a list of spelling suggestions rather than the topic context menu. Should this happen, just ignore the displayed menu and right-click the callout shape.

4. **Choose the shape and colors you want for your callout and click OK.**

   MindManager redraws your callout to conform to your specifications.

You can use your own custom image if you have prepared one. It needs to be some kind of border with the center color formatted as transparent if it is to work properly. If you use a custom image, MindManager will not be able to show a connecting line between your callout and the topic it is attached to.

In those relatively rare cases where I need to make more extensive com-ments, I can create subtopics to make my comments more easily read. Just click on the callout and press Insert. You can build as complex a topic tree as you want, just as if the Callout Topic were the Central Topic on a new map. Refer back to Chapters 2 and 3 if you need to review any details.

Figure 7-2 shows the map I used to build this chapter. I've built a callout with subtopics as I describe in this section.

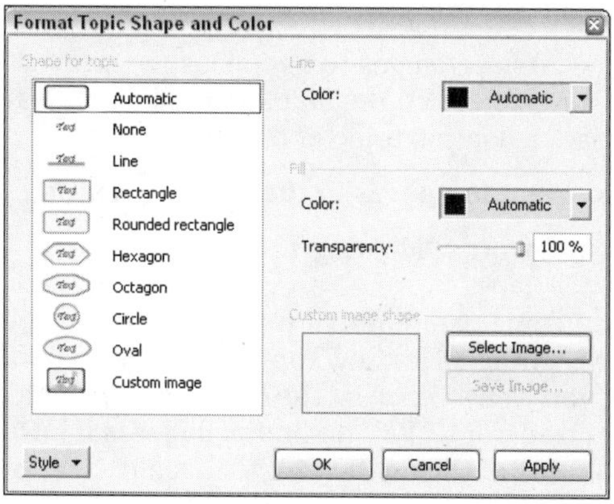

Figure 7-1:
The dialog box you use to format the shape and color of your callout.

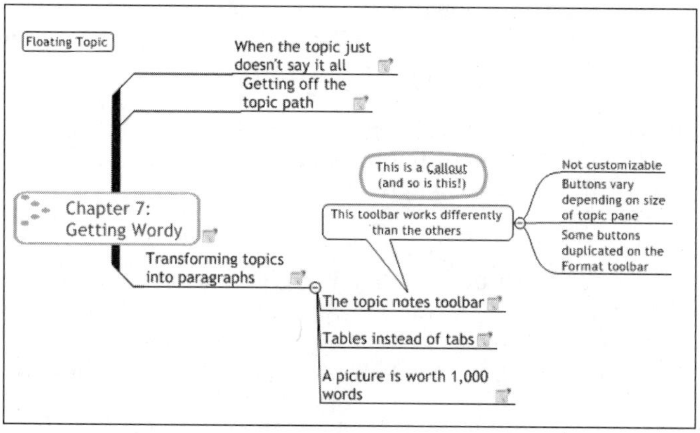

Figure 7-2:
A callout with associated subtopics.

Getting Off the Topic Path

I sometimes want to add a few words to my map that aren't associated with a single topic but rather with a group of topics or even the entire map. I do this by creating a floating topic:

1. **Right-click any blank place on your map and select Insert Floating Topic.**

   MindManager changes the mouse cursor to Floating Topic insert mode.

2. **Click the location on the map where you want your floating topic to appear.**

   MindManager draws a rounded rectangle containing the words "Floating Topic" at the point you clicked.

   The plus sign on the cursor changes to a red slashed circle whenever you point to an existing object on the map. MindManager is telling you that you cannot create a floating topic at that point.

3. **Type the words you want to appear in the floating text.**

   Your words replace the words "Floating Topic."

You can drag the Floating Topic to a different point on your map, but be a little careful. Anytime you drag a Floating Topic near any Fixed Topic, MindManager will think you want to covert the Floating Topic into a subtopic attached to that nearby Fixed Topic. When MindManager is in Attach mode, it displays a red shadow outline of the floating topic box any time your cursor points to a valid attachment point.

This can be a useful functionality — but only if it is what you want to do! To turn off Attach mode, hold down the Shift key while you are positioning the Floating Topic.

If, despite your care, MindManager captures your Floating Topic and converts it into a subtopic, you can turn it back into a Floating Topic again by clicking the newly created subtopic and then selecting Edit⇨Convert To Floating Topic.

One of the powerful features of MindManager is its *Central Topic* model that shows the relationship of all the topics and subtopics to this central theme. However, if there are complex relationships between topics, the Central Topic model may not be the best way to present my ideas. If I want to represent a series of processes that proceed in a cycle, with the last process feeding back into the first one, Floating Topics without any main topics at all are a better choice. See Figure 7-3 for an example.

I attach subtopics to my Floating Topic by clicking on the Floating Topic and then pressing Insert. I can build as complex a topic tree as I want, just as if the Callout Topic were the Central Topic on a new map. Refer back to Chapters 2 and 3 for further details.

Figure 7-3:
Example of
floating
topics used
to show
cyclical
process
flow (project
manage-
ment
processes
as defined
by the
Project
Manage-
ment
Institute).

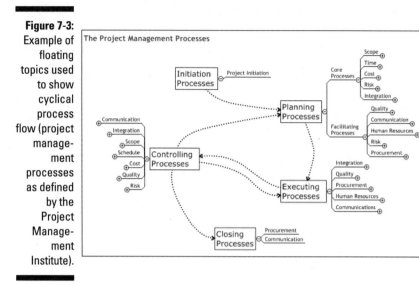

Transforming Topics into Paragraphs

I have worked long and hard on my map, the organization is exactly to my liking, and I've added all the comments that will be useful — now I need to get down to the work of putting some real meat on the bones of my map structure. I right-click the topic I want to write about and select Insert Notes. (If the topic already contains notes, I select Edit Notes.)

MindManager opens the Topic Notes panel (if it wasn't already open), copies the topic description onto the top line, and is ready for me to begin typing.

The Topic Notes toolbar

The Topic Notes toolbar that appears at the top of the panel is, in most respects, like any other toolbar. Unfortunately, the Let's Do Something Really Snazzy geeks at Mindjet got out of their cages for a while, so there are a few things that really confused me:

✔ There is a long and a short version of the toolbar (see figure 7-4 and 7-5). If you click the left-most button you toggle from one version to the other.

✔ Clicking on the "A" button on the short toolbar (the second button from the left) brings up a dialog box that gives you access to all the additional button functions on the long version.

✔ You can't customize either of these toolbars.

✔ Some of the buttons on the long version appear to be duplicated on the Formatting toolbar at the lower left-hand corner of the screen. Don't be fooled! The buttons on the Formatting toolbar apply to the text of the currently selected topic. Use the formatting buttons on the Topic Notes toolbar to modify formatting in your text notes.

Figure 7-4:
Short version of the Topic Notes toolbar.

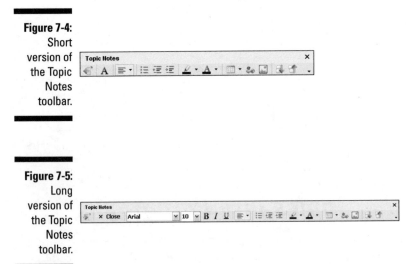

Figure 7-5:
Long version of the Topic Notes toolbar.

All of the buttons on the left side of the toolbar through Font Color function in the same way as those in Microsoft Word. MindManager does not, however, give you any options with regard to the shape and position of bullets, nor can you define tab stops.

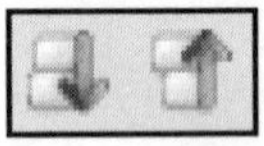

The right-most two buttons allow you to scroll forward and backward through the successive topic notes on your map. A gray rectangle highlights the topic on the map whose notes are currently displayed in the Topic Notes panel.

Hyperlinks can be inserted into Topic Notes just as they are inserted into your map. See Chapter 12 for details.

I discuss the Table button in the next section and the Insert Image button in the last section of this chapter.

Tables instead of tabs

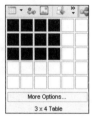

The Table button allows you to insert a table into your topic note, and in this respect it functions just like the corresponding button in Word.

Tables serve an additional function in MindManager. You can't control the setting of tabs in the Topic Notes panel, and the Tab key only inserts a fixed number of spaces. If you need to align columns or in any other way control the appearance of your text other than relative to the left margin, you must type your text into a properly formatted table. Follow these steps to insert and format a table:

1. **Click the position in the Topic Notes pane where you want the table to be inserted.**

   MindManager displays a flashing vertical line and the point where the table will be placed.

2. **Click the Table button, then click the square representing the desired number of rows and columns.**

   A table corresponding to your specification is inserted at the point selected in step 1. Figure 7-6 shows the specification of a table containing four columns and three rows just before the second mouse click.

Figure 7-6:
Selection graphic showing the size of the table to be inserted.

If you need a table larger than 5 rows by 6 columns, click More Options and enter the exact number of rows and columns desired. Once the table has been created, you can add or delete rows or columns as necessary by clicking the Table button again and selecting the appropriate option from the drop-down menu.

Tables your way

MindManager creates your table initially with thin lines marking the outline of all cells in the table. You can, however, eliminate these lines entirely or substitute any variation in borders (and the thickness of those borders) as you wish.

If you want to change the borders on only a portion of the cells in the table, you must first select the cells to work with. Point your mouse to the upper-left cell that you want to change, click and hold the mouse button and drag to the lower-right cell that you want to change. MindManager will temporarily change the background color to black to show that those cells are selected. If you want to apply changes to the entire table, click any cell in the table. Once you have made your selection, click the Table button and select Format Table.

MindManager displays the Format Table dialog box (Figure 7-7). As soon as you change any setting in this dialog box, MindManager changes the button text at the bottom of the dialog box from Cancel to Close.

If you want to change the parameters for the entire table, click the Table radio button. If you selected a group of cells before starting the format process, MindManager will automatically select the Cells radio button.

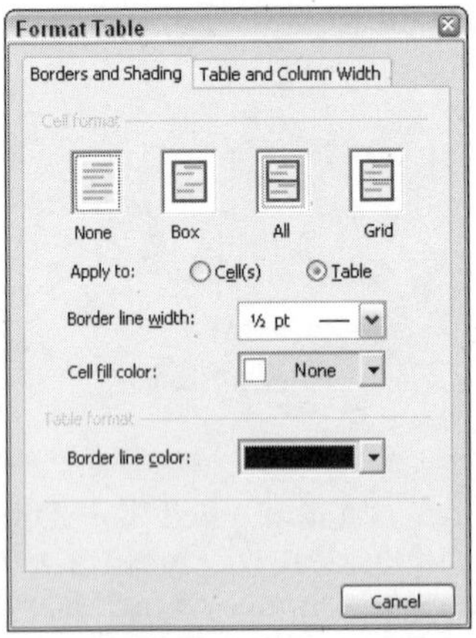

Figure 7-7:
The Format
Table
dialog box
(Borders
and Shading
tab).

The cell format settings and the border line width work together as shown in Table 7-1.

Table 7-1	Defining Table Borders	
Cell Format	*Outside Border*	*Inner Border*
None	None	None
Box	Border line width	None
All	Border line width	Border line width
Grid	Border line width	1/2 point

MindManager will still show the outline of your table cells with a dotted line even if you have turned off solid borders. If you don't want even the table gridlines to be visible, click the Format Table close button, then click the Table icon and select Hide Gridlines.

The cell fill color and border line color settings apply to either your selected cells or to the entire table depending upon the Apply To setting.

The Table and Column Width tab (Figure 7-8) is used only if you plan to export your topic notes to a Web page (see Chapter 17 for details). Use the *Assign a fixed width setting* if you know the screen resolution at which your Web page will be viewed (or you don't care if the viewer has to scroll to see your entire table). Use the *Adjust table width setting* if you want the viewer's browser to adjust the width of your table so it always fits in the viewing area.

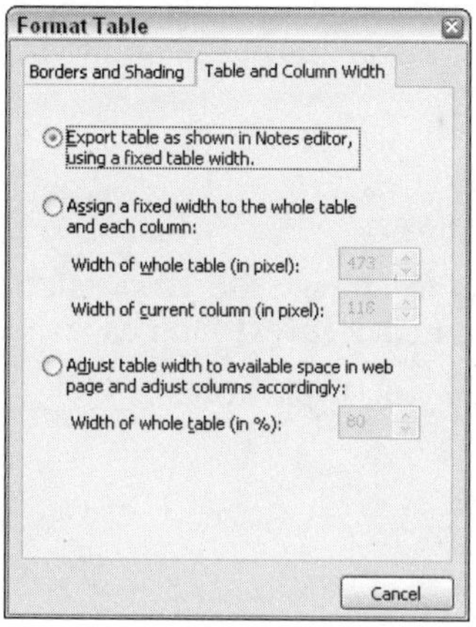

Figure 7-8:
The Format Table dialog box (Table and Column Width tab).

Format Table

Borders and Shading | Table and Column Width

⦿ Export table as shown in Notes editor, using a fixed table width.

◯ Assign a fixed width to the whole table and each column:

Width of whole table (in pixel): 473

Width of current column (in pixel): 118

◯ Adjust table width to available space in web page and adjust columns accordingly:

Width of whole table (in %): 80

Cancel

In order to properly position text or images, you may need to combine some (but not all) columns on one or more rows, or to combine some (but not all) rows in one column. You can do this as follows:

1. **Select the cells to be combined in the table.**

   The selected cells are shown with a black background.

   You can only select cells that are contiguous and make up a rectangular area for merging.

2. **Click the Table button, then select Merge Cells.**

   The selected cells are merged into one cell. Any contents of the cells are also merged together.

A picture is worth a thousand words

All of the images and icons available in MindManager, as well as your own images, can be included in the topic notes. If you need to position the image somewhere other than at the left margin, or if you want to add text to the right or left of the image, you should first create a table and then insert the image into the proper cell of that table. Refer to the prior section, "Tables Instead of Tabs," for details on how to do this. Follow these steps to insert and format an image:

1. **Click the point in your topic notes where you wish the image to be inserted.**

   MindManager displays a flashing vertical line at the point you have selected.

2. **Click the Image button.**

   The Insert Image dialog box is displayed.

3. **Browse to the location containing the image file you wish to insert, click the image filename, and then click Insert Image.**

   The selected image is inserted into your topic notes.

Chapter 8

Catapulting Your Creativity

*T*he telephone rings just as I am getting ready to leave for lunch. It is my boss. "Paul just called and told me that he has to leave on an urgent business trip immediately and won't be able to attend the dinner tonight," he says, sounding like the anchor on the six o'clock news.

"That's too bad," I reply cautiously, not really sure what this has to do with me.

"He was going to do a 20-minute talk by way of introducing the Chairman of the Board," continues my boss, "and I need you to step in for him tonight."

"Uh, what was Paul going to talk about?" I inquire with a sinking feeling in the pit of my stomach.

"Darned if I know. But the Chairman is going to be talking about international trade issues, so something on the Euro would be good. Thanks for taking this on."

A click lets me know the conversation is over. Deciding that maybe I'm not so interested in lunch after all, I start up MindManager and begin a new map. The first thing that MindManager demands from me is the title of my Central Topic (well, it doesn't actually *demand* anything, but "Central Topic" isn't exactly inspiring for a dinner presentation).

I type in "Euro", hoping that this will lead to some kind of exciting title for my talk. When nothing brilliant shows up, I try leaning back in my chair, musing over possibilities (intermixed with not so kind thoughts about my boss), and getting a cup of coffee. One of these techniques works, somehow, and I decide that something about the connection between the new shared currency and the current political trends in Europe might be of some interest.

It's a small step forward, but now I'm really stuck and face-to-face with one very unavoidable fact about MindManager: It is a fabulous tool for organizing and extending ideas, but unfortunately, you have to have something to organize first! What I need now is a tool to just capture ideas without bothering me about organization and spelling.

Fortunately, MindManager is still the right tool. I have an option to tell MindManager to get completely out of my way and just capture my ideas as I engage my creativity. I can invite others to join the process and contribute their ideas as well. When the creative flow subsides, I use MindManager to edit and organize my (our) ideas and then integrate them into my map. In this chapter, I tell you how.

Filling the Idea Pipeline

The act of creation is one of the most marvelous characteristics that make human beings unique among all the living creatures on earth. First, there is nothing; then somehow, out of the recesses of our consciousness, something appears and is molded into something quite new and different. Man has been seeking ways to facilitate this process for millennia.

Walt Disney invented one such technique in the late 1920s when he created the first animated cartoon film, "Steamboat Willie" (the first appearance of Mickey Mouse). He called it *storyboarding*. He simply drew a series of sketches that he pinned to a *board* to show the essence of the *story* that he wanted to tell. When he showed this to his co-workers, they of course began to draw their own sketches and pin them where they thought they should go (and unceremoniously taking down some of the boss' sketches in the process). The end result was that the entire group collectively evolved the story and made entertainment history. This technique continues to be one of the mainstays in film and television to this very day.

The storyboarding idea evolved over the years into a process called *brainstorming,* where a group of people (or an individual) seeks to generate lots of ideas in a short period of time, free of comment or criticism. When it is done well, the process generates a *storm* of new ideas with everyone shouting out their ideas at the same time.

Modes ▼ You can enter Brainstorm mode in MindManager at any time. Simply click Modes (far right-hand side of the workspace) and select Brainstorm. MindManager shifts the map display so that Floating Topics can be automatically inserted at the bottom of the map and displays two entry fields at the top (see Figure 8-1).

Guidelines for Effective Brainstorming

Encouraging and supporting the creative process is a challenging task. Creativity is a bit like a shy child. She wants to play, but is very afraid of the mean old bullies, Editing, Analyzing, and Criticizing. At their first appearance, she runs away and hides, and can be coaxed to return only with great difficulty.

If you are moderating a brainstorming session, explain these guidelines to everyone at the start of the session and then do your best to adhere to them. If you are privately brainstorming, keep yourself in line as well!

✔ **Do not allow criticism or debate.** Remember that many ideas sound foolish at first. Criticism is the censor that kills creativity and debate can get you off on tangents. There is time later on for evaluation.

✔ **Let your imagination soar.** Make the meeting a safe place to be silly. Remember that creativity is fostered by humor and relaxation. If it is relevant, use props to encourage participants to assume different "personalities." Above all, discourage commentary that is overly serious or derisive.

✔ **Generate a large number of ideas.** The truly great ideas, like beautiful diamonds, are usually hidden in a lot of fairly useless material. The more ideas you generate, the greater the chances of finding the "gem." Set aside a fixed amount of time for brainstorming; then use all the time allotted. The flow of ideas is not like a water spigot but rather like a geyser that spurts, subsides, and spurts again. Be patient with silence and wait for the next eruption.

✔ **Encourage mutation and combination.** An initial idea might not be worth much, but a small variation might be. Two or three very silly ideas might combine to suggest something very useful. Restate the idea in its negative form (instead of "it must not take longer than three seconds", consider "it must take at least three seconds") and see if that suggests anything new.

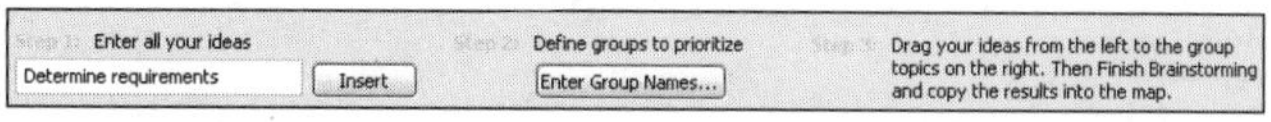

Figure 8-1:
Special fields displayed in Brainstorm mode.

Click the Entry field under the heading Step 1 and begin typing your idea just as it occurs to you. Don't worry about grammar, spelling, or anything other than just getting the idea out of your head and onto the screen. When you are finished, either click Insert or just press Enter. You can begin typing the next idea immediately.

You can, of course, just repeatedly create new Floating Topics yourself (see Chapter 7) without entering Brainstorm mode, but this has several disadvantages:

- ✔ You must select the point in the map where the Floating Topic is to be inserted, and create it with a click. (In Brainstorm mode, MindManager positions and inserts the topic automatically.)

- ✔ MindManager informs you of any misspelled words with a red wavy line. You are tempted to fix the spelling error immediately and this disturbs the creative flow of ideas. (MindManager does not mark spelling errors in the Brainstorm idea entry field.)

- ✔ If you start to type something and decide it doesn't make sense, you are tempted to start fixing the topic you have created. (In Brainstorm mode, you just press Enter and start over.)

- ✔ Brainstorm mode sets up an easy rhythm — enter an idea, then press Enter; enter an idea, then press Enter — that just encourages everyone to just call out ideas and keep going.

Figure 8-2 shows my map after I have created several topics. Notice that they are in no particular order.

Figure 8-2: Brainstorm mode after entering several ideas.

Organizing Your Ideas

After the flow of ideas has subsided, I look at the list of topics I have generated. As I scan through them, I may see several entries that no longer make sense or were mistakes. I select these and press Delete. I may see two entries that are slightly different statements of the same idea. I edit one to better state the idea and delete the other one.

The ideas that are left are probably the ones that I want to integrate into my map. I begin by defining the group headings that I want to use:

1. **Click the box that says "Enter Group Names . . ."**

   MindManager displays the dialog box shown in Figure 8-3.

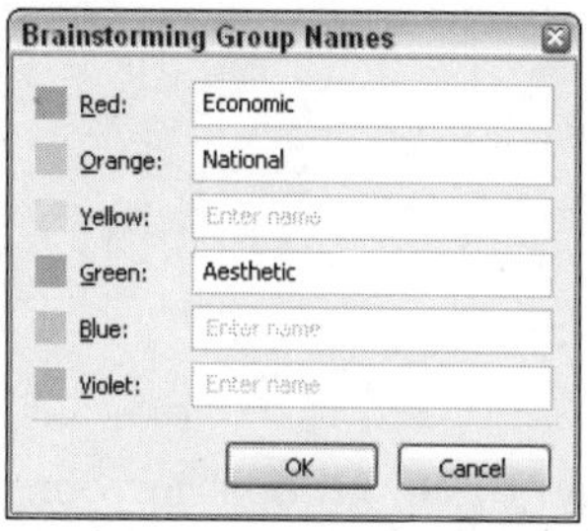

Figure 8-3:
Dialog box used to specify group names in Brainstorm mode.

Brainstorming Group Names

Red:	Economic	
Orange:	National	
Yellow:	Enter name	
Green:	Aesthetic	
Blue:	Enter name	
Violet:	Enter name	

[OK]   [Cancel]

2. **Type in the names of the headings you want next to the colors you want to use and click OK.**

   A Floating Topic called "Groups" is created in your map and the headings you define are attached as subtopics.

TIP You can skip a color that you don't want to use (see Figure 8-3), but you are limited to six headings and to the colors shown at this point. After you exit Brainstorm mode, you can create more headings and change the colors. You can change the names of your groups at any time or even eliminate them by simply deleting them in the Brainstorming Group Names dialog box.

Attach your ideas to the proper group heading by clicking the topic and dragging it to the appropriate heading. You can create subtopics or rearrange your brainstorming topics at any time just as you can on your main map. See Figure 8-4.

You exit Brainstorm mode by clicking Finish Brainstorming in the upper-right corner of the workspace. Click and drag the finished brainstorming group to the desired place on your map. MindManager attaches it to the point you specify.

TIP You can't drag the brainstorming group to a new place in your map until you quit Brainstorm mode.

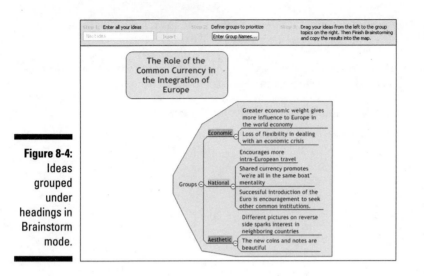

Figure 8-4:
Ideas
grouped
under
headings in
Brainstorm
mode.

You probably don't want the MindManager topic "groups" in your map. To eliminate this without disturbing your topics, right-click the "groups" topic and select Remove Topic. Your group headings now become the topics on your map. See Figure 8-5.

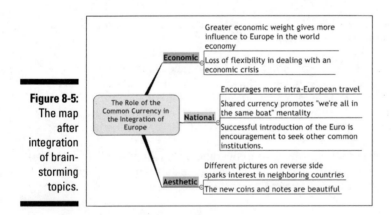

Figure 8-5:
The map
after
integration
of brain-
storming
topics.

Part III
Maps and Buried Treasure

When Leroy's brainstorming session deteriorated to stick figures, he decided to give MindManager a try.

In this part . . .

Want to know a secret? MindManager has buried treasure hidden inside! In this part, you find out how to use the buried treasure to help enhance your maps beyond your wildest dreams. Wizards appear, size matters, and plans are built. Enrich your map-making toolbox with a visit to MindManager's hidden cave of wonders. The secrets are just ahead.

Chapter 9

Putting Plans in Place

· ·

In This Chapter

▶ Recording planning information in the Task Info panel

▶ Using Map Markers to identify and differentiate tasks

▶ Filtering topics on your map to show only tasks you are interested in

▶ Tracking progress and completion of tasks

· ·

*O*ne of the most frustrating moments in my entire professional career occurred when a proposal, in which my staff and I had invested a long, 80-hour week, was immediately rejected because it was two days late and we had never submitted a deadline extension request form. What made it so frustrating, you see, was that when we decided to prepare and submit the proposal, we knew we would need extra time. I clearly remembered assigning Jim the responsibility of preparing and mailing the request for additional time, but he equally clearly remembered that I had said I would do it. The net result was that the task didn't get handled and a lot of time, money, and effort went out the window.

My initial response was to say that team meetings are just a waste of time (I'm not known for being particularly rational when I'm upset). Fortunately, after the pain had subsided a bit, I saw again the many ways in which team meetings are valuable. We all sit around the table and talk about what we are currently working on, the problems we are trying to deal with, and what our plans are for the coming week. We mix that with goodly measures of coffee and doughnuts, and leaven it all with a little side conversation about the game last Sunday and how, sometimes, teenagers are just impossible to live with. The result is an invaluable feeling of camaraderie and of everyone being on the same team.

Even so, what good does it do to identify action items if they don't get handled? After my proposal disaster, I became a real pain in the you-know-what about meeting minutes and action item follow-up. Since then, I have managed to avoid another catastrophe on the same scale as that one, but the cost has not been inconsequential. These are some of the problems I have run into:

✔ **Who will prepare the minutes?** Doing them right takes a significant amount of time and I have rarely had the luxury of a team secretary. (This is a particularly difficult issue for me because doing them "right" usually equates to doing them myself!)

✔ **What was really said and agreed to?** I'm a long ways away from being the best note taker in the world. I get too involved in the conversation and end up relying on my memory — always an unreliable source.

Furthermore, people react differently to the written word than the spoken one. Seeing things written down always inspires comments and corrections from the other participants. The result is that the review and revision of meeting minutes adds a lot more time and cost to the process.

✔ **What am I responsible for?** If my action items are intermixed with everyone else's over two or three pages, I may just miss one of my items. It is much better if everyone can get a list that has only their personal action items. But creating several lists out of the meeting minutes requires even more time.

MindManager offers a fantastic solution to these problems, although it is only available in the X5 Pro version. In this chapter, I tell you all about it.

There are two circumstances where a different solution might be appropriate:

✔ If your map consists almost exclusively of tasks that must be done in a particular order, save your map as a Microsoft Project plan (see Chapter 22) and use that software tool to polish and publish the work to be done.

✔ If you are interested in managing only your own action items, just link your items to Microsoft Outlook (see Chapter 21) and manage your tasks along with your mail.

The Task Info Pane

Effective planning with MindManager begins with a complete and accurate map of what was discussed and agreed to. If you are responsible for creating this initial map, bring your computer to the meeting. If possible, arrange for a projector or large monitor so that everyone can see your map as you create it. In this way, everyone participates in its creation (and, by implication, acknowledges its accuracy and completeness).

Figure 9-1 shows a map that has captured the key topics and action items from a team meeting of software application developers. There are several action items scattered throughout the map, and I want to now add planning information to each of these.

TIP

If you want to use the same basic structure for your meeting minutes, you can save time when you create your next meeting map by saving your basic structure as a template. (Using the example in Figure 9-1, I would always have the same four main topics with the team member names as subtopics of "Review activities since last meeting.") When you use this template to start a new map, your map is automatically loaded with your basic structure. You just start supplying the specifics. I tell you how to do this in Chapter 14.

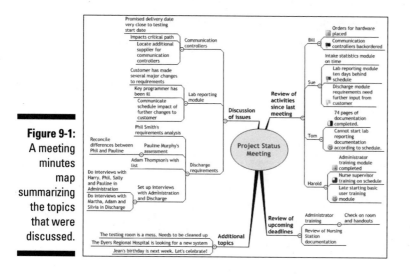

Figure 9-1:
A meeting minutes map summarizing the topics that were discussed.

To add planning information to a topic on your map, follow these steps:

1. **Click the Task Info tab at the far right-hand edge of your workspace.**

   The Task Info panel is displayed (as shown in Figure 9-2). All the fields on this panel are grayed out until you select a topic on your map.

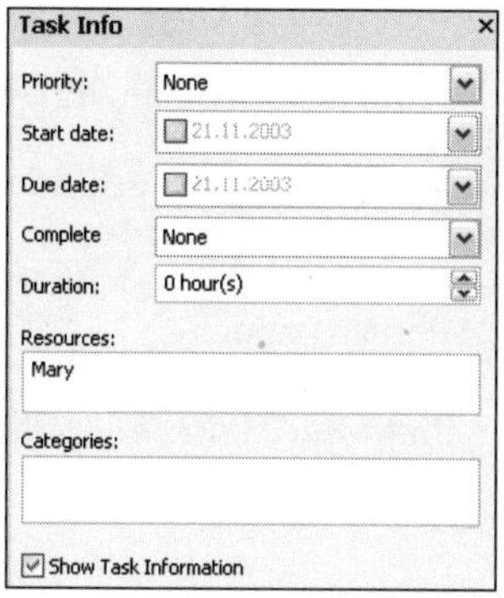

Figure 9-2:
The Task Info panel with Mary assigned responsibility for this action item.

2. **Click a topic on your map that you want to identify as a task or action item, and enter the name of the person responsible for this item in the Resources field. You can also complete any other fields for which you have the information.**

   If *Show Task Information* is checked, MindManager displays a small, tan box just below all topics on your map that have any task information, showing all the information you have entered. If you uncheck *Show Task Information*, nothing is displayed on your map.

3. **Repeat step 2 for each action item on your map.**

   Figure 9-3 shows my map after I have entered all the responsibility assignments.

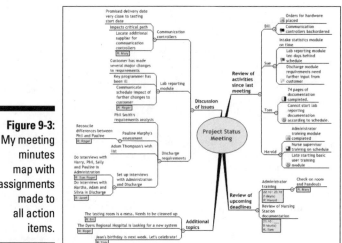

Figure 9-3:
My meeting minutes map with assignments made to all action items.

Defining Map Markers

Map Markers are used to add visual interest and non-verbal information to your map. If you want to review these topics in more detail, see Chapter 4. A second and very powerful function of Map Markers is to provide a basis for filtering topics to show (or, optionally, to hide) selected topics. I tell you more about filtering in Chapter 13. In this section, I tell you how to define and use Map Markers to facilitate planning in MindManager.

Figure 9-4 shows the default Map Markers that MindManager loads when you create a new map.

To enter or not to enter — that's the question

This innocent looking Task Info panel can be a lot harder to use than one would first imagine. I am usually satisfied with just identifying things that need to be done during the meeting and prefer not to disrupt the free flow of ideas by asking about a task's priority or how long it will take. In fact, the person just made responsible for this task often has not a clue until he or she has had time to think about it and, perhaps, check other information sources.

I am assuming that your map will be placed in a shared folder that all team members can access and update as necessary. Here are some guidelines for effectively using these fields:

✔ **Priority.** If a task is truly urgent, by all means assign a high priority during the team meeting. As a general rule, however, let the person responsible for the task assign the priority. Check it later and talk to your colleague if you disagree. To use this feature properly, assign a clear meaning to each priority level. I show you one possibility in the next part of this chapter. Although MindManager provides up to nine different priority symbols, I have never needed more than five or six.

✔ **Start Date.** Leave this field blank during the meeting. The person responsible for the task should fill this in when he or she actually begins work on the task.

✔ **Due Date.** Enter a date here if you know of a specific deadline. Otherwise, don't get distracted by the question during your meeting. Let the person responsible for the

item enter a projected completion date later and talk to that person if you have a different opinion.

✔ **Complete.** The person responsible for the task fills this in. MindManager lets you specify progress down to the nearest percentage point. If percent complete actually means something ("I'm 47 percent finished with a task to write and mail 100 letters" presumably means that you have completed and mailed 47 letters), use this capability. In most cases, however, it is sufficient to simply leave it at 0 percent until it's completed, and then change it to 100 percent.

✔ **Duration.** Let the person responsible for the action item complete this field. If the estimate is a bit generous, talk to that person later about an adjustment.

✔ **Resources.** Enter the name of the person responsible for the item here. MindManager will let you enter as many names as you want, but don't do it! Remember that if more than one person is made responsible for a task, no one is responsible for it. Attach other topics to this task instead and make one person responsible for each "assistance" topic. On the other hand, do enter any non-human resources that will be required such as equipment, supplies, and meeting room reservations.

✔ **Categories.** This is a free-form field that you can use for any other task management information such as the type of work (writing, telephoning, and so on).

 If you can't see the Map Marker pane, click the Map Markers tab at the far right-hand side of your workspace. To see all the icons, click the plus sign next to each category heading.

Figure 9-4:
The default
Map Marker
groups.

MindManager gives you almost unlimited flexibility in defining the meaning of icons and grouping them in any way you like (see Table 9-1). Define a different icon for each person on your team and group all of them under their own group name (for example, "Resources").

Table 9-1	Customizing Your Map Markers
To Do This	*Follow These Steps*
Delete the definition of a single icon.	1. **Right-click the icon.** 2. **Select Delete.** There is no warning message when you delete the group definition of a single icon.
Delete the definition of an icon group.	1. **Right-click the group.** 2. **Select Delete.** MindManager displays a query dialog box asking if you are sure you want to delete the whole group. Click Yes unless you made a mistake. The definitions of all icons in that group are also deleted.

To Do This	Follow These Steps
Rename an icon group or icon definition.	1. **Right-click the group name or the icon.** 2. **Select Rename.** 3. **Type the desired new name.**
Create a new icon group name.	1. **Click *Add new icon group* at the top of the Map Marker pane.** 2. **Type the name you want this group to have.** Your new group appears in alphabetical order in the Map Marker pane.
Assign an icon to a group.	1. **Click *Add new marker* at the top of the Map Marker pane.** The Map Marker Properties dialog box is displayed. 2. **Select the group that your icon is to belong to in the Group combo box.** A third combo box appears labeled *Icon.* 3. **Type the name you want to use for this icon in the *Name* field.** 4. **Select the icon you want from the icon combo box.** 5. **Click OK.** Your icon appears under the group heading with the name you specified.

MindManager will not allow you to define an icon in more than one group. If you want to use an icon in your own group that MindManager has already defined in the default Map Marker template, you must first delete MindManager's definition. You are not deleting the icon itself, only its association with an icon group.

You can also use fill colors or text colors to represent assignments, status, and other task planning characteristics. I have found, however, that colors are more useful to highlight groups of topics; therefore, I don't recommend using them for the planning characteristics.

If you have a larger organization, consider investing in one of the software packages that allows you to design your own icon packages. Chapter 14 tells you how to add your own icon collections to those already in MindManager.

Figure 9-5 shows my completed customization of Map Markers for my meeting map. This process took a bit of time, and I certainly don't want to have to repeat this process each time I want to create another meeting map. The solution is to save these Map Markers as a template by following these steps:

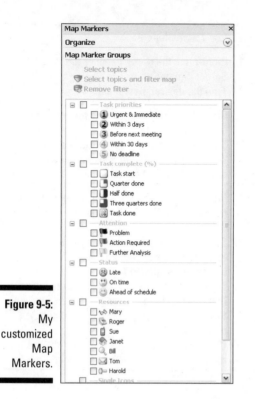

Figure 9-5:
My
customized
Map
Markers.

1. **Select Tools⇨Template Organizer from the menu bar.**

   MindManager displays the Template Organizer dialog box.

2. **Click the Map Marker Lists tab.**

   MindManager displays a list of all the currently defined Map Marker templates and displays the current definition of the first template.

3. **Click Add New Marker List.**

   A drop-down menu appears (see Figure 9-6).

4. **Select From Current Map.**

   Your Map Marker definitions are saved in the template file under the name of your current map.

5. **Click Rename and type the name you want to use for your definitions.**

   Your typing replaces the name of your current map.

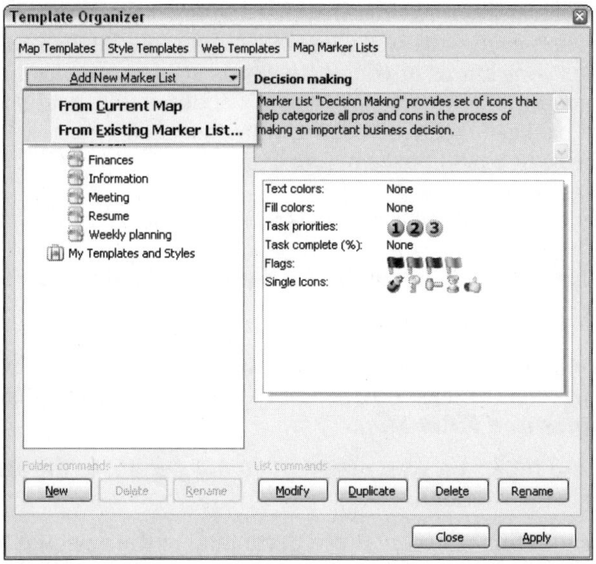

Figure 9-6:
I am ready
to add my
custom Map
Markers to
the template
directory.

All that is left to do is to associate the icon defined for each team member with the action items they are responsible for. Do this by clicking a topic that is an action item; then click the icon defined for the responsible person. That person's icon appears next to the description of the action item. Repeat for all action items on your map. Now, even without displaying the information from the Task Pane on your map, it is apparent who is responsible for what.

If you select several topics (by holding down the Ctrl key while clicking each topic), the icon you select will be added to each selected topic.

If this were the only benefit, I might question whether it was worth the effort — but there is more magic to come in the next section!

For any one topic, you are allowed to associate only one icon out of each group. If you click a different icon in the same group, it will replace the one you previously selected. You can, however, use an icon from as many of your groups as you want on any topic.

Working with Assignments

The meeting is nearly over, and people are starting to shift in their chairs and gather their papers and materials together.

"Before we go," you say in a clear and authoritative voice, "let's be sure we are all clear about what each of us is responsible for completing before our next meeting." As everyone stares at you and marvels at your organizational skills, you filter your map to show each participant's action items, get his or her agreement, and package the selected map into an e-mail. The work assignments are in the right e-mail boxes before everyone gets back to their desk.

This marvelous result is accomplished as follows:

1. **Click the Map Markers tab at the far right-hand side of your workspace.**

   The Map Marker pane is displayed.

2. **Click the checkbox next to the icon you have defined for the first team member who has at least one action item on your map; then click** *Select Topics and Filter Map.*

   All paths and topics on your map that do not pertain to the selected team member are hidden.

   If all paths and topics *except* those pertaining to the selected team member are displayed, click *(Show)* on the Map View toolbar and select *Show selected topics.*

3. **Ask the team member to verify his or her understanding of all the action items and to acknowledge his or her responsibility for its completion.**

   This may very well provoke further discussion!

4. **Click File⇨Send To⇨Mail Recipient (for review).**

   MindManager creates a mail message with the filtered map as an attachment.

5. **Add the recipient's name and any desired message; then click Send.**

   The mail message is dispatched. When the recipient opens the attachment, MindManager will display it in filtered form with just the recipient's tasks. He or she can, however, remove the filter and work with the full map as desired.

All team members must update the shared map with their information about how they will complete their assignments. Figure 9-7 shows the completion of one of Roger's tasks. When the action item is complete, any documents created can be linked to the map so that it becomes a complete reference for the team's activities.

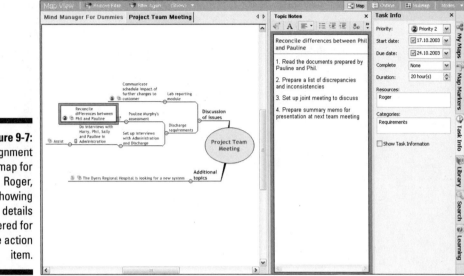

Figure 9-7:
Assignment
map for
Roger,
showing
details
entered for
one action
item.

Chapter 10

Big Maps for Big Ideas or Projects

● ●

In This Chapter

▶ Navigating around big maps

▶ Breaking apart big maps

▶ Pulling together big maps

▶ Sending big maps to others

● ●

MindManager maps have a way of becoming too big in a hurry. Defining "too big" is a bit of a problem, albeit a small one. You know when you've reached "too big." Your eyes strain to see all the topics. The map size percentage continues to decrease in an effort to keep the entire map on the screen. You get lost in one section of the map, knowing that you need to be somewhere else. You can't see the trees because the forest has overtaken you. Stop now if you are prone to anxiety attacks. There is a solution. Big maps can be tamed. How do you eat an elephant? That is a really dumb question. You should never want to eat an elephant. A big map may have hundreds of topics with numerous levels. I am going to use examples that have more than 800 topics and four levels.

Big maps can develop as one map that gets very large or as a combination of linked maps.

This chapter uses examples involving the Civil Air Patrol (CAP), which is the Auxiliary of the United States Air Force. The members of CAP are volunteers. CAP works well as an example because it mirrors the real world of business. Cross-functional teams are used, depending on the mission. There is an abundantly adequate bureaucracy. Rules and regulations are lurking around every corner. A clear, although plodding, pathway to advancement exists. Getting things done can sometimes be like mating elephants. Done at a high level, with lots of grunting and groaning, and taking two years to get results. The pay is pretty low, too. Sound familiar? Don't get me wrong — involvement in CAP is a very rewarding activity. Check out the CAP Web site at www.cap.gov. I am the Professional Development Officer for a CAP squadron. My job is to take the complexity of the organization and simplify it to help people progress. Therefore, my MindManager maps tend to be very large.

The following sections take you through the big map taming process.

Fixing Maps That Are Too Big for the Screen

A big map tends to hang over the edges of the screen. A little overhang isn't much of a problem. Chapter 2 is a good reference for some of the basics of map navigation. The vertical and horizontal screen scrollbars are the first tools to use on a big map. Pretty soon the scrollbars get worn out from overuse. The map can be reined in by adjusting the size. The size of the map is altered by changing the map size percentage. The margin art shows the map size percentage box. Click the selection arrow to drop down standard choices. Select the percent size you desire. The smaller the number, the smaller the map size. The 50 percent size is about all my bifocals can stand.

Don't forget to collapse items that don't need to be open. Use the + and - click points between topics and subtopics to open and close the levels in the map.

The map layout can also be useful in working with the almost-too-big map. I like to use the layout where all the topics are to the right of the central topic. The result is a map that climbs vertically like a rocket. To change the layout of the topics, first select the central topic, and then click Format⇨Topic Layout⇨Subtopics Layout. Choose a subtopic layout that balances your map around the central topic. A circular pattern works best.

You are going to use these simple taming methods until the map is just too much to handle. MindManager has a feature called Map Overview. Map Overview allows you to easily look at different portions of the map. Think of a satellite taking pictures of the earth.

Using Map Overview

The following steps show you how to use Map Overview to create a map that has a bit of bigness to it:

1. **Click the Map Overview icon on the toolbar.**

   The margin art shows you the toolbar button. The Map Overview bar appears on the map.

2. **Place your cursor over the Map Overview bar and the Map Overview window opens.**

   Figure 10-1 shows both the closed and opened Map Overview bar.

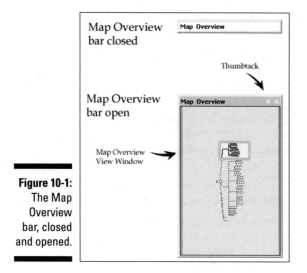

Figure 10-1:
The Map
Overview
bar, closed
and opened.

3. **Click on the thumbtack, as shown in Figure 10-1.**

   The thumbtack rotates to the vertical position. This little feature is cute, because the thumbtack keeps the Map Overview window open. The Map Overview window closes when you move your cursor off of the Map Overview bar if you don't click/stick the thumbtack. Click again to unstick the thumbtack. Figure 10-2 shows the Map Overview window on top of a MindManager map.

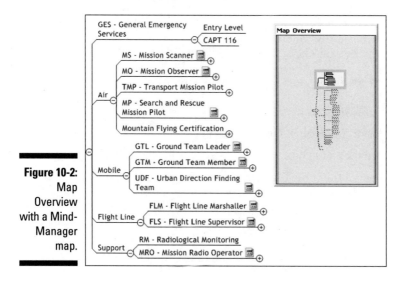

Figure 10-2:
Map
Overview
with a Mind-
Manager
map.

4. **Place your cursor near the Map Overview view window. (Refer to Figure 10-1.) Move the cursor around the view window.**

   Small arrows or a hand appear. The hand indicates that you can move the view window. Use the little arrows to adjust the size of the view window. Get back to the hand. Click and drag the window around on the MindManager map.

   The Map Overview shows the whole MindManager map. Any part of the map not under the view window is shaded. Move the view window over the shaded portions of the box. The MindManager map moves around as you move the window.

5. **Move the cursor near the map until an arrow appears. Click and drag the arrow and the view window size changes.**

   The view window size changes, but in reality the size of the map underneath also changes. For example, making the window larger decreases the map size. Making the window smaller increases the size of the underlying map.

The Map Overview view window can be very small if the map is very large. Change the size of the window by changing the size of the Map Overview box. Go to the edge of the box with the cursor. Click and drag the sizing arrows. The box gets bigger. The view window also gets bigger. Less map is visible, but it is easier to move the view window.

Cheap indexing with bookmarks

I can get lost in a big map. I start working in one area, and I want to go somewhere else. Hmm . . . Now where is it I need to go and how do I get there? Bookmarks help. Bookmarks are location holders in the map.

The following steps show you a way to use bookmarks to navigate in a big map:

1. **Select a topic in your map.**

2. **Select Insert⇨Bookmark from the menu.**

   The Bookmark dialog box appears, as shown in Figure 10-3.

   I have selected the topic *Communications* from the MindManager map. The name of the topic appears in the Bookmark name box. You have the option of changing the title of the bookmark or keeping it as the title of the topic. MindManager links the bookmark name to the topic location in the map.

3. **Click Add to add the bookmark name to the bookmark list.**

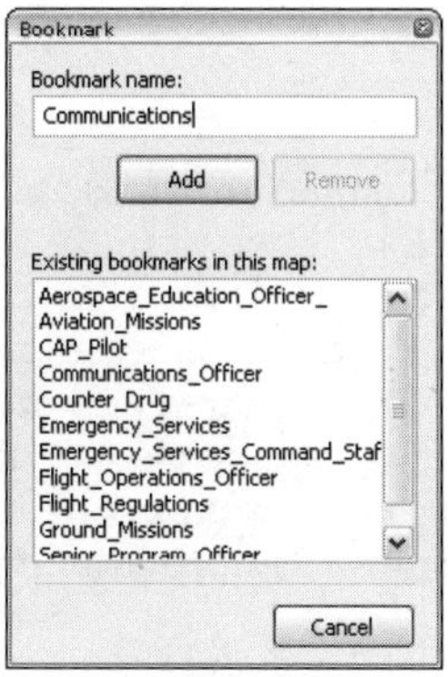

Figure 10-3:
The
Bookmark
dialog box.

4. **Select other topics in your map and add bookmarks to the list.**

   You can add as many as you desire. The Cancel button changes to a Close button after you have added a bookmark.

5. **Click Close.**

   You have an option to choose how you use the bookmarks in your map. I like the quick and dirty non-documented way. Notice the list of bookmarks shown in Figure 10-3. The list represents an index of map locations. I use the list as a Go To list. Unfortunately, you won't find a Go To command in the toolbar.

6. **Select Insert⇨Bookmarks.**

   The Bookmark dialog box appears again (refer to Figure 10-3).

7. **Select one of the bookmarks in the list.**

   You are immediately transported to the location of the bookmark in the map.

8. **Click Cancel.**

   You have arrived at the desired location in the map with minimal keystrokes.

The other way to use a bookmark is to establish a link from one topic to a bookmarked topic. You click on the link icon and are transported to the bookmarked topic. You may want to use the link technique if you have a repeatable path that you take through your map. Refer to Chapter 12 for info on adding bookmark links to a topic.

Breaking Up a Big Map

My Civil Air Patrol MindManager map is big. The map grows as I add specialty tracks, emergency services, and regulations. Each of these additions adds hundreds of topics. I like a large map. All the topics are available. I dig through and mine the topics I need. For example, the CAP organization and members are very safety-conscious. Flying is not a risk-free activity, so minimizing the risk is always a goal. I take my large map and select all the topics related to safety. I send the selected topics off to a new map. The safety process improvement team works with the topics to improve safety.

Rather than mining topics from all over the map, I may want to have a team work one section of the map. I break off a branch of the map and send it. The team performs their magic, and I bring their work back into the map.

The following sections show you how to select tasks to make a new map and how to break a branch off the map to create a new map.

A topic here, a topic there

You can create a new map by selecting topics from the big map. I recently had a call from a prospective CAP member — a retired airline pilot who would like to join CAP. She has numerous instructor ratings and is interested in maintaining an active role in aviation. I am going to use the big map to create a smaller map specific to her interest in flying. Refer to Chapter 3 for some of the basics of expanding and collapsing topics.

The following steps show you how to grab topics and create a smaller map from a big map:

1. **Select the central topic, and collapse the map to show only one level of topic.**

   You can use the Level of Detail button in the toolbar. Refer to the margin art.

   You can start anywhere in the map. I like to begin at the center with a very small map and increase its size in the direction I need.

2. **Open one of the main topics, and continue opening topics until you have reached an area where you want to grab a topic or two.**

3. **Select a topic and then Ctrl-click other topics to be included in a map.**

   The selected topics have a highlighted square around them. Don't lower the level of the map after you select a topic. The topics are no longer selected if you do.

4. **Open other areas of the map and select a few more topics.**

   You don't have to select all the topics at one time. You can return and grab more later. The first batch of topics is used to create a new map.

5. **Select File⇨Send To⇨MindManager (As New Map).**

   A new map is created with your selected topics. Subsequent visits to the big map to get more topics can't use the same *Send To* technique. A copy and paste method is required for adding more topics.

6. **Go back to the big map to select additional topics. Use Step 3 as a guide. Right-click the last topic selected, and click Copy.**

7. **Return to the new map. Right-click the Central Topic, and click Paste.**

The new MindManager map contains all the pertinent topics gathered from the big map. In the case of the prospective CAP pilot, a map is created that includes performance requirements, job descriptions, regulations, and mission activities. Figure 10-4 is derived from a map having over 800 topics. I am going to create a PowerPoint slide show directly from the map and send it to her. Be back in a minute.

Sometimes it is desirable to send an entire section of a map to a new map. The process is very similar to the one you just read, but there are differences. The next section sends one part of the big map to a new map.

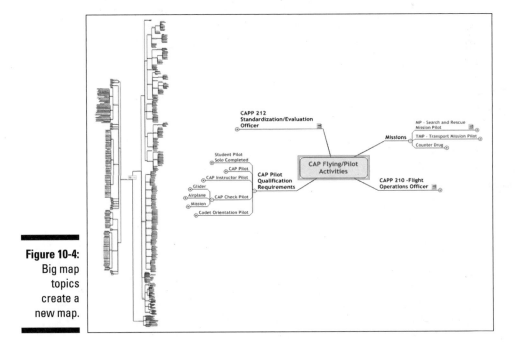

Figure 10-4:
Big map
topics
create a
new map.

Breaking the branch

Imagine a big apple tree being analogous to your big map. In the last section, you took the apples from all parts of the tree to make an apple pie. In this section, you are going to remove a branch of the tree to become a new tree.

Your team doesn't need the entire big map. Send the team only the topics and series of subtopics they need. Perhaps your map is a large work breakdown structure of a software project. Send the Development team only the topic branch that relates to their work. Later in the chapter, you are going to bring their work back into the big map.

Alert! Alert! A new search-and-rescue training mission has just been assigned. One of the first tasks is to decide who is going to do what. I am going to break the big Civil Air Patrol map at the Emergency Services Command Staff topic and send it to a new map. The topics and subtopics in the new map help assemble the right team from a resource base of hundreds of CAP members.

The following steps show you how to break the map at a topic and send it to a new map:

1. **Select a topic in the map.**

2. **Click Files⇨Send To⇨MindManager (As New Map).**

   The Send To MindManager dialog box appears, as shown in Figure 10-5. You have the choice of making the excised topic a main topic or a central topic in the new map. The central topic is the one in the center of the map, and the main topic is the first level topic off of the central topic.

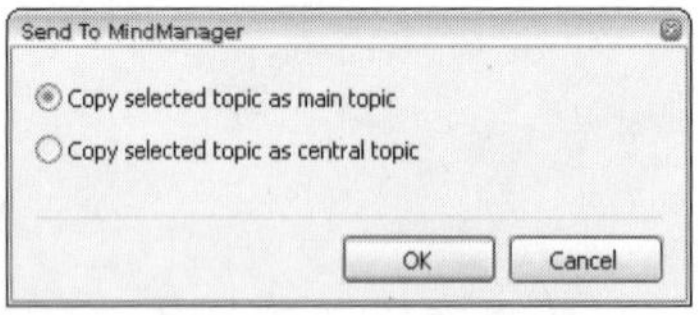

Figure 10-5:
Choose a main or central topic.

3. **Click *Copy selected topic as main topic* and click OK.**

   The topic and subtopics are now transported to the new map. Figure 10-6 shows the new map.

You can add additional topics to the new map, but you can use *Send To MindManager (As New Map)* only once. You have to copy topics from the big map and paste them into the new map if you want to add additional branches to the new map. See Steps 6 and 7 in the preceding section.

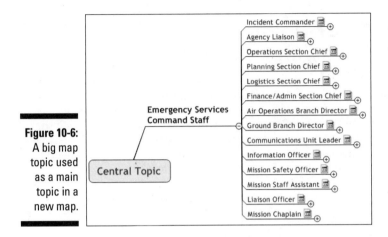

The next section works with maps that are connected by links. MindManager calls it the Multimap mode.

Configuration management

Configuration management is making sure that all parts, including information, of a product or system are linked together. Changing any one part alters the configuration. You buy a new operating system for your computer and find that half your programs don't work any more. The configuration of your computer has changed and the results are painful. Configuration management can be affected by breaking off a part of a big MindManager map and creating a new map.

Sending a MindManager topic over to a new map does not remove the topic or subtopics from the big map. They remain in the big map. You must decide whether changes made in the new map should be reflected in the big map. How do you manage the configuration?

I have two suggestions. The first suggestion is to place an icon on all the topics in the big map

that are sent to the new map. I use the eyeglasses icon and change the name to *look for change*. The icons are transferred to the new map. A link should be established between the big map and the new map. The link lets you easily transport to the new map to check on changes. Make changes in the big map as necessary to maintain the configuration.

My other suggestion is a bit more invasive. You delete topics from the big map after they are sent to the new map. Add a link between the two maps. I add topic notes to remind myself what I have done. You bring the topics back into the big map by cutting the topics from the new map and pasting them back into the big map as needed. You may not even need to bring the topics back into the big map. The links serve as a way to maintain the configuration.

Making the Most of the Multimap Workspace

The show *Star Trek* has a very nasty villain called the Borg. The Borg is a collection of linked individuals. Borg enemies are assimilated into the Borg collective. Think of MindManager's Multimap workspace like a view screen that can see all the linked Borg elements at one time. From the screen, a message can be sent to Starfleet describing all the individuals in the linked collective. What would Captain Jean Luc Picard do for a tool like that?

MindManager maps are linked together by hyperlinks. Many, many maps can be linked together. The only way to see all the linked maps at one time is with the Multimap workspace.

Entering the Multimap workspace

The following prerequisites must be in place before you use the Multimap workspace:

- ✔ **The individual maps must be saved:** Multimap workspace only works with saved maps. You can work on a linked map, but changes are not carried into the Multimap workspace until the linked map is saved. See Chapter 2 for information on saving your map.

- ✔ **The maps must be connected by hyperlinks:** The hyperlinks must exist in all the saved maps. The hyperlink specifies the connection between two or more maps. Refer to Chapter 12 for information on setting up hyperlinks. Map hyperlinks found in Topic Notes don't count.

- ✔ **One map to many works best:** Multimap workspace does not show a series of circular links. For example, Map A links to Map B, which links to Map C, which links to Map D, which links back to Map A. The Multimap workspace would show only two maps. A one-to-many link means that Map A links to Maps B, C, and D. All four maps would be shown in the Multimap workspace.

The following steps show you how to enter the multimap workspace:

1. **Open the map that links to all the other maps.**

   I am using a map titled CAP Senior Squadron. The map links to Operations, Specialty Tracks, Regulations, and New Member information. The map started as a big map that I broke apart. Figure 10-7 shows the hyperlinks in the map.

Figure 10-7:
A Multimap
workspace
map with
hyperlinks.

2. Select Multimap on the toolbar. Refer to the margin art.

The map view changes to Multimap workspace. Figure 10-8 shows the
workspace with the linked maps. The base map has a blue background.

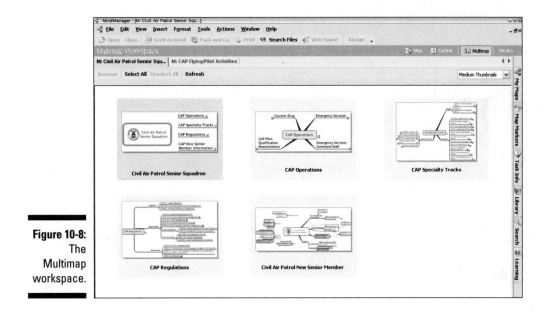

Figure 10-8:
The
Multimap
workspace.

Working in the Multimap workspace

Use the Multimap workspace for the following purposes:

✔ Applying a common style to all the maps.

✔ Creating an e-mail .zip file.

✔ Packing the maps into a .zip file or a self-extracting .exe file.

✔ Creating a Web export file.

✔ Opening all the linked maps.

The following steps show you some of the basics of using the Multimap workspace. Your map, with the links to other maps, should be open as shown in Figure 10-8:

1. **Click Select All.**

   A box appears around all the maps. The Select All method is a faster way to select maps than using the Ctrl-click method or double-clicking on an individual map.

2. **Click Open to open all the linked maps.**

   You can work on the open files by selecting them. Return to the Multimap workspace by selecting the base map. The base map has an *M:* in front of the file name.

3. **Click Refresh.**

   You have to hit Refresh every time you change and save one of the linked maps.

Don't forget to save the linked maps when you work on them. The Close command saves the linked files. You can click Select All⇨Close⇨Refresh to ensure that the Multimap workspace has the most up-to-date files.

The Multimap workspace treats all the selected maps as one. The easiest way to export or make Web pages with multiple maps is to use the Multimap workspace. The Pack and Go and Send as E-mail commands are covered in Chapter 17. Web Export is covered in Chapter 18. Assigning a style is described in Chapter 14.

Use Assign⇨Style Template with caution. The style is assigned to the selected maps in a permanent way. The style is saved to the map file, so you can't undo the change.

Chapter 11

Adding Supplemental Information

*I*n this chapter, you use different MindManager features to add supplemental information to a MindManager map. The next few paragraphs describe the building blocks.

I am not scatterbrained, but thinking about one thing at a time seems a bit boring. The standard MindManager map has one track called the central topic. I am going to show you how to expand your topical horizons beyond the one central topic theme. You are going to add floating topics to your map.

There are times when the few words of a topic just aren't enough. Remember those cute little balloons that come out of people's heads in the comics? MindManager has them, too. You insert a callout topic — the comic strip balloon — to add clarification or information to a topic.

As a pilot, I love good weather forecasting. Have you ever looked at a detailed weather map? I am not talking about the local TV weatherman or for the masses stuff. I am talking about the map that makes you say, "Huh? What's all this stuff?" I look at the legend of the weather map first. I still don't understand the map, but at least I know the names of the parts. MindManager makes it simple to include a legend in a map. Add clarity to your meaning by adding a legend.

Have you ever needed the advice of a friend or a trusted colleague? MindManager has a review mode. Review comments get added to the map. Be careful, because the advice givers can screw up your map with their goofy ideas, but at least you have a trail of their actions. You are going to review a MindManager map so that you can reject the comments that you don't want but not hurt your friend's feelings while doing it. Did that make sense? I guess I need some review.

The central topic is the topic at the center of the map. Topics and subtopics emanate from the central topic. I use the term *topic* to describe a topic or an attached subtopic.

Chapter 7 is a good reference, because it describes callouts and floating topics. You will start building the map with floating topics and callouts.

The premise for the next series of activities is derived from my participation in the Civil Air Patrol (CAP), which is the United States Air Force Auxiliary. I am responsible in my squadron for orienting new senior members and starting them on their specialty tracks. To orient the newcomers, I can put 10 pounds of regulations in front of them, or I can put a well-structured MindManager map in their hands. Not surprisingly, putting 10 pounds of regulations in front of them never seems to work.

Topics Floating in Space

Let's make a MindManager map with a central topic and a number of subtopics. Use the map shown in Figure 11-1 as a start. Refer to Chapter 2 for the basics of putting a map together.

Figure 11-1:
A basic Mind-Manager map.

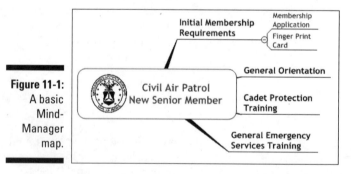

The map describes the initial steps that a new CAP senior member takes. Stating the steps to be taken does not answer many questions that a prospective member may have. Many organizations stop at the basic steps. The new employee or team member is given a set of actions to take, but behind-the-scenes questions are not answered. Perhaps Human Resources departments can benefit from using MindManager. Policy and procedure manuals would be much more informative. Sorry, back to the map. You are going to add floating topics to the MindManager map.

Floating topics do not attach to the central topic or its subtopics. Floating topics float around the periphery of the MindManager map. You can treat a floating topic the same way as any other topic. You add subtopics and link relationships to them. Adding a floating topic takes a bit of strategy. You can always add a floating topic, but it may be difficult to move.

MindManager has a black hole in the center of the map. It is called the central topic. The central topic sends out gravitational tractor beams to any topic that gets near it. You can try to fool the central topic by inserting a floating topic. You insert the floating topic right next to the central topic or its subtopics, and it remains unattached. Try to move the inserted floating topic, and the attach mode from the central topic or subtopic sends out the red tractor beam. Keep your floating topics just out of reach of the central topic or its subtopics. If you do, you can move them wherever you like.

Put floating topics in a vacant area of the map. Try to avoid the direction that the map is building. I place floating topics on the opposite side from where the map is building. Change the growth direction layout by right-clicking the central topic. Click Layout and then click a growth direction other than centered. Floating topics can now be put on the opposite side of the growth direction. The red tractor beam of the central topic attach mode is neutralized on that side. You can also hold the Shift key while inserting or moving a floating topic and the tractor beam is turned off.

The following steps show you how to add a few floating topics to the map:

1. **Click the Floating Topic tool (refer to the margin art).**

2. **Place the floating topic a couple of inches from the central topic or on the opposite side from where the map is growing.**

3. **Test the location by trying to move the newly inserted floating topic.**

I like to test the location of a floating topic by trying to move it. Frustration can set in if you place a floating topic in just the right spot and then try to move it. The central topic attach mode grabs it.

The topics that I have added to the map are shown in Figure 11-2. I have spruced up the map just a little by adding a boundary and some relationship links. Check out Chapter 6 to get a refresher on adding relationship links and boundaries.

I like to add invisible boundaries. Make boundaries invisible by choosing a border color that matches the background. The relationship link can now connect to a grouping of subtasks rather than to a specific task. A visible boundary doesn't have to show. In Figure 11-2, the Membership Application and Fingerprint Card are surrounded by an invisible boundary. The relationship connects to the invisible boundary rather than to one of the subtasks.

Reducing the subtasks by clicking on the plus sign doesn't eliminate the relationship line. Reduce a subtopic, and the relationship line disappears. Sometimes I forget where I put the invisible boundary. You can find it by clicking Edit⇨Select⇨Select All. The boundary becomes visible with a blue box around it.

Figure 11-2:
Floating
topics
added to
the map.

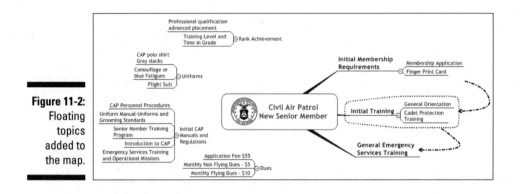

Floating topics add information to the map that may not be connected to the logic of the central topic.

Informing with Callout Topics

Callout topics add information to a specific element in the map. The element may be a boundary, a topic, or an image. Callout topics can have subtopics attached.

The following steps show you how to add callout topics to various map elements:

1. **Select a topic in your map.**

2. **Click the Insert Callout Topic tool (refer to the margin art).**

   A comic strip style balloon is now attached to the selected topic.

3. **Change the characteristics of the balloon by right-clicking the balloon and clicking Shape and Color.**

   Make the changes you desire. You can change text size by using the Increase and Decrease Text tools. The margin art shows the tools.

4. **Reposition the callout topic by dragging it to a different location.**

   It remains connected to the original topic. The string-like thing under the balloon moves also.

5. **Select a relationship line. When the red dots and yellow handles appear, click the Insert Callout tool.**

   The callout topic straddles the relationship line. The transparency is set to 22 percent, so some of the line shows through. Nice touch.

Attaching a callout topic to an image or other map element follows the same pattern. Figure 11-3 shows the callout topics added to the map. I have taken the floating topics out of the figure so that you don't need bifocals to see the fine print.

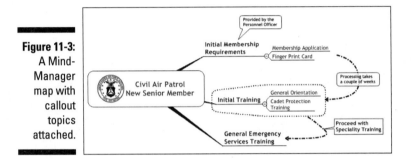

Figure 11-3: A Mind-Manager map with callout topics attached.

Don't forget that you can add subtopics to the callouts. I didn't do it in my map, but you can in yours. Adding callouts continues the process of adding supplemental information to the map. Next stop: legends.

Becoming Legendary

The map legend contains a description of the icon, text color, text fill colors, priorities, and a few other components. Chapter 4 describes how to add icons, text color, and text fill color to a map. Chapter 9 discusses placing priorities. A map legend contains information that describes elements of a map that are not self-explanatory or may need specific clarification. A smiley face that has a large open mouth has a default definition of furious. It could mean that the topic should be announced with vigor. The legend clarifies the definition. The map I have created is a bit boring. My engineer side is showing again. I am going to add some icons, colors, and priorities — the stuff legends are made of.

The following steps show you how to add a legend to the map. If you haven't added the icons, colors, and priorities, sprinkle some in:

1. **Open the Map Markers menu by clicking the Map Markers menu tab on the right side in the vertical menu.**

   The map markers are shown. The map markers include what you have put into the map and the default markers. Figure 11-4 shows the Map Markers menu.

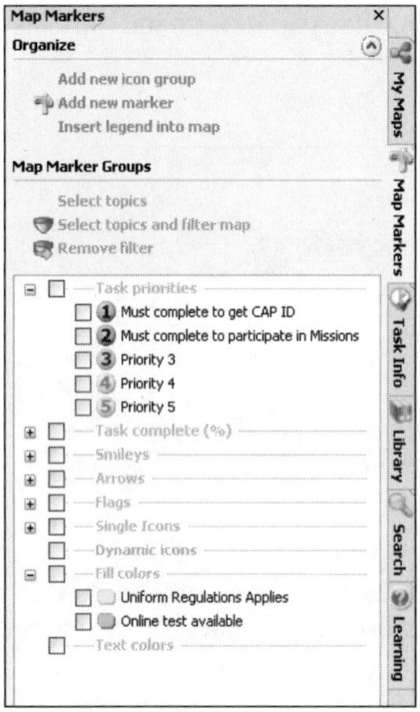

Figure 11-4:
The Map
Markers
menu.

2. **Right-click the marker name. Click Rename, and rename the marker as appropriate.**

   I changed the name of the priority icons and the Fill colors. It is especially important to add a legend if you change the marker names. Your audience may be familiar with the default meanings, and you can surprise them. Clarify your intentions with a legend.

3. **Go to the top of the Map Markers menu (shown in Figure 11-4), and click *Insert legend into map*.**

   The Insert Map Marker Legend dialog box appears, as shown in Figure 11-5. I always click the button *Insert only map markers that are used in the map somewhere*. I haven't figured out why you would want to put in a bunch of map markers that aren't even used.

4. **Click OK.**

5. **Select the legend topic and drag the legend to the location of your choice.**

The legend is now added to the MindManager map. Figure 11-6 shows how all the pieces fit together. There shouldn't be any confusion, but you know how that goes. Getting comments from a reviewer adds another pair of spectacles to help find the blind spots.

Figure 11-5:
The Insert
Map Marker
Legend
dialog box.

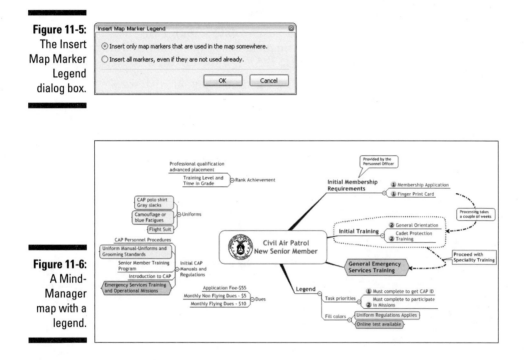

Figure 11-6:
A Mind-
Manager
map with a
legend.

Reviewing the Map

The MindManager review mode is pretty basic on the surface. You send the map to someone for review. That person makes changes or comments in the map and returns it. You then examine what the reviewer had to say and ignore most of the goofy ideas. Getting input from others is not the only use. The review mode is a tool that *you* can use. I make notes to myself by using the review mode. You can view the comments or hide them. I remind myself where I left off or identify places in the map where more research is needed. I use the review mode to capture ideas that need to germinate before being added to the map.

The following steps show you how to add your own review comments. You are going to add a feature to the map and send the map to someone for review (refer to Figure 11-6):

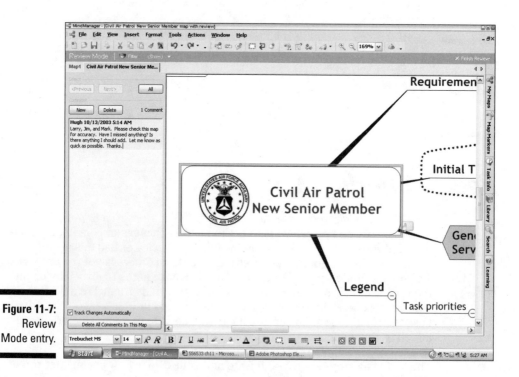

Modes ▼

1. **Enter the review mode, and click Modes on the toolbar. (The margin art shows the tool.)**

   The Modes dialog box appears.

2. **Click Review to bring up the blank review screen.**

3. **Select a topic in the map and click New.**

   Your name appears with a time and date stamp. The yellow background indicates that the review comment has not been added. Notice that the Entry Mode icon is placed to the lower right of the selected topic.

4. **Type a comment, such as instructions for your reviewers.**

   Use the central topic as your repository for instructions to others. The review mode starts with the central topic selected, so it is the first place a reviewer looks.

5. **Press Enter after typing your comment.**

   The yellow background changes to blue. The comment is now attached to the topic and is saved with the map, as shown in Figure 11-7.

Figure 11-7:
Review
Mode entry.

6. **Select a topic on the map to continue entering comments.**

   A blank review screen is created for each topic selected.

7. **Enter a new topic into the map.**

   An entry in the review screen appears identifying that a new topic has been entered.

Notice the check box at the lower-left side of the review screen shown in Figure 11-7. The Track Changes Automatically check box is checked by default. This feature adds comments to the review section when changes are made to the map. I leave it checked because I want to see changes made to the topics in the map. The track changes feature doesn't track all changes made to a map. The only ones tracked are adding, changing, or deleting topics. Topic movement and relationship changes are not tracked.

Your review instructions have been entered into the map. The map is a work of art. Time to bare your soul to someone else. Time for a review. MindManager makes an assumption that all of us are connected to the great Internet. Therefore, solicitations for review are sent via e-mail.

Click File⇨Send To⇨Mail Recipient (for Review). A new e-mail is generated using your default e-mail program. Figure 11-8 shows the e-mail that is generated.

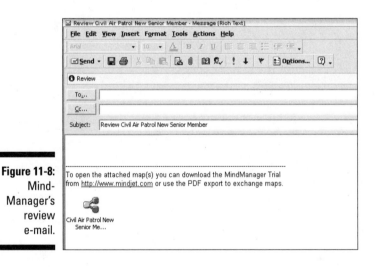

Figure 11-8:
Mind-
Manager's
review
e-mail.

Did I mention that anyone that reviews your map must also have MindManager? The folks at Mindjet didn't miss this one. They send out a link to the MindManager download site with each review e-mail.

All the files necessary to view the MindManager map are included. The recipient opens the map and makes comments. Threaten dire consequences if anyone unchecks the Track Changes Automatically button. The review sends it back to you the same way you sent it to them.

You can also have others review your map at your workstation. Any changes they make at your computer have your name attached to the comment though. Make their names appear on the review comments by clicking Files⇨Options⇨ User Information. Change your name to the reviewer's name. Review comments now have the reviewer's name instead of yours. Be sure to change it back when the review is over.

What pearls of wisdom have you received from your reviewers? Use the Previous and Next buttons to browse through the comments. Click the All button to highlight all the topics having comments. You can also select individual topics that have the review icon attached. The map can be sent back and forth as many times as you like.

The review mode is the final building block of adding supplemental information into the MindManager map.

Chapter 12

Putting the World at Your Mouse Click

*I*t was a beautiful spring evening in late May. My wife and I had just served a great BBQ to three other couples, all long-time friends. The food was abundant, as was the beer and wine. We came to a moment of silence, everyone relaxing and enjoying that quiet closeness among friends. Suddenly, a tiny thought arose in my head and rushed out my mouth without checking with my brain first: "We all love the outdoors so much. Why don't we go on some kind of expedition together this summer?"

Everyone thought this was a grand idea and immediately invoked the standard rule that the person who came up with a grand idea was responsible for managing its implementation. So I passed out assignments for gathering information, compiling comparative costs, checking out transportation and lodging possibilities, and other such things. It was the last time on that particular endeavor that I had any illusion about having things under control.

Within a few days I was flooded with brochures, flyers, e-mails, spreadsheets, unending lists of Web site addresses, airline and rail schedules, equipment catalogues, and all kinds of other stuff. In addition, there were lots of phone calls with their associated odd-sized pieces of paper with hastily scribbled notes. My computer files swelled, my file cabinet swelled, my desk acquired mountain ranges of paper, and my head swelled to the bursting point. Conversations with my friends began to increasingly contain the phrase, "I know I've got something on that here . . . somewhere." I think we based our final decisions much more on what I managed to find in that mess than on any sort of "optimal" choice.

If I had known about MindManager then, the process would have been quite a bit less hectic. Today I create maps to show where, and in what form, I can find all the information pertaining to a particular project. I can include links to important Web sites, identify folders on my computer where I keep relevant data, tie detailed maps into summary maps, and launch any other program directly from my map with a single mouse-click. In this chapter I tell you how.

Putting Pointers to Information on Your Map

If I am working with a simple topic, I use my map to show the structure of the information as well as the information itself. As the complexity of the topic increases, I find it more and more difficult to show the structure of the information in the topic/subtopic format. I can use relationships (see Chapter 6) to show how one topic relates to another, but if I put too many relationships on my map, they become confusing rather than helpful. If my topic becomes even more complex, I start moving the information to external documents and use the map just to show structure.

A Flying Leap through Time and Space

At the beginning of the twentieth century, Albert Einstein turned the scientific world on its head when he published his Special Theory of Relativity. One of the more surprising aspects of his theory was that time is not a fixed and invariant dimension but rather one that expands and contracts depending upon the speed of the observer. Mathematicians recognized that, in theory at least, there was no restriction at all on the number of dimensions that could be defined, even though such a space was impossible to visualize. Needing a word to describe these strange constructs, they invented *hyperspace*.

(A brief comment to any theoretical mathematician or physicist who — however improbable — may deign to read this: Please don't write and explain why this is a ridiculous oversimplification. I'm trying to tell a story here!)

Einstein and his colleague, Nathan Rosen, later extended the Special Theory to predict the existence of something called *wormholes.* Although strictly theoretical, they predicted that wormholes could offer a shortcut through space and time that would allow communication (or possibly even physical travel) from one side of the universe to the other in the time it would take to fly a distance of a few miles.

Science fiction writers found a bonanza in this notion. The theme surfaced repeatedly in novels, television (*Star Trek*), and movies (again, *Star Trek* and, more recently, *Contact*). After the World Wide Web began its exponential growth, the ability to go from one side of the information space to the other in a few seconds echoed this theme as well. Needing a word to describe these portals to Otherwhere, the IT folks invented *hyperlink.*

In this section, I show you how to use hyperlinks to capture pointer information so that a user can move quickly to any desired piece of information, no matter where it may be located:

✔ Somewhere else on your current map.

✔ Somewhere on a different map.

✔ In a file on your computer or your network.

✔ A Web site anywhere in the world.

The place where you define a hyperlink is called the hyperlink *origin*. The place you go to when you click a hyperlink is called the hyperlink *destination*.

You can place a hyperlink either on a topic itself, or in the notes that are attached to that topic. The appearance and behavior of hyperlinks is somewhat different depending on their location:

✔ **If you place the hyperlink on a topic:** MindManager places an icon that represents the nature of the destination file next to the topic description (I'll explore several of the possible icons later in this chapter). MindManager allows you to place only one hyperlink on any given topic on your map. If you point your mouse to the hyperlink icon, MindManager paints a red line around the icon, changes the background to pale red, and displays the link destination. If you click this icon, you go to the hyperlink destination (if it is a folder or a Web site) or launch the application that created the destination file as is appropriate.

✔ **If you place the hyperlink in a topic note:** MindManager does not place an icon in your text but rather inserts the text of the hyperlink destination, underlines it, and displays it with the color blue. For example, a link to the next topic in this chapter would appear as follows:

It's on my map

But a link to Wiley's Web site would appear as follows:

http://www.wiley.com/WileyCDA

MindManager always uses the topic title or full path name to the destination file to represent the hyperlink in topic notes. These insertions are, however, just text. You can edit them and incorporate the edited text into a sentence to make its purpose clearer. For example, in the sentence "Double-click here to see other books available from Wiley," the word "here" still contains all the hyperlink information, but it is more obvious to readers why they should (or should not) double-click the link.

Nothing happens if you point your mouse to a hyperlink in a note. To go to the hyperlink destination from a topic note, you must *double*-click the underlined link. You can, however, place an unlimited number of hyperlinks in the note that is attached to that topic.

It's on my map

It's possible to directly create a hyperlink to any topic on your current map by following these steps:

1. **Right-click the topic that you want to be the hyperlink origin, and select Insert Hyperlink.**

   The Insert Hyperlink dialog box appears (see Figure 12-1).

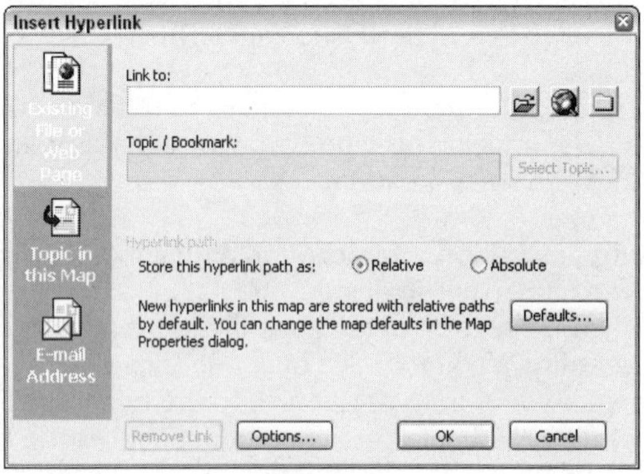

Figure 12-1:
The Insert
Hyperlink
dialog box.

2. **Click *Topic in this map*.**

   A list of all map topics will appear (as shown in Figure 12-2).

   If you have created at least one topic on your map but do not see anything in the *Select topic to link to* field, click the *Show all topics* radio button.

Figure 12-2:
Listing of all
the topics in
the map of
this chapter.

3. **Click the topic you want to be the hyperlink destination, and then click OK.**

   The Insert Hyperlink dialog box closes and MindManager adds the hyperlink icon to the display of your origin topic. If you now point your mouse to the hyperlink icon, MindManager will display the text of the destination topic.

As your map grows larger, the list of all topics on your map will become somewhat lengthy and the topic you want to link to may be buried three or four levels deep in the topic tree displayed when you select *Show All Topics*.

You can make this process easier by creating *bookmarks*. Repeat these steps for each topic you want to be a hyperlink destination:

1. **Click the topic that you want to bookmark; then click Insert⇨Bookmark on the Menu bar.**

   The Bookmark dialog box is displayed with the text of the topic to be bookmarked automatically entered in the Bookmark Name field.

2. **Change the bookmark name to something shorter or more descriptive if you want; then click OK.**

   The dialog box closes and your bookmark name is associated with the topic you selected. There is no visible change in your map, however.

When you create hyperlinks, click *Show only Bookmarked Topics* (see Figure 12-2) at step 2. You now see only your bookmarked topics.

To edit your bookmarks, follow these steps:

1. **Click any topic on your map, and then click Insert⇨Bookmark on the Menu bar.**

   MindManager displays the bookmark dialog box with all bookmarks that you have defined for your map shown in the lower field.

2. **Click the bookmark you want to edit.**

   MindManager inserts the name of the bookmark into the Bookmark Name field and changes the text of the *Add* button to *Modify*.

3a. **To delete the bookmark, click *Remove*.**

   MindManager deletes the selected bookmark from the list and displays the text of the topic you used for step 1 in the Bookmark Name field.

3b. **To change the name of the bookmark, type the new name in the Bookmark Name field and click *Modify*.**

   MindManager redisplays all defined bookmarks, now using your changed name. The bookmark's new name is selected in the list.

4. **Repeat steps 2 and either 3a or 3b until you have completed all your editing; then click Close.**

   MindManager stores your edited bookmark list with your map.

If you delete all bookmarks, the text of the *Close* button changes to *Cancel*. In this case, *Cancel* does not mean to ignore all the changes you made to your bookmarks but rather means that you do not want to bookmark the currently selected topic and you do want to exit the dialog box.

It's on another map

I find that my single map just doesn't offer the flexibility I need in cases such as these:

- ✔ My map has grown too large to manage as one file.
- ✔ I want others to take over responsibility for portions of the map.
- ✔ My project team has already created separate maps, and now I need to integrate them all together.

In order to deal with the first two problems, I need to be able to create a new map from a portion of my current map. I do this as follows:

1. **Click the topic you want to have as a separate map. Select Actions⇨ Level of Detail⇨Show whole topic from the menu bar.**

   All subtopics associated with the selected topic are displayed.

2. **Select File⇨Send to⇨MindManager (as new map).**

   MindManager displays the *Send To MindManager* dialog box.

3. **Choose the format desired for the new map and click OK.**

   MindManager creates a new map according to your specifications (see Figure 12-3).

4. **Click the tab corresponding to your origin map and delete the subtopics that were exported to the new map.**

   MindManager displays your simplified origin map.

5. **Click Window on the menu bar and select the new map that you just created.**

   MindManager displays your new map.

6. **Save your new map by clicking File⇨Save as. . . from the Menu bar and typing in the desired filename.**

   MindManager saves your new map. It is now available for you to specify as a hyperlink destination. I tell you how in a couple of paragraphs.

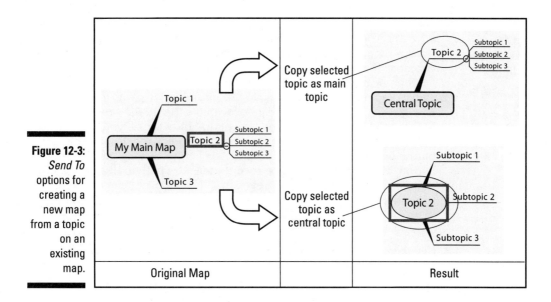

You can select and send more than one topic to a new map. If you select more than one topic, however, you will not see the Send To MindManager dialog box and the new map will always be created with the selected topics as main topics.

If an exported topic contains hyperlinks, those hyperlinks will probably not work from the new map. See the section "Keeping Your Links Fit and Healthy" for details on how to repair broken links.

I may have at this point a mixture of maps:

✔ From the procedure just described.

✔ Other maps that I created.

✔ Maps created by someone else.

This is the third problem situation I described at the beginning of this section. I solve it in a simple and elegant way by creating links to all my related maps, using these steps:

1. **Right-click the topic that is to be the hyperlink origin on your original map and select *Insert Hyperlink*.**

   MindManager opens the Insert Hyperlink dialog box.

2. **Click the File Browse button.**

   MindManager opens the File Select dialog box.

MindManager records, by default, the location of the destination file relative to the location of the main file. For this reason, the path is called a *relative* path. The advantage of this choice is that you can transfer the directory that contains your main map (and all subdirectories) to another location on your computer, or to a different computer entirely, and all your links will still work. In order for relative paths to work, however, your destination files must be located either in the same directory as the main file, or in a subdirectory of that directory. If you cannot do this, or simply do not **want** to for any reason, click the *Absolute* radio button on the Insert Hyperlink dialog box before clicking the File Browse button. MindManager will then record the entire path to the file from the root directory. Remember, however, that if you move the main directory to another location or computer with this option selected, you will have to repair all of the hyperlinks before being able to use the map hyperlinks again.

 3. **Navigate to the folder containing your new map, click the file name, and then click OK.**

    MindManager displays the path to your selected file in the Link To field.

4a. **If you want the destination to be the entire map, click OK.**

MindManager closes the *Insert Hyperlink* dialog box and inserts the MindManager application icon next to the topic description on the main map. If you point your mouse to the icon, MindManager draws a red border with red shading around the icon and briefly displays the path name stored in the hyperlink.

4b. **If you want the destination to be a particular topic on the map, click** *Select Topic*.

    MindManager opens the Select Topic dialog box and displays all the topics defined in that map. If you have bookmarked topics in the destination map, you can click *Show only bookmarked topics* to restrict the display to your identified topics.

    a. **Click the topic or bookmark that you want to be the hyperlink destination and click OK.**

       MindManager closes the Select Topic dialog box and displays the name of the topic or bookmark that you selected in the Topic/ Bookmark field.

    b. **Click OK.**

MindManager closes the Insert Hyperlink dialog box and displays the hyperlink to topic icon next to the topic on your main map. If you point your mouse to the icon, MindManager briefly displays the path to the destination file and the title of the selected topic.

To edit your hyperlinks, right-click the hyperlink icon and select *Edit Hyperlink*. You can change any fields just as if you were creating a new hyperlink. Click *Remove Hyperlink* to delete the hyperlink entirely.

MindManager has a fantastic option for working with maps containing hyperlinks to other maps. Figure 12-4 shows a meeting minutes map with two large topics presented in separate maps. I have set up hyperlinks to *Review of activities since last meeting* and *Discussion of issues*.

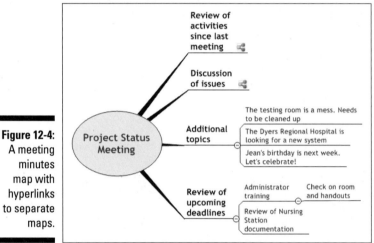

Figure 12-4: A meeting minutes map with hyperlinks to separate maps.

If I click on the Multimap Workspace button with this map displayed, MindManager shifts to multimap mode. In this mode, MindManager does the following:

- Displays the base map as a thumbnail in the upper-left corner of the display.

- Displays all hyperlink destination maps that have the base map as their origin, also as thumbnails.

- Provides a drop-down combo box that you use to change the size of the thumbnails.

- Displays a toolbar and four action tabs that you use to carry out a number of functions involving all of these related maps.

Figure 12-5 shows MindManager's display of my meeting map in multimap mode.

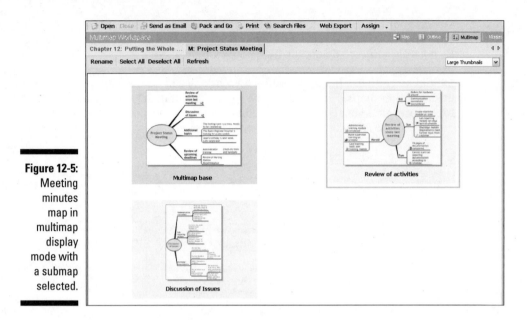

Figure 12-5:
Meeting
minutes
map in
multimap
display
mode with
a submap
selected.

Select any map by clicking it. Select two or more maps by holding down the control key while you click on each desired map. Click *Select All* to select all maps with a single click.

With the exception of *Rename* (active only if one, and only one, thumbnail is selected), all commands are executed on each selected map. This is particularly useful if you want to use the *Assign* command to make all maps uniform in style and color (see Chapter 14 for more detail on this).

I want something besides a map

Information exists in myriad forms and with MindManager I can access any file (for which I have permission, of course) on my computer, on my network, or on the World Wide Web:

- ✔ A Word document
- ✔ An Excel spreadsheet
- ✔ A PowerPoint presentation
- ✔ An Acrobat .pdf file
- ✔ A database
- ✔ An image
- ✔ And much more

When you double-click the hyperlink, MindManager automatically launches the proper application to display the destination file (assuming you have it installed on your computer). For example, if you create a link to a Web page, MindManager knows to launch your Web browser in order to display it. To create a link to a file or Web page, follow these steps:

1. **Right-click the topic (or the place in a topic note) that is to be the hyperlink origin and select Insert Hyperlink.**

   MindManager displays the Insert Hyperlink dialog box (refer to Figure 12-1).

   Click *Existing File or Web Page* if you do not see the page pictured in Figure 12-1.

2. **Type the name of the file, the path to the directory, or the Web address that is to be the destination of the hyperlink in the *Link To* field, or do one of the following:**

   a. **Click the File Browse button, navigate to the destination file's directory, click the file name, and click OK.**

   b. **Click the Web Browse button and navigate to the desired Web page. Right-click the Web address on your browser and select Copy. Right-click the *Link To* field on the Insert Hyperlink dialog box and select Paste.**

   c. **Click the Directory Browse button, navigate to the desired destination directory, and click OK.**

   MindManager displays the address of the destination file, Web site, or directory in the *Link To* field.

   Set the hyperlink path option to Absolute if you are linking to a file or directory that is not in (or in a subdirectory of) the directory where the origin map is located. This setting doesn't matter if you are linking to a Web page.

3. **Click OK.**

   MindManager closes the dialog box and displays an icon next to the topic that you have specified as the hyperlink origin. The icon will tell you what type of file you will link to (the example shown indicates that a Word document would be opened). If you point your mouse to the icon, MindManager displays the name of the file that will be opened.

Starting Other Things from Your Map

Suppose you are building a map to organize digital pictures from your vacation. You create main topics for each day, subtopics for the various places you visited each day, and sub-subtopics for captions to go with each individual picture. Finally, you want to drop each digital picture onto its caption to complete your map.

The problem is, the pictures frequently require a bit of work. This one has red-eye, that one needs to be vertical rather than horizontal, and another one needs to have the contrast adjusted a bit. You can, of course, start your photo application each time, process the picture, save the corrected picture, and then return to MindManager again. After a while, this might get to be a bit tiresome. An alternative is to create a topic called "Photo App" (or whatever you like) and attach a hyperlink to launch the photo application. As you finish adjusting a picture, you can just drag it from the Photo App to the appropriate topic.

You can set up MindManager to launch any application installed on your computer by following the steps described in the previous section, except that you select the program file itself (for example, WINWORD.EXE) rather than a data file in the Link To dialog box.

What if you wanted to build a map that contained key information about several people? You might include a small picture that you actually display as an image on the map along with addresses, telephone numbers, and e-mail addresses. You can, of course, create an extra topic to launch your mail program just as you can with any other application, but MindManager offers an even better solution: e-mail links. With an e-mail link, you just click the E-mail icon and an e-mail is created, addressed, and ready for you to type in the message. You set up this feature by following these steps:

1. **Right-click the topic (or location in a topic note) that you want to be the link origin and select Insert Hyperlink.**

   MindManager displays the Insert Hyperlink dialog box.

2. **Click E-mail Address.**

   MindManager displays the E-mail Address page (as shown in Figure 12-6).

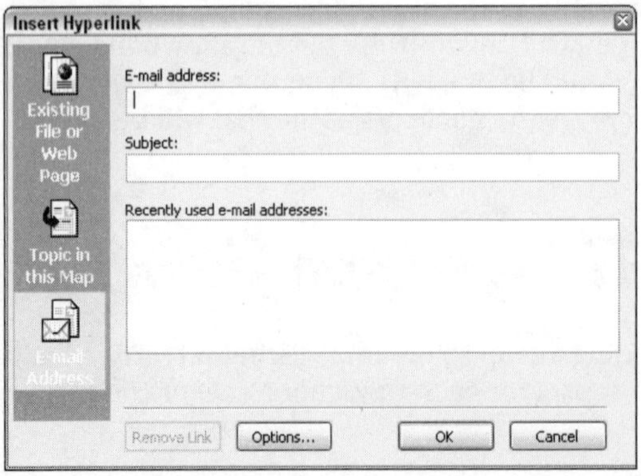

Figure 12-6:
The E-mail Address page of the Insert Hyperlink dialog box.

3. **Type the desired e-mail address in the first field.**

If the desired address is displayed in the *Recently used e-mail addresses* field, click the address. MindManager will insert it into the *E-mail address* field.

4. **Type the subject of the e-mail message in the *Subject* field.**

The subject field of your e-mail will always contain this text. If you want to type different subject lines on each e-mail, leave this field blank.

You need a "MAPI-compliant" e-mail client on your system (such as Outlook or Outlook Express) to use this. If you use web-based mail (through your web browser), these e-mail hyperlinks won't work.

A hyperlink attached to a topic is launched by clicking the icon. A hyperlink that is inserted into a topic note is launched by double-clicking the under-lined text.

Keeping Your Links Fit and Healthy

If you move, rename, or delete a document that is a link destination, all hyper-links to it will be "broken." MindManager tells you that a link is broken by replacing the original hyperlink icon with the Broken Hyperlink icon (shown here in the margin). If you click this Broken Hyperlink icon, you'll get a message that offers you the opportunity to repair it (as shown in Figure 12-7). If you know that many, or all, of your links are broken because you moved the file, click Tools on the menu bar and select *Repair Broken File Links*. MindManager will then automatically detect all broken links and display the Broken Hyperlink dialog box for each one in turn.

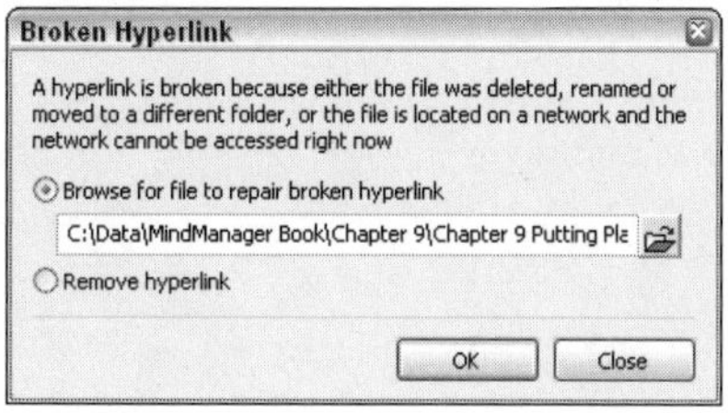

Figure 12-7:
The Broken
Hyperlink
dialog box.

> **Broken Hyperlink**
>
> A hyperlink is broken because either the file was deleted, renamed or moved to a different folder, or the file is located on a network and the network cannot be accessed right now
>
> ⦿ Browse for file to repair broken hyperlink
>
> C:\Data\MindManager Book\Chapter 9\Chapter 9 Putting Pla
>
> ◯ Remove hyperlink
>
> OK   Close

To delete the hyperlink from your origin map, select *Remove hyperlink* and click OK.

To repair the broken hyperlink, click the File Browse button, navigate to the current location of the desired file, click Open on the File Select dialog box, and then click OK on the Broken Hyperlink dialog box.

In Case You Were Wondering . . .

If you are wondering about what I did with all those vacation brochures, they stayed piled up on my desk for quite awhile. I kept stacking them higher and higher, and pushing them more toward the edge to make room for other things, but I was unwilling (or unable) to get rid of them. One day my cat decided to take a nap on the corner of my desk and, in the considerate and helpful manner of all felines, pushed the whole pile onto the floor. The unexpected racket terrified her, and she exited the room in one leap. In obedience to *Newton's* law, my desk pad and just about everything on it flew off my desk in the opposite direction. Mumbling unprintable things about this creature that had taken over my house, my papers went back on my desk and the brochures went in the trash can.

Today, I avoid collecting paper brochures at all costs. I use MindManager to collect Web links instead!

This dialog box always repairs the link with an absolute rather than a relative path. If you want to use relative paths (for example, because you just renamed the destination file and still want to preserve the directory relationships between the origin map and all linked destination files), right-click the broken link and select *Edit Hyperlink*. MindManager will display the current hyperlink information and you can update the destination filename (as a relative path). When you click OK, the hyperlink will be repaired.

Chapter 13

Finding and Filtering the Information You Need

*F*iltering topics is a great way to reduce the visual overload that happens with a large map. You work on topics that meet specific criteria. The rest of the map is still there; you just don't have to look at it. The reverse also works well. You select the topics that you don't want to see. For example, if you are done scheduling 20 percent of the tasks, hide the ones you are finished with. Filtering fine-tunes your map for delivery to the outside world. Only visible topics are exported.

I feel the need for filter speed. Too much time is spent locating and selecting topics one by one in a complex map. Plan your map to make selection easy. MindManager has a plethora of possibilities to choose from to select topics. Filtering your map is a snap when the topics are selected.

In this chapter, you get a grasp on controlling your map by using filtering. You sort through the selection techniques. The filter is engaged when topics are selected. The goal is to filter your map to get what you want — showing the topics you choose and hiding the rest. The filtered map acts like a new map. The topics shown are printed, exported or sent. The filtering process starts by selecting topics. You choose whether to show or hide the selected topics. For example, you have completed half the tasks in your map. You select the completed tasks. You then opt to hide them. The filter is engaged and the resulting map shows all the tasks that are not yet completed.

I have severe bite marks from the travel bug. I get an itch once or twice a year to hit the international road. I am trying to add to my list of 41 countries that I have worked in or visited. Join me on a trip to one of my favorite European stomping grounds. Slovenia is a wonderful little country nestled into the corner of Austria and Italy. The people are friendly, and costs are reasonable. This chapter shows you how to use a MindManager map for trip planning.

Selecting Topics to be Filtered

Selecting topics is the start to filtering your map. Filtering involves pushing a button while selecting topics takes a bit of strategy. You use various techniques to select topics in the following sections.

Understanding selection criteria

You determine the way the elements of the map are selected for filtering. I use the Map Markers placed with topics as an easy way to select topics to be filtered. The Map Markers that can be used for filtering include icons, priorities, task completion %, smileys, flags, fill, and task colors. Topic location in the map is another way to select topics for filtering. Callouts and floating topics are selectable for filtering. I hope you are getting the idea that almost any selectable element in the map can be used for filtering.

You have to make a decision about your selections. Do you want to show or hide the selected items when the filtering is complete? The Show button and the Hide button are on the Map View toolbar. Either the word *Show* or *Hide* is visible on the toolbar. Click on *Show* or *Hide* and the selection menu pops up. Click on Show Selected Topics or Hide Selected Topics. Your selection determines how the filter processes the selected elements in the map.

Selection criteria are not applicable in multimap mode. You have to pull the maps together into one map to use filtering. Refer to Chapter 10.

I have added some icons, a callout topic, and a floating topic to the travel-planning map shown in Figure 13-1.

Using icons to select topics

Look through your map and try to envision which topics you would like to be able to select for filtering. Add an icon to the topic. You may want to add different icons depending on the meaning. Topics can have multiple icons. They are very easy to add and remove. Refer to Chapter 4 to brush up on the use of icons. You don't need to attach an icon to every topic. Figure 13-2 shows how filtering works with an icon. The icons are attached to topics as shown on the left side of the figure. The topics are selected and the filter is turned on. The result is shown on the right side of the figure. Many topics remain even though the dollar icon isn't attached. Anything downstream of the icon stays.

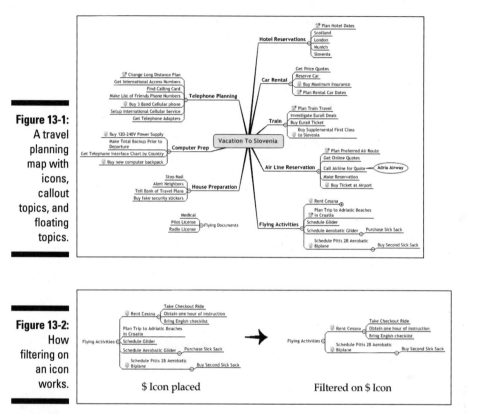

Figure 13-1:
A travel planning map with icons, callout topics, and floating topics.

Figure 13-2:
How filtering on an icon works.

$ Icon placed   Filtered on $ Icon

Any Map Marker acts the same way as the example with the icon. A Map Marker attached to a topic can be used to select the topic for filtering.

Using text search to select topics

The following steps show you how to use a text search to select topics for filtering:

1. **Click Edit⇨Find.**

   The Find and Replace dialog box appears, as shown in Figure 13-3.

2. **Click the check boxes for Topic text, All topics, and Find whole words only.**

3. **Enter the search word in the Find What box (for example, the word *Plan*).**

4. **Click Find All.**

5. **Click Close.**

   All the topics with the word Plan are identified. The selected topics are surrounded by a blue box.

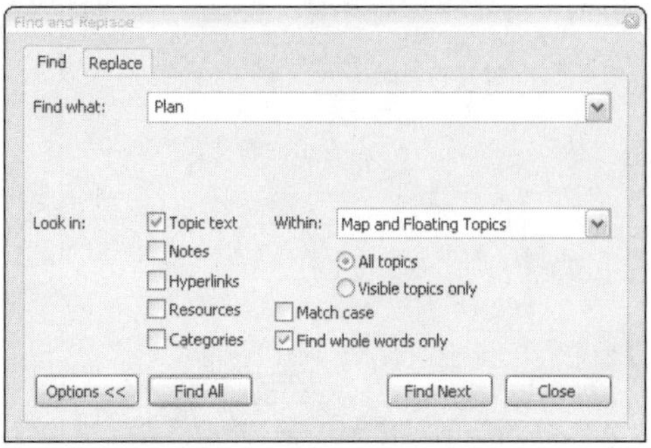

Figure 13-3:
The Find
and Replace
dialog box.

Selecting by location on the map

The click-and-drag method works to select topics. Move your cursor to a blank section of the map. Click-and-drag the cursor over part of the map. A light blue square appears as you drag the cursor. Any topic touching the square is selected. Release the click, and all the selected topics are wearing blue boxes.

Selecting by floating and callout topics

I use floating topics and callouts for supplemental information in a map. Sometimes it is nice to be able to look at just this information. Follow these steps to use a filter:

1. **Click Edit➪Select➪Select Special.**

2. **Click Select floating topics and callouts.**

3. **Click OK.**

   The Select Special dialog box appears, as shown in Figure 13-4.

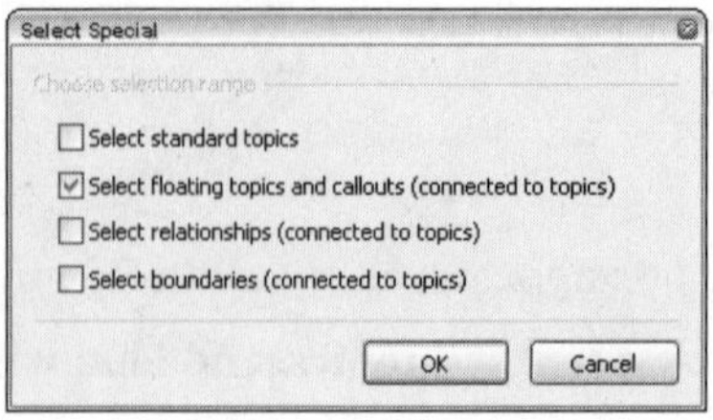

Figure 13-4:
The Select
Special
dialog box.

All the floating topics and callouts are selected. After topics are selected, you can invoke the filter.

TIP

When you have topics selected, don't lower the level of the map by clicking the minus sign between topics. The topics lose their blue box and are no longer selected.

Filtering the Selected Topics

This chapter covers selection separately from filtering because initiating a filter is easy. The tough part is getting the right topics filtered. The filter symbol is shown in the margin art.

To begin filtering, start in the Map Marker menu. Figure 13-5 shows part of the Map Marker menu. The filter symbol is at the top.

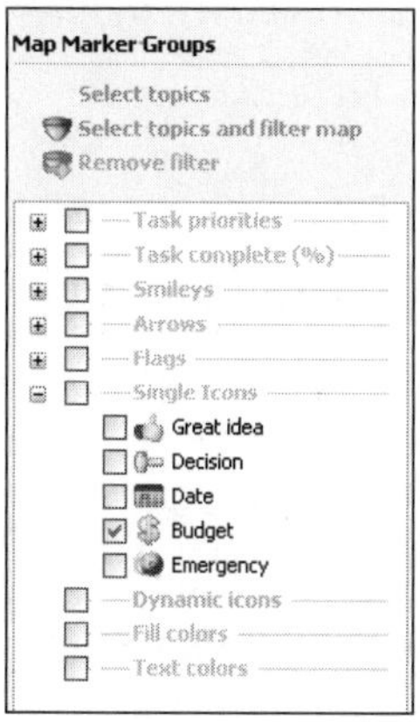

Figure 13-5:
The Map
Marker
menu.

> **Map Marker Groups**
>
> Select topics
> Select topics and filter map
> Remove filter
>
> ⊞ ☐ ──── Task priorities ────
> ⊞ ☐ ──── Task complete (%) ────
> ⊞ ☐ ── Smileys ──
> ⊞ ☐ ── Arrows ──
> ⊞ ☐ ── Flags ──
> ⊟ ☐ ──── Single Icons ────
>   ☐ 💡 Great idea
>   ☐ Decision
>   ☐ Date
>   ☑ 💲 Budget
>   ☐ Emergency
> ☐ ──── Dynamic icons ────
> ☐ ── Fill colors ──
> ☐ ── Text colors ──

In Figure 13-5, the icon with the dollar sign and the word Budget is checked. A checked icon is used as a filter. Click Select Topics at the top of the menu, and all the topics with the dollar sign icon grow blue squares. You can use the toolbar Filter icon. You usually skip this step and use menu selection with the filter symbol. Click Select Topics and Filter Map. The effect on the Slovenian travel map is shown in Figure 13-6.

Figure 13-6:
A map
filtered by
the $ icon.

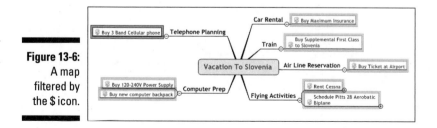

All the topics I am going to spend money on are extracted. You might be working on a large project and need to pull out tasks associated with capital expenditures. This is the technique you would use.

The blue selection boxes are still present. Send them away by clicking anywhere on a blank section of the map.

Remove the filter by clicking the Remove Filter icon. The icon is shown in the margin art.

Next to the filter symbol on the toolbar is a drop-down menu. You can choose to either hide or show selected topics. In the previous example, the Show setting is selected. You can also choose to hide the selected topics. All the topics in the map *except* the selected topics are shown. I hide the cost items in my Slovenia vacation map because they are depressing.

The Toolbar Filter symbol shown in the margin art is used to filter all other selected topics.

Getting the Most Out of Filtering

I use filtering to pull out specific information found in the map. My team can work better because the screen is less cluttered. I can also see what I have missed. The capital elements in the project are spread everywhere in your plan. Pull out the capital items using a filter. Does it match the capital budget? Are all the items there? The team is finished. The capital items have been examined and missed items have been added. Presentation time!

The filter is a tool to prepare your map for giving to someone else. The interface with Word, PowerPoint, Outlook, Project, and Web export uses only the filtered topics. Refer to the Vacation Map shown in Figure 13-1. I added an icon to each of the topics involved with planning. The Planning icon is used to filter the map. I could filter on the word *Plan* and get the same result. The filter is engaged and the effect on the MindManager map is shown in Figure 13-7.

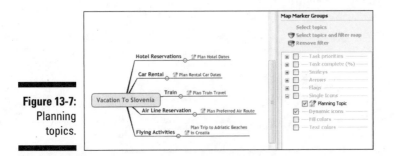

Figure 13-7:
Planning
topics.

The export to Word produces the outline shown in Figure 13-8. Refer to Chapter 20 for information on how to create a Word document from a MindManager map.

Figure 13-8:
A Word
document
with
planning
topics.

Vacation To Slovenia

Hotel Reservations

Plan Hotel Dates

Car Rental

Plan Rental Car Dates

Train

Plan Train Travel

Air Line Reservation

Plan Preferred Air Route

Flying Activities

Plan Trip to Adriatic Beaches in Croatia

The PowerPoint export is one of my favorite MindManager features. I use a filter combined with a PowerPoint export to create presentations that target the audience. The filter produces the PowerPoint slides shown in Figure 13-9. Jump over to Chapter 19 to see how to make PowerPoint presentations from a MindManager map.

The other export tools follow the same pattern. Use filters to make your MindManager map export more powerful.

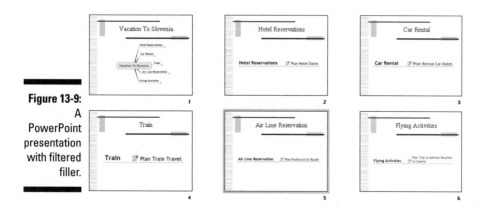

Figure 13-9:
A
PowerPoint
presentation
with filtered
filler.

Chapter 14

Getting a Fast Start with Templates and Styles

My father started working for IBM in the days when they really made *machines* — big, noisy printers, punches, and sorters the size of a small car — and when every male employee who went to a customer's place of business was required to wear a suit, white shirt, and tie. No exception was made for my father despite the fact that he was hired to repair and maintain these grease and oil filled monsters. Inevitably, he would come home from time to time with grease or oil on his clothes that simply could not be removed. My parents never discarded anything (perhaps because of their experiences during the Great Depression), so the clothes were stored away in rag bags to be used for some other purpose that would somehow become clear sometime in the future.

One day, at the age of five or six, I discovered this stash hidden away in a corner of our basement (as you may imagine, the cache grew far faster than my parents could find uses for rags). Delighted with the find, I decided to dress up "just like dad." Well, you can imagine what I must have looked like. The clothes had been wadded up for months or years, were many sizes too big, and had large grease spots here and there.

In my eyes, though, I looked just like my hero and went running up the stairs so he could see me. I never gave a thought to the fact that my parents were actually quite busy at the moment, hosting a party for several IBM families. When I suddenly ran into the room, it was a total conversation stopper — for about five seconds. Then, with a roar of laughter, they started teasing my father unmercifully: "That suit never looked better!" "He's ready to take over your job now!" "Now you won't have to take night calls." On and on. My father laughed, too, but I never saw him with such a red face as he had that day.

Does your map look to you like I must have looked to my father that day? Does it just not fit well with your message? Does it look old-fashioned, droopy, and not ready for prime time? This chapter has the answers you need! In the next pages, you will discover how you can dress up your maps so that they really capture the look and mood that you want to convey to your audience. Even better, you will see how you can save both your style and your subject ideas so that you (and others) can reuse them again on future maps with just a few mouse clicks.

Making It Look the Way You Want

I seldom know exactly how I want my topics to appear — I just know that the way they look now isn't quite right. MindManager makes it very easy to experiment. Almost all the dialog boxes have thumbnail sketches that show you what that choice will look like, and they all have an Apply button that you can click to see the result of your choice without closing the dialog box. So explore, investigate, and experiment!

MindManager groups style changes under one of the following headings:

- ✔ Font
- ✔ Shape and Color
- ✔ Layout

Each group has its own dialog box. I discuss each of these in the following sections.

To change the appearance of any map element, first right-click the element you want to change and then select the format group (Font, Shape and Color, or Layout) you want to work with.

Fonts

MindManager displays the Format Font dialog box shown in Figure 14-1 if you select *Fonts*. Although the choices are more limited than those available in Word, the dialog box functions in exactly the same way.

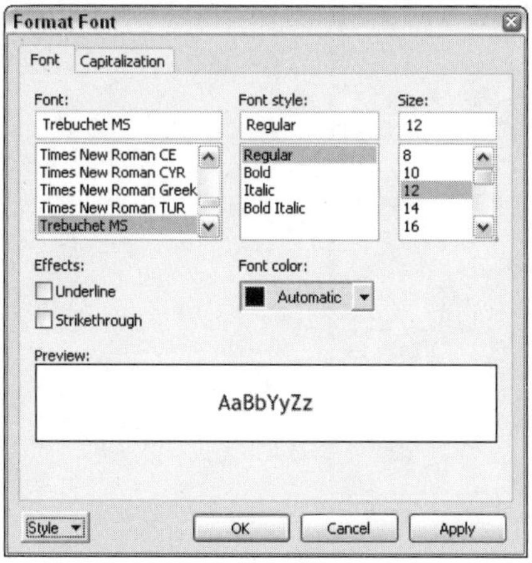

Format Font

Font | Capitalization

Font:
Trebuchet MS

Font style:
Regular

Size:
12

Times New Roman CE
Times New Roman CYR
Times New Roman Greek
Times New Roman TUR
Trebuchet MS

Regular
Bold
Italic
Bold Italic

8
10
12
14
16

Effects:
☐ Underline
☐ Strikethrough

Font color:
■ Automatic

Preview:

AaBbYyZz

Style ▾ | OK | Cancel | Apply

Figure 14-1:
The Format
Font dialog
box.

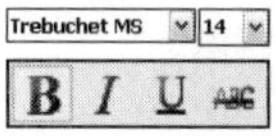

You can also make any of these font changes using the formatting toolbar on
the lower left-hand corner of your workspace (after selecting the desired
topic).

Shape and color

MindManager displays the Format Topic Shape and Color dialog box shown
in Figure 14-2 if you select *Shape and Color.* Selecting *Automatic* means that
the shape and color will be defined by the Map's style sheet (I tell you all
about style sheets later in this chapter). With any other selection, MindManager
ignores the style sheet for the selected topic and uses the settings you enter
here.

Strictly speaking, MindManager uses style *templates* rather than style sheets,
but that makes it rather awkward to distinguish between those templates that
only contain style elements from those that contain specific structured topics
and subtopics — I would have to call these topic templates or something like
that. So, to make things simple, I will use the term *style sheet* in this chapter
and in the rest of this book. However, for those of you who plan to further
modify a Web page exported from MindManager (as discussed in chapter 18)
with a Web editing tool such as Microsoft FrontPage, the Web style sheet does
not inherit any information from the MindManager style template.

The line color and fill color drop-down combo boxes display a palette of colors.
Select the color you want by clicking on the color sample. MindManager displays your color choices in the drop-down combo boxes. If you want a darker
fill color with a black font, set the Transparency slide bar to around 30 percent
to make your text readable.

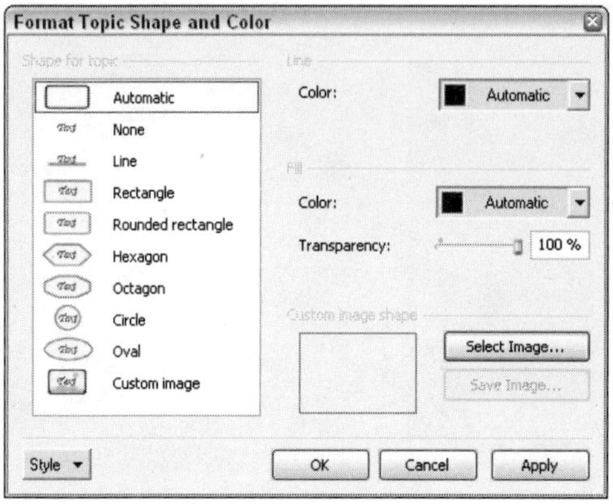

Figure 14-2:
The Format
Topic Shape
and Color
dialog box.

 Line, Fill, and Font colors can also be modified using the Formatting toolbar.

The shapes shown in Figure 14-2 can also be selected by clicking the tiny arrow on the toolbar button and then selecting the desired shape. Custom shapes can be used by clicking the Select Image button, selecting the desired image file, and then clicking Custom Image. The image must usually be specifically prepared for use as a shape to achieve satisfactory results (see the next section for more).

I want my own shape!

MindManager does not provide any tools for creating or working with your own shapes, so you will probably need some kind of graphics software. If you want to just create something simple, use the normal Paint program that is part of Windows. Regardless of the source of the image, you must ensure that its size is not greater than 180 x 180 pixels, and that the file type is one of the following:

- ✔ .bmp (Windows or OS/2 bitmap)
- ✔ .emf (Windows Enhanced Metafile)
- ✔ .wmf (Windows Metafile)
- ✔ .gif (CompuServe Graphics Interchange)
- ✔ .jpeg or .jpg (JPEG or JFIF compliant)
- ✔ .pcx (Zsoft Paintbrush)
- ✔ .png (Portable Network Graphics)

Prepare your custom shape for use by following these steps:

1. **If you have not already done so, create a package folder for all resource types on your hard disk.**

   (See "Making a Place for My Stuff," later in this chapter, for details on how to do this.)

2. **Navigate to your Package folder and save your image in the subfolder called Shapes.**

   You can create sub-subfolders within Shapes to further organize your shape images if you wish.

3. **Right-click the folder in the Library page of the task pane where you saved the shape and select Refresh.**

   MindManager reloads the library information from the selected folder.

4. **Click the Library tab, click Shapes and then click your Package folder.**

   Your custom shape is displayed in the lower half of the Task Pane.

   If you created subfolders under Shapes, you need to click the subfolder where you saved your image in order to see your custom shape.

5. **Right-click your image and select Edit Content Margins.**

   MindManager displays a dialog box similar to that shown in Figure 14-3. If you add text to this image in your map, the text will appear only in the space within the black rectangle.

6. **Point your mouse to any of the small, black sizing squares on the Content Margins box and drag the boundary to the position of your choice.**

   Figure 14-3 shows my shape after I have completed this step.

7. **Click OK.**

   Your shape is saved in your Package folder and is now ready for use.

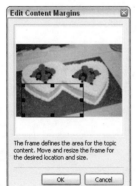

Figure 14-3: Adjusting the text area in a shape.

Edit Content Margins

The frame defines the area for the topic content. Move and resize the frame for the desired location and size.

OK   Cancel

To apply the shape, click your central topic and then click your custom icon in the Library. Figure 14-4 shows the start of my map to plan my son's wedding. If you are not pleased with the placement of text and the sizing of the image (MindManager does all of this automatically based on the Content boundaries you set in step 5), right-click the topic, select Layout, and then click the Size and Margins tab. See "The Size and Margins page" section, later in this chapter, for details on using these settings.

Figure 14-4:
The final appearance of my custom shape in a new map.

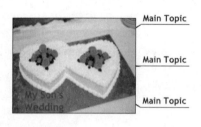

Layout

MindManager displays the Format Topic Layout dialog box shown in Figure 14-5 if you select Layout. This is the most complicated dialog box of the three choices, and the tabs (and the content of some of the tabs) varies depending upon whether you have selected the central topic or a main or subtopic, and whether the selected topic has an associated image or not. So grab something cold, pull up a comfortable chair and let me take you on a quick tour.

Figure 14-5:
The Alignment page of the Format Topic Layout dialog box.

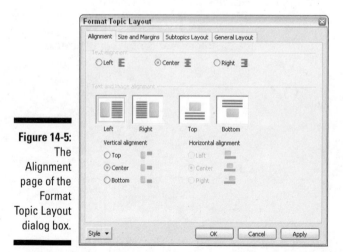

The Alignment page

You use this page if you have more than one line of text or you have added an image to a topic.

The Text alignment radio buttons at the top of the page control the visual relationship between two or more lines of text. The small illustrations next to each radio button show how the text lines will be displayed. Your setting here is still used for the text part of your topic even if you make an additional selection in the lower part of the page.

The Text and image alignment section controls the position of your image relative to the text. The Vertical Alignment radio buttons are only active if you have chosen to position your image to the left or to the right of your text. The Vertical Alignment choice then controls how the *text* is positioned relative to the image. If, however, you have chosen to position your image above or below your text, you chose a horizontal alignment. This setting controls how the *image* is positioned relative to the text.

The Size and Margins page

If you have already added an image to your selected topic and you click the Size and Margins tab, MindManager displays the page shown in Figure 14-6.

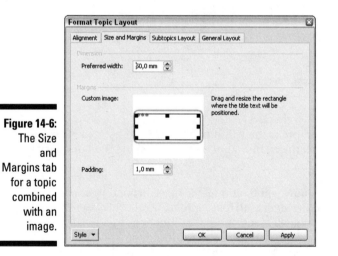

Figure 14-6: The Size and Margins tab for a topic combined with an image.

The preferred width setting functions only to force MindManager to compress the image (make it less wide relative to its height). Any setting larger than the one calculated by MindManager is ignored.

Adjust the position of the topic's text by grabbing one of the tiny black sizing squares on the black rectangle with your mouse and moving it to your desired position. The Padding setting is ignored by MindManager unless your topic contains both an image and text. In this case, increasing the Padding setting will increase the space between your text and your image.

If you make the text rectangle smaller, MindManager will make the image larger in order to accommodate your topic's text. The reverse is also true.

If your selected topic does not have an added image, MindManager displays the Size and Margins page shown in Figure 14-7. The Preferred width setting again allows you to compress the width of the topic (and thus force the text to appear on two or more lines) but has no effect once the setting exceeds the maximum width calculated by MindManager for the topic's text.

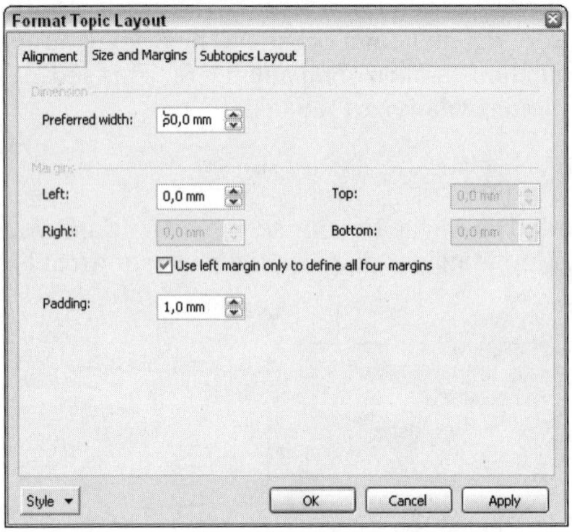

Figure 14-7:
The Size and Margins tab for topics without an image.

[Format Topic Layout dialog box showing:]

Tabs: Alignment | Size and Margins | Subtopics Layout

Dimension
Preferred width: 50,0 mm

Margins
Left: 0,0 mm   Top: 0,0 mm
Right: 0,0 mm   Bottom: 0,0 mm
☑ Use left margin only to define all four margins
Padding: 1,0 mm

Style ▾   OK   Cancel   Apply

It is much easier to compress the width of a topic's text by clicking the topic, pointing your mouse to the right boundary, and dragging the boundary to the left.

The margins settings allow you to add blank space around your topic's text. If the *Use left margin only to define all four margins* box is checked, the added blank space is uniform on all sides of the text. Uncheck this box if you want the text to be positioned other than in the center.

The padding setting is ignored by MindManager.

The Subtopics Layout page

If you click your central topic before selecting the Subtopics Layout page, MindManager displays the page as shown in Figure 14-8. The Connect From settings control the appearance of the lines that connect the central topic to the main topics. See Table 14-1 for illustrations of each possibility. Depending on your other choices, this setting can result in quite dramatic differences. Explore this yourself!

Table 14-1	The Connect From Settings
Connect From Setting	*Result*
Outside	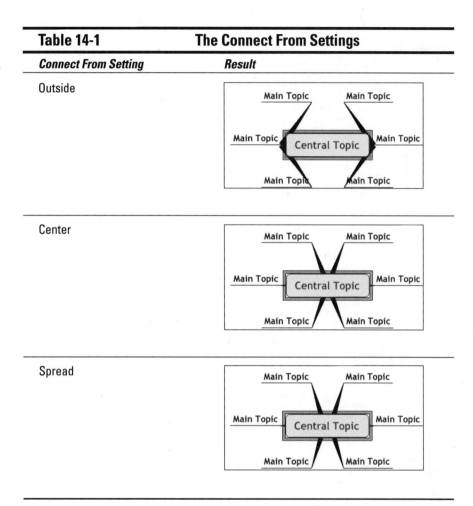
Center	
Spread	

The Growth Direction setting controls the placement of topics and subtopics relative to the central topic. The Connection Style controls the shape of the lines connecting the main topics with the central topic. Because the final appearance of your map depends on the interaction of these settings, there are literally thousands of possible map appearances. Look at the thumbnail sketches of the MindManager built-in Styles (see the section on "Using style sheet masters," later in this chapter) to get ideas; then have some fun and try out different combinations on your own.

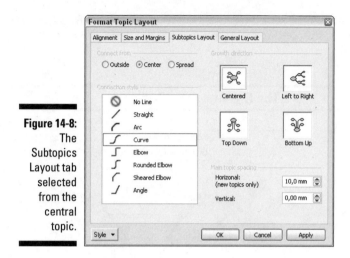

Figure 14-8:
The Subtopics Layout tab selected from the central topic.

The Horizontal spacing allows you to force new topics (that you add *after* changing this setting) to be spaced farther away from the central topic. The Vertical spacing allows you to force MindManager to space topics vertically farther apart from one another than originally calculated by MindManager. In both cases, if this setting is less than that calculated by MindManager, the setting is ignored.

If you click any topic other than your central topic before selecting the Subtopics Layout page, MindManager displays the page as shown in Figure 14-9.

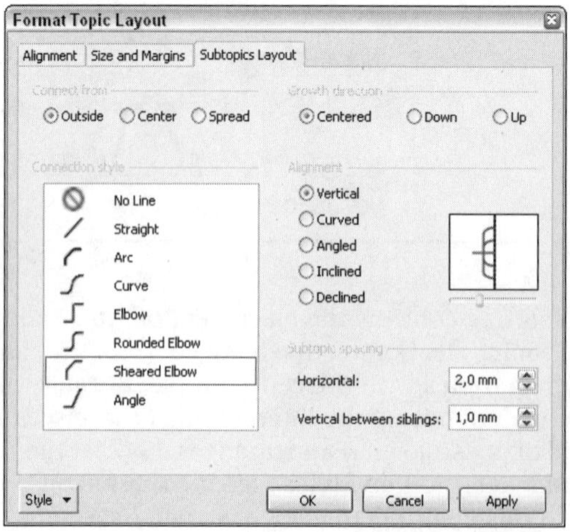

Figure 14-9:
The Subtopics Layout tab selected from a topic other than the central topic.

The Connect From and the Connection Style settings work in the same way as for the setting for the central topic. The Vertical Between Siblings and Horizontal settings function the same as the Vertical and Horizontal settings except that the Horizontal setting will be applied to existing subtopics as well as to new ones. Settings less than the MindManager calculated minimums are ignored.

The Growth Direction setting allows you to control the positioning of the sub-topics relative to the topic. Choosing Down tells MindManager to place the *first* subtopic at the same level as the topic and all other topics below that one. Choosing Up tells MindManager to place the *last* subtopic at the same level as the topic and all other topics above it. Choosing Centered tells MindManager to put as many subtopics above the level of the topic as below it.

The Alignment setting allows you to control the positioning of the subtopics relative to each other. The little thumbnail sketch will illustrate the result of each choice you make in the dialog box. The slider below the thumbnail is active for all choices except vertical and allows you to add more or less emphasis to your choice.

General Layout

The General Layout tab (shown in Figure 14-10) is only available if you select your central topic first. Clicking the Organic Appearance checkbox creates a heavier line under all the main topics. Clicking the Display Shadow checkbox results in a light gray duplication of the lines from the central topic to each of the main topics, creating a 3-D illusion for your map.

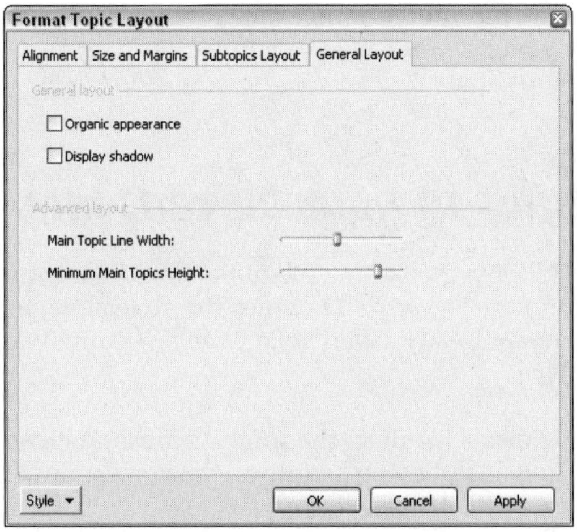

Figure 14-10: The General Layout tab.

Use the Main Topic Line Width to make the lines from the central topic to the main topics fatter (drag the slider to the right) or thinner (drag the slider to the left). Use the Minimum Main Topics Height slider to increase or decrease the empty space on your map between main topics. This slider duplicates the function of Vertical topic spacing (refer to Figure 14-8).

Reusing Styles

I had a lot of fun exploring all of these pages and seeing how much control I actually have over the appearance of a topic. It was with a bit of dismay, however, that I then noticed, after lots of mouse clicks and opening and saving of dialog boxes, that I had altered but one single topic on my map. The thought of having to go to every single topic to make all the same changes was daunting, to say the least.

Fortunately, there is an easy solution: the Style button at the bottom left-hand corner of each of these dialog boxes. Click this button, select Save As New Style Default, and voilà — every other element like the one you have changed will acquire the same style characteristics. Whew!

Another way to make the style of other topics match your current topic is to use the Format Painter button. Refer to chapter 2 for details.

Actually, the approach I describe in the previous section is better suited to making one topic appear *different* than all the others. To create a common style for all the elements in your map, you should work directly with the map style sheet. This has the additional advantage that, if you want to also use the styles for future maps, you can save your style sheet as a template. In this section, I show you how.

Changing styles in your current map

Select Format⇨Style⇨Modify. . . from the menu bar. MindManager displays the style sheet for your map. Figure 14-11 shows the style sheet for the default map. If you haven't already saved style changes, your style sheet should look very similar.

The upper left corner shows a list of all the topic elements defined by MindManager. If you click one of these headings, the corresponding element in the style sheet is automatically selected.

The middle display lets you define how many levels of topics you want to customize. In Figure 14-11, two levels have been selected. This means that you can define one style for the Central Topic, another style for main topics, and a third style for all second-level *and lower* subtopics.

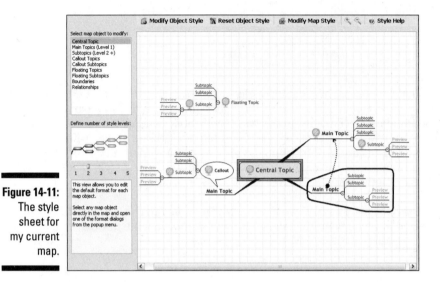

Figure 14-11:
The style
sheet for
my current
map.

When I first saw this, I got really excited and set the slider all the way over to five levels. This was not one of my more brilliant ideas. It was a lot of work defining that many different styles and I found that I rarely needed a different style for all levels below level 3. (I still can change one element using the tools in the previous section.) Try working with just the default two levels at first; then add more levels if you really need them.

The two style elements not accessible from the *Select map object to modify* list are the map background and the default font for topic notes. You can access these elements by clicking the Modify Map Style button at the top of the style sheet and selecting the element you want to modify.

The Reset Object Style button is your rescue lifeline in case you end up not liking your modifications. Clicking this button will restore all the settings for the selected topic element to those defined in the master style sheet (more on this in the section "Creating a style sheet master").

MindManager will display the format menu for the selected element type if you click the Modify Object Style button. It's actually easier, though, to just directly click the element you want to modify in the style sheet. MindManager immediately displays the format menu (see Figure 14-12), so you save a couple of mouse clicks and a fair amount of mouse motion (sounds like some kind of dread disease, doesn't it?).

Figure 14-12:
The Style
Sheet's
context
menu.

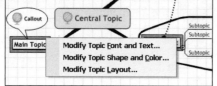

From this point on, everything works just as though you were working directly on your map. Your exit key is on the right-hand side of the gray bar just below the standard toolbar (the label says "Modify Style — Map"). If you click Cancel, everything you have done will be discarded (so feel free to play with the style sheet and explore all the possibilities). If you click Apply and Close, all of your style changes will be applied to your current map and the style sheet will be saved with the map.

The style sheet you have created is available only to the map in which you created it. If you want to make your style sheet available to other maps, continue reading!

Making a place for my stuff

You can save all the style sheets, icons, shapes, and other custom elements that you develop with the MindManager elements. If you plan to do only two or three special elements, that is probably the easiest and quickest solution.

The problem is that these MindManager elements are saved in your personal Windows folder called My Documents, where they are normally inaccessible to anyone else. Furthermore, if you should need to reinstall MindManager for any reason, your custom elements will be lost.

I suggest creating a separate set of folders to store these objects. You can create these folders on your own hard disk and then grant permission to others to access and use them. If you are working in a server environment, you (or your administrator) can create these folders on a shared drive and make them available to anyone in the company.

Create a place for your stuff (and maybe Mary's and Tom's as well) by following these steps:

1. **Select Tools⇨Package Folders . . . from the menu bar.**

   MindManager displays the Package Folders dialog box.

2. **Click New.**

   MindManager displays the New Package dialog box (see Figure 14-13).

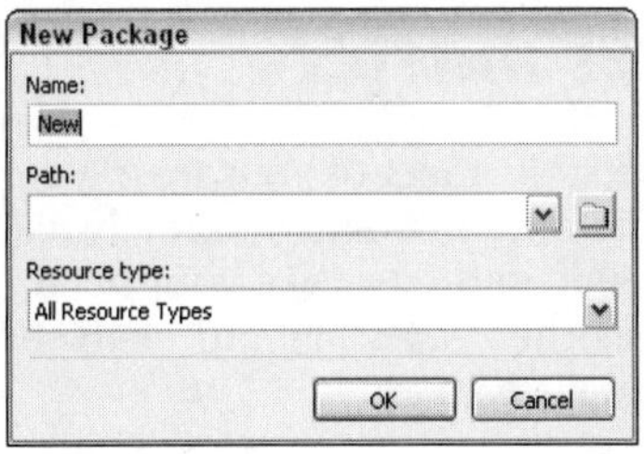

Figure 14-13:
The New
Package
dialog box.

3. Type the name you want for the custom elements master folder in the Name field.

MindManager will create specially named subfolders for various elements in this directory, so choose a name that is appropriate for a collection rather than one particular element.

4. Click the Folder Browse button and navigate to the directory where the master folder should be created; then click OK.

MindManager inserts the path into the Path field. Don't bother clicking the combo box arrow — the list is empty. The Mindjet folks must really love creating dialog box elements. If they don't get to create their quota for the day, they just make up useless ones for fun.

5. Click OK.

MindManager creates the master folder and subfolders for each type of topic element in the location you specify, returns to the Package Folders dialog box, and displays your new master folder name in the list (see Figure 14-14).

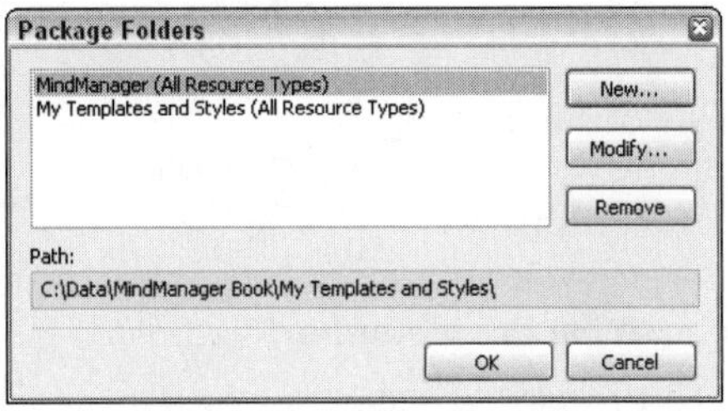

Figure 14-14:
The
Package
Folders
dialog box.

The New Package dialog box allows you to restrict the number of subfolders that MindManager creates to some subset of all the possible element types, but there is really no good reason to do this. Furthermore, MindManager will still offer you the option of saving every kind of element in this master folder and will then choke if the appropriate subfolder is missing.

You can change the parameters of your package folder by clicking the folder name and then clicking Modify.

Creating a style sheet master

OK, you've worked really hard on the style sheet of your map, you've gone back to the map itself and added more elements and you really like what you have. Now that little voice begins to sing in the back of your head, "Oh, this is wonderful. I want to save it to use for other maps!" Figure 14-15 shows the map style I had when I first heard this little voice.

To save your style sheet and make it available to future maps, follow these steps:

1. **If the map's style sheet is not already in edit mode, select Format⇨Style⇨Modify . . . from the menu bar.**

   The map's style sheet is displayed in edit mode (refer to Figure 14-15).

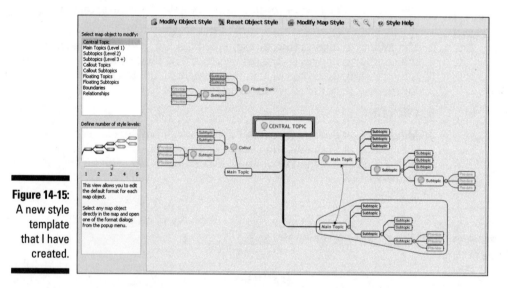

Figure 14-15:
A new style template that I have created.

2. **Select File⇨Properties . . . from the menu bar.**

   MindManager displays the Properties dialog box (as shown in Figure 14-16).

   If the Properties dialog box does not open with the Summary page displayed, click the Summary tab.

3. **Complete at least the Comments field with a brief description of this style sheet and how it should be used; then click OK.**

The Properties dialog box closes and the information is stored with the style sheet. The comments will be displayed anytime someone accesses the style sheet.

Windows provides powerful search tools based on information in the properties table. If you are going to have very many styles or several people will be creating shared styles, a bit of time invested in completing the Author, Category, and Keywords fields will yield big dividends.

Figure 14-16:
Properties
dialog box
for a style
sheet.

4. **Select File➪Save as . . . from the menu bar.**

   MindManager displays the Save As dialog box.

5. **Navigate to the Styles subfolder in your Package Folder (see the "Making a Place for My Stuff" section).**

   The Save As dialog box will be displayed as empty.

6. **Change the Save As file type to MindManager Styles (*.mmas).**

   If this is the first style sheet you have saved, the Save As dialog list box will remain empty. Otherwise, you will see the names of all the other custom styles that you have previously saved.

7. **Enter an appropriate and descriptive name for your style sheet and click Save.**

   Your style sheet is saved as a Style Sheet Master.

Using style sheet masters

To apply the style sheet master to a new map, follow these steps:

1. **Open the map and select Format⇨Style⇨Assign From Template Organizer . . .**

   MindManager displays the Select New Style for Current Map dialog box (as shown in Figure 14-17).

   You have to right-click the folder where you saved your Style Master in the library page of the Task pane and select Refresh before your new style master will be visible to MindManager.

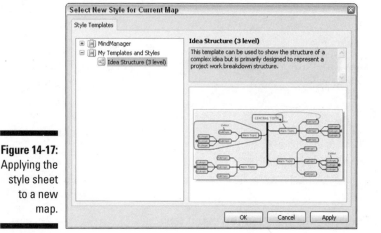

Figure 14-17: Applying the style sheet to a new map.

2. **Navigate to the desired style sheet and click Apply.**

   MindManager modifies your current map to reflect your chosen style.

You can preview all of the MindManager styles in this dialog box. Take a look at them if you want to get the creative juices flowing! By the way, *style sheet master* is not a term that MindManager itself uses — I just like the term because the result is so similar to the style sheet masters used in Microsoft PowerPoint.

Managing your style library

Anything you need to do to manage your style library begins by opening the Template Organizer to the Style Templates page. You do this by selecting Tools⇨Template Organizer . . . from the menu bar and then clicking the Style Templates tab at the top of the dialog box (as shown in Figure 14-18).

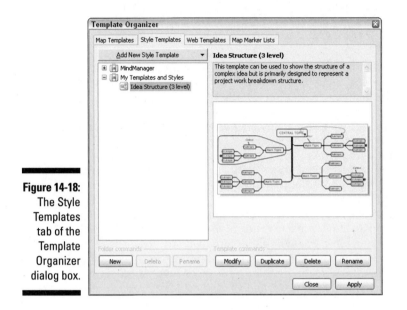

Figure 14-18:
The Style
Templates
tab of the
Template
Organizer
dialog box.

If you only have two or three style masters that you like and want to use again, don't worry about the New, Delete, and Rename buttons at the lower left — just store everything in the root Style folder and be done with it.

If you start accumulating many style masters, however, you will probably find it helpful to group them into appropriately named folders. The New, Delete, and Rename buttons allow you to create, organize, and name folders however you like. If you look at the Shapes directory in your Package Folder with File Explorer, you will see that you are just creating ordinary folders. The advantage of doing this from the Template Organizer is that the library display is also updated so that you don't need to right-click and then choose Refresh.

The Modify button opens the selected style master in edit mode. You can make any changes desired and then resave the master. If the master is already good and you plan to make it even better (everyone hear the warning buzzer and see the flashing red light?), it would probably be a good idea to first click the Duplicate button and make a backup. If it *really* is better, you can delete the backup by clicking the Delete button. (Okay, now everyone try to guess how many times *I* didn't make a backup before making something "better," only to find that I had made it much worse instead. It's a big number.)

You can create a style template master from your current map by clicking the *Add New Style Template* button and then selecting "From current map."

Subject Templates

I started my own managing consulting company almost 30 years ago. It was a little silly in the beginning, because the only creature I was managing was my cat. (I think I actually have that backwards.)

I made an introductory call one day on a prospect who clearly had no real interest in my services, but for the sake of politeness he accepted my business card and brochure. As I was getting ready to leave, the phone rang. It turned out that a prospect of *his* suddenly needed someone for a meeting — that afternoon, and more than 100 miles away.

He put his hand over the receiver, told me he had no interest in doing the work, and asked if I would take over for him. Being young and foolish (also desperate to win my first client), I said, "Sure, glad to." He passed this on to the client, telling them that this "experienced professional" would be coming in his place. After hanging up, he told me three or four sentences about what was wanted, gave me the address, and wished me luck.

I jumped in my car and went roaring down the highway, arriving at the client's office just as the meeting was starting. The President of the group began the meeting by introducing me and then saying that I was there to now "tell all of them what was necessary to get their project started."

I can assure you, it was 100 percent style that afternoon without a trace of substance! But style can only take you so far, and the same is true of your MindManager maps. A pretty map will get noticed, but it is its substance that holds attention. In this last section of this chapter, I tell you how you can also save your great ideas and topic organizations as Subject Templates that will give you and your colleagues a terrific head start on planning and managing your key business and personal activities.

Once organized, keep going

I often use MindManager to develop a structure for thinking about and working with a topic. One of the great challenges of business in recent years has been how to accomplish more and more with fewer people.

One of the greatest time wasters in business today is meetings when they are not properly planned, clear goals are not set, and time limits are not respected. Figure 14-19 shows the essential elements of a meeting planner that I have found very helpful. The meeting planner is responsible for completing all the items on the right side before the meeting starts, and the person responsible for documenting the meeting completes all the items on the left side as the meeting progresses.

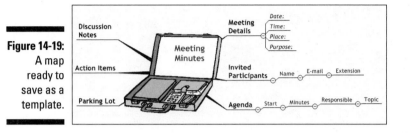

This is not a particularly complicated template, but there is still no reason to create this from scratch each time. To save this as a map template, I follow these steps:

1. **Select File⇨Properties . . . from the menu bar.**

   MindManager displays the Properties dialog box (refer to Figure 14-16).

2. **Complete at least the Comments field with a brief description of this template and how it should be used; then click OK.**

   The Properties dialog box closes and the information is stored with the template. The comments will be displayed anytime someone accesses the template.

3. **Select File⇨Save as . . . from the menu bar.**

   MindManager displays the Save As dialog box.

4. **Navigate to the Templates subfolder in your Package Folder (see the "Making a Place for My Stuff" section).**

   The Save As dialog list box will be empty.

5. **Change the Save As file type to MindManager Templates (*.mmat).**

   If this is the first template you have saved, the Save As dialog list box will remain empty. Otherwise, you will see the names of all the other templates that you have previously saved.

6. **Enter an appropriate and descriptive name for your template and click Save.**

   Your map is saved as a template.

You can also create a template from your current map by using the Template Organizer. Refer to the prior section on managing your style library for details. The Map Templates page functions identically to the Style Templates page.

To create a new map using your template, follow these steps:

1. **Select File⇨New . . . from the menu bar.**

   MindManager displays the New Map dialog box (as shown in Figure 14-20).

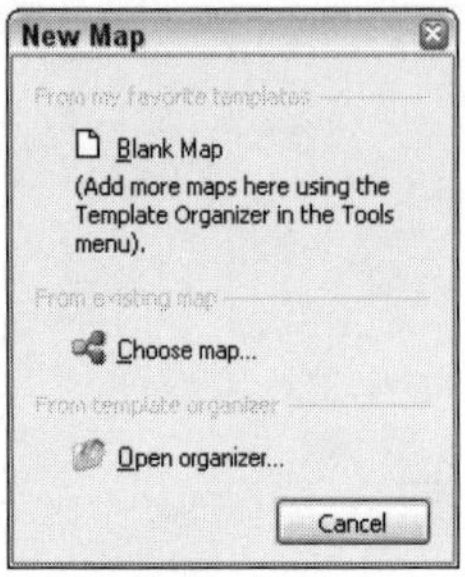

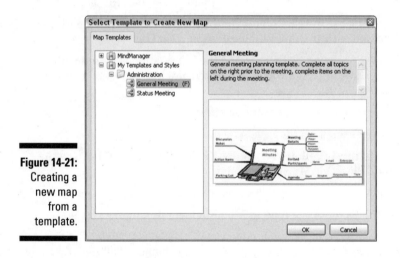

Figure 14-20:
The New
Map dialog
box.

2. **Click Open organizer . . .**

   MindManager displays the Select Template to Create New Map dialog box with the Map Templates page displayed (as shown in Figure 14-21).

Figure 14-21:
Creating a
new map
from a
template.

3. **Navigate to your template and then click OK.**

   MindManager creates a new map based on the template you selected. You can begin working on the map immediately.

If you use a particular template frequently, add it to your favorites list. Select Tools➪Template Organizer . . . from the menu bar and navigate to your template on the Map Templates page (see Figure 14-22). Check the *Show in favorite template list* box and then click OK.

The next time you open the New Map dialog box, your map template will be listed in the top section (see Figure 14-23).

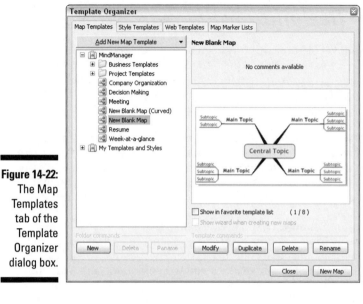

Figure 14-22:
The Map
Templates
tab of the
Template
Organizer
dialog box.

Figure 14-23:
The New
Map dialog
box with a
favorite
template
listed.

You are allowed a maximum of eight templates in your favorite list. To remove a template from your favorite list, open the Template organizer, navigate to the template to be deleted from the favorite list, uncheck the *Show in favorite template list* box, and click OK.

Using and changing the default template

If you click Blank Map in the New Map dialog box or simply click the New Map button on the standard toolbar, MindManager creates the new map using the special template called New Blank Map.

You can modify this template (make a backup first!) and, more importantly, its associated style sheet. All new maps that you create from the default template will then reflect your standard style.

Creating flexibility using map parts

Are you worn out yet? I know this has been a really long chapter, but there is just one more, very exciting thing I need to tell you about: You can create and use templates for parts of your map just like you can for an entire new map! This wonderful facility goes by the very straightforward name of *Map Parts*, because — well — they become parts of a map.

The Meeting Minutes template (refer to Figure 14-19) is a great example. It's important to have the e-mail address and telephone number of all the participants at hand (in part because I want to e-mail them their to-do list directly from my Map), but I will plan lots of meetings with the same participants. I sure don't want to enter the same information over and over again.

The solution is quite simple. First, I create a map that just has all of the company employees as topics. Figure 14-24 shows a start for "Dizzy" Bill. (You don't actually need an image of course, but creating a caricature for each employee can be a lot of fun and enables you to avoid doing any work for a little while.)

Figure 14-24:
A topic
ready to
save as a
map part.

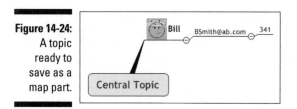

As soon as you have finished the map, you are ready to begin creating your Map Parts. Follow these steps:

1. **Click the Library tab on the Task pane.**

   MindManager displays the library page in the Task pane.

2. **Click Map Parts and then click your package folder.**

   If your package folder contains subfolders, click the subfolder where you want to save the Map Parts.

   Even if you don't create a lot of other custom objects in MindManager, you are likely to create lots of map parts because they are so useful. I strongly recommend using folders. Right-click your package folder and select New Folder. Give it an appropriate name for each group of map parts.

3. **Click the topic that should be the root topic in the Map Part.**

   MindManger indicates that the topic has been selected. In my example, I would click Bill.

4. Right-click the folder or subfolder where the Map Part is to be saved and select Add Selected Topic(s) and new map part(s).

MindManager saves the selected topic as a Map Part and displays a thumbnail in the lower half of the Task pane.

To apply a map part to an existing map, select the topic on your main map where the map part is to be attached as a subtopic (see Figure 14-25); then click the desired Map Part. MindManager adds the Map Part as a topic to your map (see Figure 14-26).

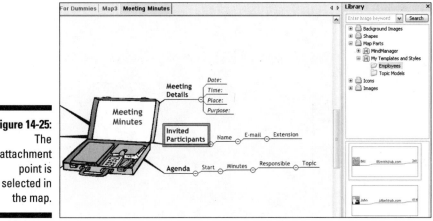

Figure 14-25:
The attachment point is selected in the map.

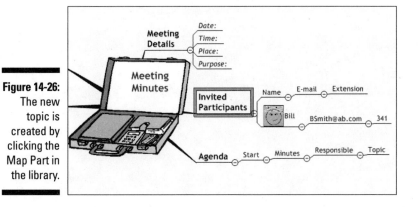

Figure 14-26:
The new topic is created by clicking the Map Part in the library.

MindManager provides a number of useful map parts (as shown in Figure 14-27). You can use these as they are or modify them by right-clicking the map part and selecting Modify.

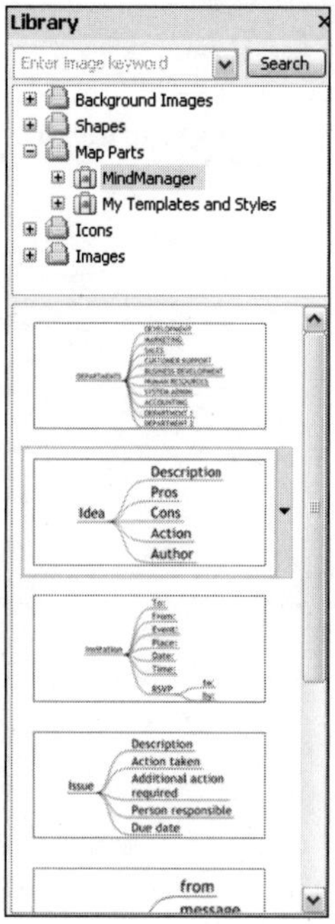

Figure 14-27:
Some of the
map parts
provided
with Mind-
Manager
with *Idea*
selected.

Chapter 15

Letting a Wonderful Wizard Guide You

*F*inding your way to your goal is always a challenge. Consider the case of the simple farm girl Dorothy and her little dog Toto, who are swept into the Kansas skies by a powerful tornado and carried far away to the magical land of Oz. It's a most unfortunate situation for Dorothy, who has no clue what to do next, although it was perhaps even more unfortunate for the poor, unfortunate witch who was just out for a quick spin on her broomstick.

Lacking any better idea, Dorothy steps out onto her front porch (the house having apparently survived the journey with no structural damage) in hopes of finding some inspiration. Instead, she is greeted by small, strange people in big hats, who are singing and dancing because they are so happy about this accident. Dorothy, appalled at the indifference to the death of this poor, inno-cent woman (after all, remember that this was the kinder and gentler time we've been told about), observes, "Toto — I've a feeling we aren't in Kansas any more."

How are Dorothy and Toto to get home? It soon becomes clear from the Munchkins (so the strange little people are called) that Dorothy needs a wizard to show her the way, and there just happens to be one in downtown Oz with time available on his calendar a week from Friday.

After a long and hazardous journey to the Emerald City (which is what hap-pens when you don't have wizards), she finally gets the guidance she needs and quickly and easily achieves her goal of getting home again.

The truth is, we all need magic slippers and guidance from time to time. Templates (which I cover in Chapter 14) can be your magic slippers, but if you don't have something to tell you to click your heels together three times in order to invoke the magic, you may not be able to use them.

MindManager wizards are exactly the "something" that you need. With them, you can guide the user step by step through the creation of a new map from a template. Users need to focus on only a few questions at a time and can always go backward and forward through the questions until they are satisfied with the answers. I tell you all about it in this chapter.

Creating a Wizard

When I first learned about MindManager wizards and the things that I could do with them, I got so excited that I fired up MindManager and tried to create a wizard from scratch. I may have learned a bit about how to create wizards, but what I produced was just about worthless.

As I gained more experience working with MindManager, I discovered that I absolutely had to begin with a dynamite (but wizard-less) map that I had used a few times and had perhaps modified a bit as I discovered more clearly exactly what it was that I really needed.

Figure 15-1 shows a map that I had used several times for status meetings on various projects. I really liked the concise way it laid out the essential things that I wanted to accomplish and my team members always knew what was expected of them in the meetings. We often finished ahead of schedule and had a good sense of accomplishment.

Figure 15-1:
A successful map used to run a project status meeting.

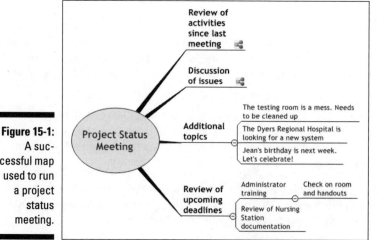

I had noticed all the things that I needed to delete from the previous status meeting map in order to reach my starting point for a new meeting, and I had created a template using this base map. (See Chapter 14 if you want to know more about this process.) I realized that it would be helpful to have the purpose, date, time, and place clearly stated on the map, so I added places to show this information in a callout. My final template looked like the one shown in Figure 15-2.

Wizards are available only in the X5 Pro version, and you can only use wizards with templates. MindManager runs the wizard one time when you create a new map from the template and deletes all of the wizard information from the map that is created. This also means that, once you have exited the wizard, you cannot restart it again without creating an entirely new map and starting over.

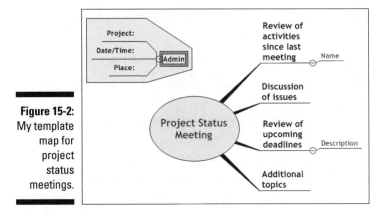

Figure 15-2: My template map for project status meetings.

Wizards only guide users to the entry of information so that they don't get confused or distracted by all of the topics that may be in your template. It's really important, then, to create your wizard so that it asks for information in a logical sequence. MindManager does not provide any mechanism to change the order of wizard elements to something other than the order in which you created them, so investing a little planning time before you start will save you a lot of rework later on.

I decided with my status meeting template that the most logical order of entering information would be to begin with the purpose, date, time, and place information. I could then add the invited participants and finally add the upcoming deadline topics.

A wizard will *replace* all the topic text on the template with the text that the user enters unless the topic text ends with a colon. If the topic text does end with a colon, the wizard will *append* the user's entry after the colon.

MindManager wizards can ask one, two, or three questions in a single dialog box. If I want the user to complete more than three topics, MindManager repeats the dialog box with the additional questions until all questions have been presented. If you remember this "rule of three," your wizards will feel much more user-friendly. For example, I could have chosen to have the meeting date and meeting time as two separate topics, but this would have meant that the user would have had to work with two dialog boxes (with only one question on the second one) rather than just one.

The phrase *Wizard Customization dialog box* refers to the dialog box you use to *build* your wizard (see Figure 15-3). The phrase *Wizard dialog box* refers to what MindManager constructs from your wizard settings when you create a new map from your template. You will see examples of these Wizard dialog boxes in the "Using a Wizard" section, later in this chapter.

In each of the following sections, I assume you have already completed the following steps:

1. **Select Tools⇨Template Organizer . . . from the menu bar.**

   MindManager displays the Template Organizer dialog box with the Map Templates page selected.

2. **Navigate to the template to which you wish to add a wizard and then click the Modify button.**

   MindManager opens the selected template in edit mode.

3. **Select Tools⇨Wizard Customization . . . from the menu bar.**

   MindManager displays the Wizard Customization dialog box (as shown in Figure 15-3).

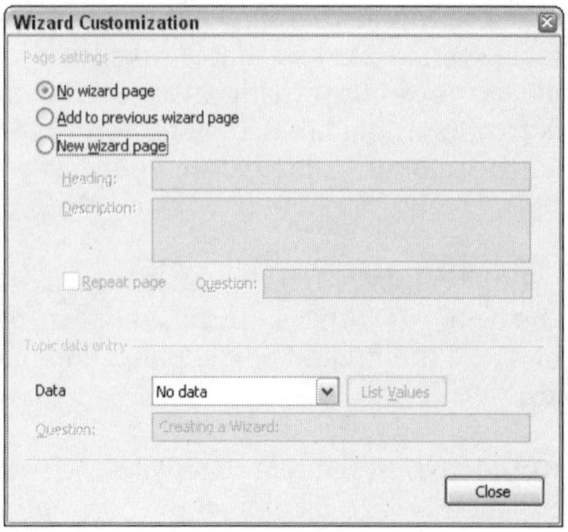

Figure 15-3:
The Wizard Customiz-ation dialog box.

I divide this wizard-creation process into three distinct parts, each of which requires a slightly different combination of wizard settings, so that you can easily find the description you need. However, when you do this on your map, you don't need to close and re-open the Wizard Customization dialog box. Just click the next topic to which you want to add wizard components and continue on. Close the dialog box and save your template only when you have entered all of your wizard components.

Adding multiple subtopics to an anchor topic

Completing the Admin callout in Figure 15-2 is an example of this category of wizard task. The main callout topic will still be called "Admin" when the wizard finishes, but I want to create a wizard to help the user complete the other three topics. To do this, follow these steps:

1. **Click the topic that is to be the anchor topic.**

   MindManager displays the current wizard settings for the topic in the Wizard Customization dialog box. If there are no current settings, the *No wizard page* radio button will be selected and the rest of the fields will be empty.

2. **Click the *New wizard page* radio button and enter the heading and description for the new page (as shown in Figure 15-4).**

Figure 15-4: Completed dialog box settings for a new wizard page.

Wizard Customization	☒

Page settings

○ No wizard page (resets all other settings)
○ Add to previous wizard page
◉ New wizard page

Heading: Meeting Administration

Description: Please enter the project name and the date, time and place of the meeting.

☐ Repeat page   Question:

Topic data entry

Data   No data ▾   List Values

Question: Admin:

Close

MindManager uses this information to build the Wizard dialog box when your map is loaded. The top line will include your heading entry (in bold) followed by your description (the figures in the Using a Wizard section later in this chapter show the results of these settings).

Do not click the Repeat Page check box, but *do* leave the Data selection set to No data.

3. **Click the first subtopic you want to attach to your anchor.**

   MindManager displays the current wizard settings for the topic in the Wizard Customization dialog box.

4. **Click the *Add to previous wizard page* radio button.**

   MindManager grays out the entire *Page settings* section because the page settings from the prior dialog box will be used.

5. **Select the Data Type for the subtopic (see Table 15-1) and enter the prompting question you want MindManager to display in the Wizard dialog box.**

   MindManager outlines the subtopic with a contrasting color to indicate that it is bound to the anchor topic.

6. **Repeat steps 3, 4, and 5 for each additional subtopic you want to bind to your anchor topic.**

   MindManager updates the map display to show all topics bound to the anchor topic (see Figure 15-5).

Table 15-1		Wizard Data Types
Selection	*Allowed Entry*	*Wizard Behavior*
No Data	None allowed	Skips the subtopic.
Text	Any	Allows entry of any characters up to a maximum length of 255.
List	Only items included on the list	Displays combo drop-down box for selection; does not permit editing or entry of items not on the list.
Date	Only a date in long format (day of week, month, day, year)	Displays a calendar that can be scrolled to month desired. Entry is created by clicking the desired date on the calendar display.
Hyperlink	A valid path to a stored data item	Provides a browse button that enables navigation to the desired data item. Path can be entered directly as text if desired.
Time	Only time in long format (hh:mm:ss)	User can select any one of the three fields (hours, minutes, or seconds) and type a new value, or can use the up/down arrows to adjust with mouse clicks.

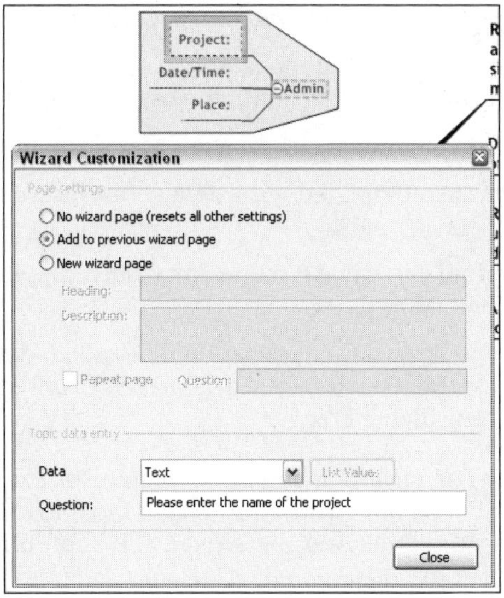

Figure 15-5:
Completed
wizard
page for
the Admin
anchor
topic.

The wizard pages are indicated on the template map only when the Wizard Customization dialog box is visible.

7. **If you have completed all the wizard pages for your template, click Close and then save your template.**

   MindManager closes the Wizard Customization dialog box, deletes the boundary indicators for the wizard pages, and makes your template available to the File⇨New dialog box.

Adding repeating variable subtopics

I will not always know the number of subtopics that I might want to create on my map, and I may not always have an anchor topic either. Using my status meeting template as an example, I may have only two or three people attend one meeting, and perhaps six or seven will attend the next one. I can add a repeating variable subtopic as follows:

1. **Create one model subtopic on your template to indicate where the wizard is to attach the variable number of subtopics.**

   In Figure 15-6, my model subtopic is *Name*. It is a subtopic of *Review of activities since last meeting*.

2. **Create a wizard page for the model subtopic as described in the previous section.**

   MindManager highlights the model subtopic with color to indicate that it has an associated wizard page.

3. **Click the Repeat Page check box and enter a prompting question.**

During execution, MindManager will repeatedly display the same wizard page, adding a new subtopic each time, until the user clicks the No button.

4. **Complete the Data and Question fields in the Topic data entry section.**

MindManager displays the completed wizard page (as shown in Figure 15-6).

5. **If you have completed all the wizard pages for your template, click Close and then save your template.**

MindManager closes the Wizard Customization dialog box, deletes the boundary indicators for the wizard pages, and makes your template available to the File⇨New dialog box.

You can combine both types of wizards if you like. Assume, for example, that in addition to each participant's name, you want to also include the title of his or her topic and the allotted time. Add these fixed sub-subtopics to your model subtopic, and then use the *Add to previous wizard page* radio button setting for each sub-subtopic. During execution, MindManager will then repeat the entire sequence of Name, topic, and time questions, creating the branches on your map each time, until the user clicks the No button.

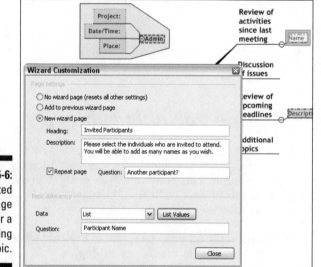

Figure 15-6:
Completed wizard page for a repeating subtopic.

Adding fixed subtopics from a list

To limit the text entry for a subtopic to items only on a specific list, select List as the data type (refer to Figure 15-6) and then click the List Values button. MindManager then displays the dialog box shown in Figure 15-7.

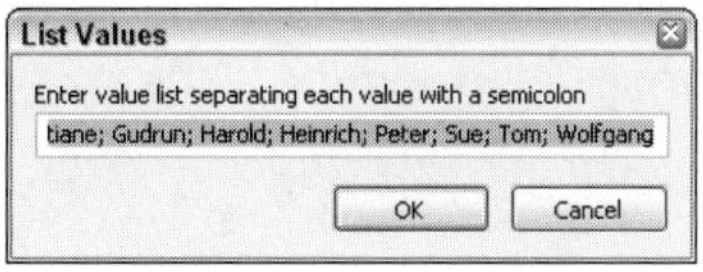

Figure 15-7:
The List
Values
dialog box.

List Values

Enter value list separating each value with a semicolon

tiane; Gudrun; Harold; Heinrich; Peter; Sue; Tom; Wolfgang

OK   Cancel

Enter the list of valid choices in the value list field, separating each value with a semicolon. The drop-down combo box that MindManager creates is approximately the same width as the entry field, so if there is any choice that cannot be completely displayed in the list field, the user will not be able to see the entire item either.

This tool is only suitable for relatively short lists (the maximum number of characters for all choices, including the semicolons, is 255) that change only occasionally. The list cannot be modified except by loading the template again in edit mode and manually changing the list.

MindManager displays your list in the exact order you enter it, so if you want the list to be alphabetized or in numeric order, you must enter it that way.

Changing a Wizard

You can modify your wizard in the same way that you created it: Load the template containing the wizard from the Template Organizer as described in the "Creating a Wizard" section, select Tools➪Wizard customization . . . from the menu bar, click the topic whose wizard parameters you want to modify, and make the modifications you want.

Unfortunately, there is no easy way to modify the sequence of wizard pages. New wizard pages are always added after those already created, so if you want to insert a wizard page, you must first delete all the wizard pages after the insertion point, create your new wizard page, and then re-create all of the other wizard pages that you deleted. The same approach is necessary if you want to change the order of wizard pages.

To delete a wizard page, follow these steps:

1. **Open the template and the Wizard Customization dialog box as described at the beginning of this section.**

   MindManager displays the Wizard Customization dialog box.

2. **Click the first subtopic that is to be added to the Wizard dialog box on your map.**

   MindManager displays the wizard parameters for the subtopic in the Wizard Customization dialog box (refer to Figure 15-5).

3. **Click the *No wizard page* radio button.**

   The entries for all other fields are deleted and the fields are grayed out.

   You cannot undo this action. If you make this choice in error, you must re-enter all of the parameters.

4. **Repeat steps 2 and 3 for all remaining subtopics that were marked *Add to previous wizard page*.**

   MindManager deletes the colored outline and fill around the subtopic on your map template.

5. **Select the topic that contains the wizard page information and repeat step 3.**

   MindManager removes the colored outline and fill around the anchor topic.

6. **Click Close and then save your template.**

   The wizard page has been deleted from your template.

Using a Wizard

The wizard executes automatically when a new map is created from the wizard's template. The following figures show the execution of the wizard when I create a map from my Status Meeting template. Compare the Wizard Customization entries shown in Figures 15-4 through 15-7 with the resulting Wizard dialog boxes shown in this section.

Figure 15-8 shows the Meeting Administration page with questions asking for the text to be inserted on the three fixed subtopics in the callout. MindManager highlights the entry point where the answers to the questions will be inserted on the new map as shown. The user can drag the Wizard dialog box to another place on the map if desired.

In Figure 15-9, the user has completed answering the three questions and is ready to click the Next button.

In Figure 15-10, the user has clicked the Next button. The entries from Step 1 have been added to the map. Because Project, Date/Time, and Place ended with colons on the template, MindManager has appended the Step 1 answers to these descriptive headers.

The Step 2 wizard page has been displayed, and the user has clicked the arrow on the drop-down combo box to display all the names that were entered on the list (refer to Figure 15-7). The list in Figure 15-10 is hiding a "Back" button. If I realize I made an error or a typo on the Step 1 page, I can click the Back button, return to Step 1, and correct my entries.

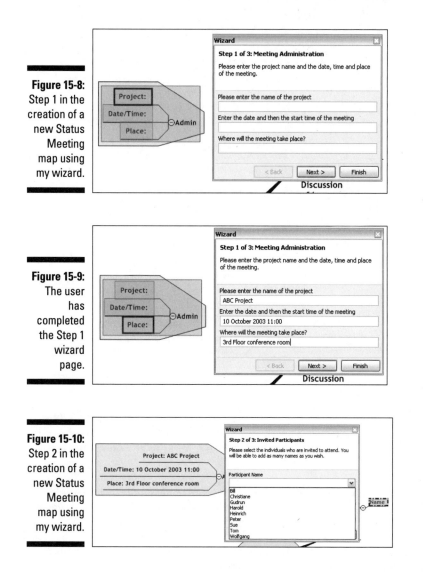

Figure 15-8:
Step 1 in the
creation of a
new Status
Meeting
map using
my wizard.

Figure 15-9:
The user
has
completed
the Step 1
wizard
page.

Figure 15-10:
Step 2 in the
creation of a
new Status
Meeting
map using
my wizard.

Notice in Figure 15-11 that the subtopic "Bill" has been created on my map. The wizard now asks if I want to create another participant. (Notice that this is the question I entered when I created this page, as shown in Figure 15-6.) If I click Yes, I will see Figure 15-10 again. If I click No, I will move on to Step 3.

In Figure 15-12, I have already added a total of four participants and then clicked the No button when MindManager asked if I wanted to add another participant. You can see how MindManager added these names to my map. MindManager now displays the wizard for Step 3. Again, I can click the Back button if I want to go back to a previous Step page to make changes.

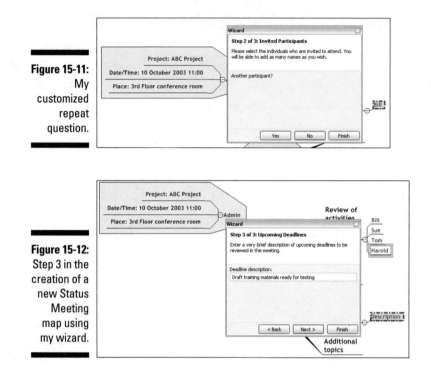

Figure 15-11:
My customized repeat question.

Figure 15-12:
Step 3 in the creation of a new Status Meeting map using my wizard.

In Figure 15-13, I have entered two deadline review topics and then clicked the No button when MindManager asked if I wanted to add another deadline review topic. MindManager has now reached the end of the wizard parameters on this template and gives me one last chance to modify any of my entries using the wizard.

If I click Finish, the wizard will close and all wizard parameters will be deleted from my map. I can still modify my map entries using the normal MindManager tools, but I cannot start the wizard again.

Figure 15-14 shows my Status Meeting map after the wizard closes. I probably have more things to add for this particular meeting, but I'm a long way down the road to being prepared!

Figure 15-15 shows a different template created to illustrate how the wizard obtains topic information if you select the Date, Time, and Hyperlink data types (refer to Table 15-1).

MindManager does not provide a wizard data type for date and time in one field like you find in the Microsoft Office applications.

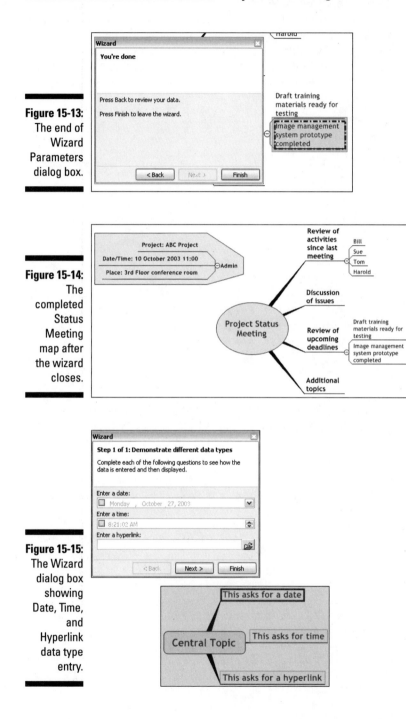

Figure 15-13:
The end of Wizard Parameters dialog box.

Figure 15-14:
The completed Status Meeting map after the wizard closes.

Figure 15-15:
The Wizard dialog box showing Date, Time, and Hyperlink data type entry.

If I click the down arrow on the Date entry field, the wizard displays a calendar, as shown in Figure 15-16. I scroll to the desired year and month, and then I click the date. The wizard automatically adds a check mark next to the date entry when I click the down arrow.

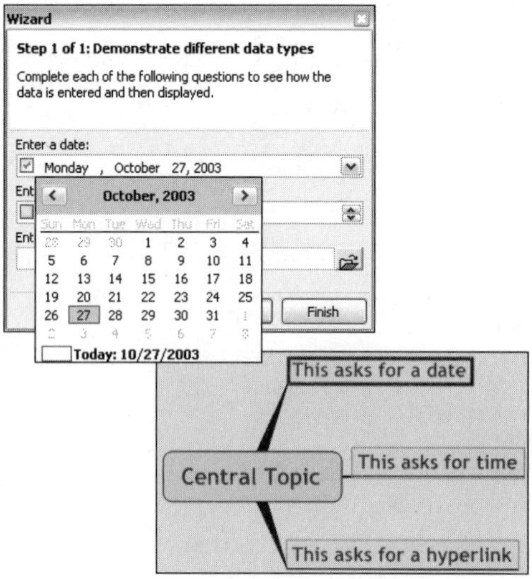

Figure 15-16:
The wizard data entry calendar tool.

Figure 15-17 shows the completion of the Time data field. I must first click the check box and then click the part of the time I want to modify (hours, minutes, or seconds). I can either type in the value I want or use the scrolling arrows at the right.

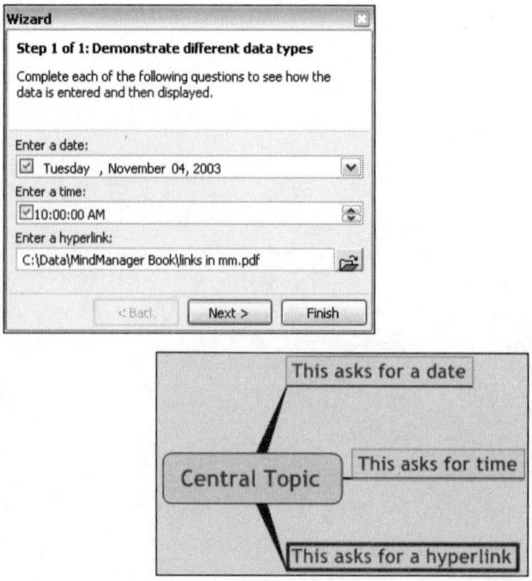

Figure 15-17:
The completed Wizard dialog box for this map template.

I can click the browse button to the right of the Hyperlink field and then browse for the document to which I want to add a hyperlink. When I click OK, the wizard inserts the path into the data field of the hyperlink, and then displays the hyperlink icon at the end of the topic line.

In Figure 15-18, I have clicked Finish in the End of Wizard Parameters dialog box (refer to Figure 15-13), and MindManager now displays my completed map. Notice that, because none of my template entries ended in a colon, MindManager has *replaced* the template topic text with my wizard entries.

The entries that the wizard created on my map are now just text entries that I can modify however I want. This means that I can use the calendar feature in the wizard without being stuck with this particular date format.

Figure 15-18:
The
completed
map.

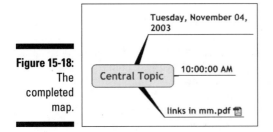

Adding Pizzazz with Smart Map Parts

You know, I really am very fond of programmers. My goodness, where would we be without these creative folks who find happiness and fulfillment in lives spent in front of a computer munching french fries and sipping a soda for a fashionably late dinner at 11pm? The only problem is, many of them cannot imagine that there are people who actually find some other source of pleasure in life. The result is that the rest of us have to put up with some pretty challenging and unfriendly barriers in order to realize the benefits of their creativity.

Smart Map Parts (SMPs), the topic of this section, are a very good example of this. We talked about plain old simple Map Parts (MPs) in Chapter 14. These are just fragments of topics that I might want to use repeatedly, so I create an MP with the structure I want and save it in the Map Parts section of my library. Then, when I want to use it, I select the anchor topic on my map and click the MP. MindManager automatically inserts the map fragment into my map.

The problem with both MPs and wizards is that they are *static*. After I have created them, they can be changed only by opening them in edit mode, modifying them, and then resaving them. If the changes are only relevant to the next map, I gain no advantage by working with the MP or the wizard. It is more efficient just to build my map from scratch.

SMPs, on the other hand, are *dynamic* wizards that are capable of modifying themselves according to the details of the current map and, in some cases, the underlying information that is to be represented on the map. Unfortunately, creating an SMP requires a knowledge of programming that is beyond most of us. (Appendix C has a very simple example. You might want to try it out, because all you have to do is copy a small amount of program code.) Given this new technology, however, I hope we can expect other developers to begin writing SMPs that we will find useful and timesaving in the near future.

MindManager includes a few very useful SMPs (and some not so useful). I describe the useful ones in this last section.

File Explorer SMPs

The File Explorer SMPs allow you to create a dynamic list of files, folders, or files *and* folders directly on your map. If the content of your folder changes, you can update your map display with just a couple of mouse clicks. You can, of course, put a hyperlink to a folder on your map without using an SMP. Clicking this hyperlink will open Windows Explorer and navigate to the defined folder so that you can see the current contents. This method, however, does not enable you to view the files directly on your map, nor does it automatically create hyperlinks to each file. File Explorer SMPs, on the other hand, accomplish both of these objectives (see Figure 15-19).

To add a File Explorer SMP to your map, follow these steps:

1. **Select the topic that you want to be the anchor point for the SMP or create a new anchor point topic somewhere on your map.**

   MindManager changes the color of the topic to show it has been selected.

2. **Right-click the anchor topic and then select Insert Hyperlink . . .**

   MindManager opens the Insert Hyperlink dialog box.

 3. **Click the Browse Folder icon, navigate to the desired folder, and click OK in the Browse To Folder dialog box.**

   MindManager inserts the path to the desired folder into the hyperlink field.

4. **Click OK.**

    MindManager closes the Insert Hyperlink dialog box and inserts the folder hyperlink icon next to your anchor topic.

5. **Click the Library tab in the Task pane and then select Map Parts⇨MindManager⇨File Explorer.**

   MindManager displays the File Explorer SMPs in the lower half of the Task pane.

6. **Point your mouse to the desired SMP.**

   MindManager displays a small down arrow on the right side of the SMP. Figure 15-19 shows examples of the output you can expect from each one. Choosing All Files and Folders will combine the two different displays into one.

7. **Click the down arrow and select Insert as New Topic.**

   MindManager will display a small progress dialog box while it obtains a list of all the files and/or folders from the location specified in your hyperlink and, after a short pause, will display a list similar to that shown in Figure 15-19. You can change the SMP text to something more descriptive if you like.

You can refresh the display so that it shows the current contents of the designated folder(s) at any time by right-clicking the SMP in your map and selecting Map Part⇨Refresh. MindManager displays a message box reminding you that the refresh process will delete any changes you made to the display and asks if you really want to refresh. I personally find this rather annoying to answer every time I want to refresh the display, so I check the Don't Ask Again box.

If you change your mind and don't want the SMP on your map anymore, just delete it as you would any other topic. This will not damage any of the referenced files or folders.

If you want to send your map to someone else without sending the underlying folder(s) and files, you first need to convert the SMP to an ordinary MP (otherwise MindManager will delete the file and/or folder list on the next refresh because it no longer has access to the hyperlinked directory). You do this by right-clicking the SMP in your map and selecting Map Part⇨Convert to Regular.

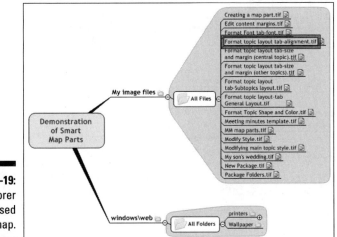

Figure 15-19:
File Explorer
SMPs used
in a map.

You cannot undo this selection. If you accidentally convert an SMP to an MP, your only choice is to delete the MP and re-add an SMP beginning with step 6 in the preceding list.

Although a right-click on an SMP shows several choices in addition to the ones normally seen on the topic context menu, none of them are of any particular use with SMPs and can simply be ignored.

Outlook Linker SMPs

You can tightly integrate your Outlook files, folders, and e-mail items with your maps using the Outlook Linker SMPs. I found the implementation of this functionality to be a bit confusing and awkward, but the value and usefulness it brings to MindManager maps makes it worth figuring out.

When using Outlook Linker SMPs, it's critical to remember that any time you add one of these SMPs to your map using MindManager, you create a *new* item in Outlook. Outlook will immediately display its own appropriate dialog box and ask you to complete the data fields. To add an *existing* Outlook item to your map, you must do so from Outlook.

Suppose I'm planning a vacation (with all the vacation planning I do, you would think I would actually take vacations more often). I've just started my map, as shown in Figure 15-20. I suddenly realize that if I decide to take a vacation in the Far East, I need to update my immunizations. Because my doctor always has a fairly full calendar, I need to be sure I don't forget to set up an appointment. I could, of course, just switch to Outlook and add a reminder task there, but then I wouldn't have a link to it from my vacation planning map.

Because I do want to create a new item in Outlook, I can add an SMP directly onto my map. To do this, I follow exactly the same steps that were required to add a File Explorer SMP: Click the Library tab, select Map Parts⇨ MindManager⇨Outlook Linker, right-click Task, and choose Insert as new topic.

Figure 15-20:
The start of my vacation planning map.

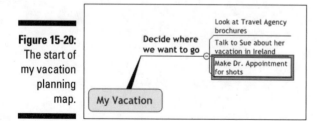

You must either select the anchor topic on your map where the SMP is to be added before starting this process or drag the SMP and drop it onto the anchor topic.

MindManager appends the Task SMP and, after a brief pause, displays the Outlook Task dialog box (shown in Figure 15-21). I complete as much information as I know about this task (which at this point is not much!). I then save and close the Outlook dialog box.

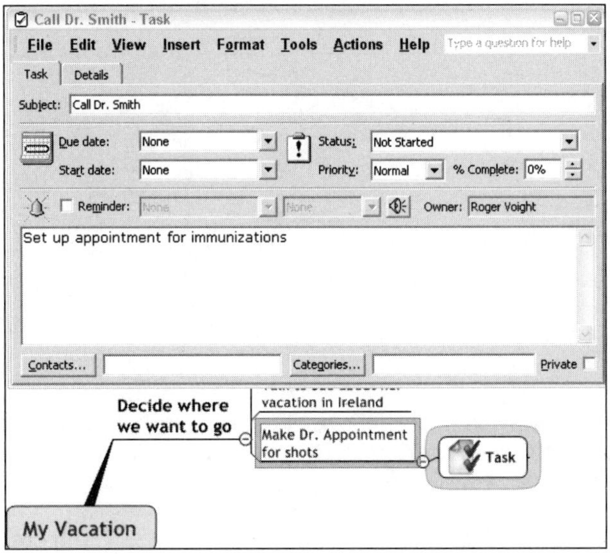

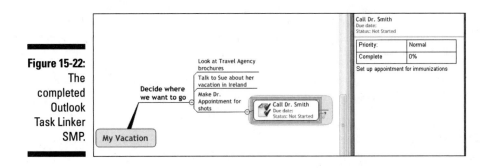

Figure 15-21: Entering task details in the Outlook Task dialog box.

MindManager then updates the SMP text and records the additional task information in the topic notes, as shown in Figure 15-22. If I switch to Outlook, I will find this task in my task list just as if I had created it directly in Outlook.

Figure 15-22: The completed Outlook Task Linker SMP.

When I manage to reach the doctor, I will want to update this task record with the date and time of the appointment and perhaps add other information as well. I can either do this directly in Outlook, or I can right-click the Task SMP, select Map Part⇨Open Outlook Item, and update the record that way.

If I update the record in Outlook, I need to tell MindManager to update the information in my map. I do this by right-clicking the Task SMP and selecting Map Part⇨Refresh. MindManager then updates the topic and topic notes information, as shown in Figure 15-23.

Figure 15-23:
My vacation planning map updated with task information from Outlook.

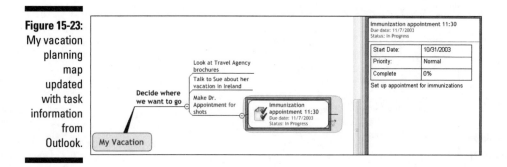

Returning to my vacation planning map, I remember that my friend Paul recently returned from a vacation in Thailand and decide that I would like to talk to him about his experiences.

If I add the Contact SMP directly in MindManager, the SMP will create a new, blank contact record in Outlook rather than allowing me to choose Paul's existing record. The addition of existing Outlook data to a map must be done from Outlook.

Because I want all the relevant information to be in this map, I want to include his contact information. I could just copy what I need from my address record, but what if his telephone number changes before I call him? I would then need to change the number in both places. (Okay, this is getting a little silly for a vacation plan, but you see the point.) I now need to switch to Outlook to locate Paul's address record.

You must select the anchor topic in your map *before* you switch to Outlook and select the record to be linked.

I click Paul's address record in my Outlook contact list and then click the Send to MindManager button on Outlook's standard toolbar. Because of all the viruses that use the Outlook address list to propagate themselves, Outlook always displays the warning message shown in Figure 15-24. You must click Yes to allow the information to be passed to MindManager. If you are planning to send several items to your map, click the *Allow access for* check box and choose an appropriate time limit. Outlook will then not display this warning again until you try to access an Outlook record after your chosen time limit has expired.

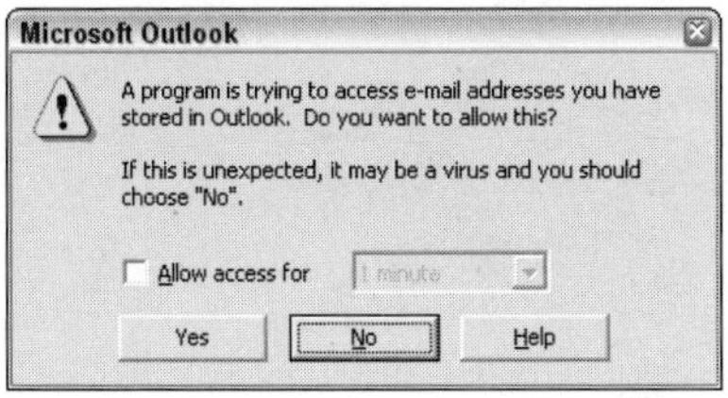

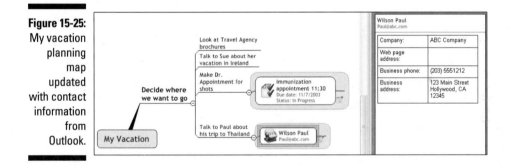

Figure 15-24:
Outlook's
file access
warning
dialog box.

All of Paul's address information is then added to my map, either to the topic itself or to the topic notes, as shown in Figure 15-25.

Figure 15-25:
My vacation
planning
map
updated
with contact
information
from
Outlook.

The Notes and Appointment SMPs function in exactly the same way. MindManager always knows the right SMP to use when you send a record from Outlook.

There is one more Outlook Linker SMP that you might find useful. Create a topic on your map to reference a folder in Outlook. Switch to Outlook, select that folder, and click the Export Folder to MindManager button on the Outlook standard toolbar.

MindManager will add the Outlook Folder SMP to your anchor topic. If you now right-click this SMP, select Map Part➪Open Outlook Item, and *then* switch to Outlook, you will find your folder selected and the contents displayed.

Chapter 16

Recombining the Building Blocks with Scripting

My grandfather was a railroad conductor for the old Illinois Central Railway for more than 30 years. One of his most prized and trusted possessions was his railroad watch, an enormous pocket watch nearly a half inch thick and two inches in diameter. Swiss made, it was the most accurate timekeeper that could be bought at any price until the electric Seikos and Rolexes appeared many decades later. For a boy of eight or nine years, it was just magic. I would ask my grandfather a dozen times a day for the time just to watch him slowly pull that marvel out of his pocket, always securely fastened to his belt with a broad, golden-chained fob, open the cover, and announce the exact time (he *never* said it was two o'clock unless it was *exactly* two o'clock). On special occasions, he would let me hold it for a short time and watch the tiny movements of the second hand.

One day, when I asked what time it was for the umpteenth time, a different pocket watch appeared — much older, but still a railroad watch. This one had a leather fob, and my grandfather fastened it to *my* belt! To this day, I can vividly remember the shock, the heart-pounding excitement, and disbelief that such a treasure was actually being entrusted to me. I practiced for hours in front of the mirror, trying to exactly mimic the way he pulled the watch from his pocket to tell time. In the weeks and months after that, it was my grandfather asking *me* what time it was when we were working in his yard. Smart man, my grandfather!

He died a year or so after that, and strangely enough, the watch stopped working at almost the same time. I was just devastated, and my father went to several jewelry stores to try and get it repaired. It was just too old and no one was willing to attempt repairs. In desperation, I decided I would try to fix it myself. I remember carefully removing the incredibly tiny screws and trying to see what I could do to make it run again — and the moment when the mainspring sprung open, flinging the gears and pieces all over the room. It was a powerful lesson for a young boy about knowing what you were getting into before you started!

Well, in this chapter I tell you what you are getting into if you decide to go under the hood of MindManager and try to get it to do some new tricks that the creators never thought of. By the way, I promise you there are no "main-springs" that will throw MindManager all over the room in tiny pieces! The examples in Appendix C will give you a little hint at how much fun it can be to just explore some possibilities.

Depending on your reason for turning to this chapter, you may not want to read every section. Here are some suggestions:

✔ If you really have no interest at all in programming but do want to use some program code (that was prepared by a friend, downloaded from some site on the Internet, or copied from Appendix C), follow the steps described in the section entitled "Getting Started with Scripts."

✔ If you already know a bit about programming but don't quite know how to get at the gears and levers of an application like MindManager, read this entire chapter.

✔ Finally, if you already have some experience with OOP, just skip right ahead to Appendix C ("Useful Scripts") and start playing with the examples to orient yourself with the MindManager Object Model. You'll find the environment very similar to what you already know from Microsoft's Visual Basic for Applications.

Creating and running MindManager programs (called *macros*) is only available in the X5 Pro version.

What on Earth is an "Object"?

This book is about all the things that MindManager can do for you through mouse clicks, dragging things around the screen, and typing. It's really a pretty impressive list. But sooner or later, you may decide you want to do something with one mouse click instead of three or four, or you want to use some of the MindManager functions in an entirely different way.

MindManager provides a way for you to do this by providing access to its many program functions through the process called *scripting*. To use the language from the World of Object Oriented Programming (WoOOP), MindManager *exposes* its information and functions to your script program. (Sounds a bit racy, doesn't it?) Programming with objects sounds pretty intimidating, but in fact it really is nothing more than a formal way of talking about the parts and pieces of something and how they all work together.

By the way, the people from WoOOP may be a bit offended by this bit of irreverence (they would just call it OOP), but the first few times I tried to work with OOP, I was saying, "woops, that's not what I wanted to do," quite a bit, so it fits somehow.

Look at Figure 16-1. It's an ordinary traffic signal, and it has several components: a support pole, a control board, different colored lights, and so on. Now, a traffic signal doesn't have anything at all to do with MindManager scripting, but there is an interesting parallel between the traffic signal's control board and MindManager's macros: Both can be programmed to make their device (traffic signal) or application (MindManager) do things the way the user wants.

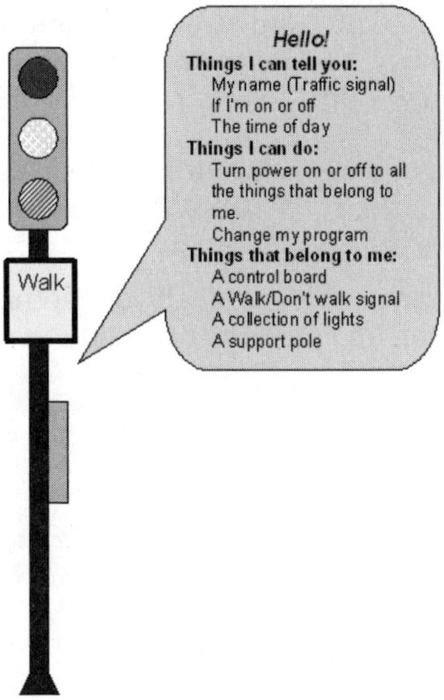

Figure 16-1:
Meet Mr.
Traffic
Signal and
learn about
the things
he can do
and tell you
about.

In WoOOP, all the things that belong to the traffic signal are called *objects* (hence the name, *object*-oriented programming), and the traffic signal is called the *parent* of all the things that belong to it. In a similar way, MindManager has topics of various kinds, buttons, menus, icons, and so on, and these are all MindManager objects, while a toolbar is the parent of all the buttons *on* that toolbar.

Some of the objects on the traffic signal can do things. For example, the green light can turn on and off and the walk signal can display "Walk" or "Don't Walk." In WoOOP, the things that an object can do are called its *methods*. The Save button in MindManager can record the current contents of your map on your hard disk, so this is one of MindManager's methods.

Objects can also store bits of information and provide this information on request. The control board on the traffic signal can "ask" the red light if it is on or off and determine the next light to turn on based on this information. Similarly, a topic on your map has the text you typed in when you created it. Your script program can "ask" for the text of the topic and make it available to your script program to change in some way (after your program changes the text, MindManager will change the displayed text on your map). The information that an object stores about itself is called its *properties*.

Okay, just how would I "ask" the traffic signal what word it is displaying on the Walk signal? Look at Figure 16-2. If I were to ask you, I might ask the question this way:

What is **My Current Display** of the **Walk Signal** of the **Traffic Signal**?

(Okay, you might conclude I was more than a little weird if I asked it this way, but stay with me here.) I "ask" the Walk Signal in my pretend traffic signal program in exactly the same way, although I must follow the WoOOP conventions:

- ✔ Any time a *property* is on the right-hand side of a statement, it is understood that a question is being asked, so "What is" and the question mark aren't needed.

- ✔ The order of the objects is always from right to left so that the most important object is shown first and the property or method is shown last.

- ✔ The words "of the" are replaced by a period.

- ✔ Spaces are eliminated.

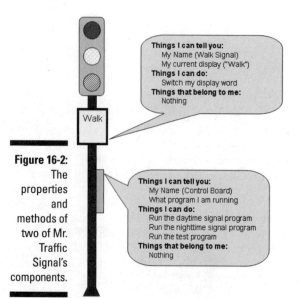

Figure 16-2:
The properties and methods of two of Mr. Traffic Signal's components.

Rephrasing my question according to WoOOP rules, I now ask the following:

```
DisplayedWords = TrafficLight.WalkSignal.MyCurrentDisplay
```

DisplayedWords is a *variable* name that I chose, and I can now use it later in my control board program. For example, if in a different part of my pretend traffic signal program I have determined that the red light is about to be turned on, I might have this program statement:

```
If DisplayedWords = "Walk" then
TrafficLight.WalkSignal.SwitchMyDisplayWord
```

SwitchMyDisplayWord is a method of WalkSignal (see Figure 16-2), and the above statement would cause WalkSignal to turn off the lights behind the word "Walk" and turn on the lights behind the words "Don't Walk." Here you can see the tremendous power of OOP (Object Oriented Programming): I don't have to know one tiny detail about how WalkSignal achieves this result!

This is a really good thing. Suppose I am writing a little macro to program MindManager, and I want my macro to add a new subtopic with the text "Hooray." Now, the Mindjet programmers have written probably hundreds of lines of code in order to achieve this result, and the last thing I want to even imagine in my worst nightmare is to have to learn enough to be able to write all this program code myself. Fortunately, I don't have to. I just include a statement in my program like this:

```
myTopic.AddSubtopic("Hooray")
```

This is all I need to add a subtopic named "Hooray" to my selected topic on my map! Furthermore, even if Mindjet decides in some future version of MindManager to completely change the program code for the AddSubtopic method, I don't care because my script code is not affected.

Now there is one more type of object that is really important in OOP, and it is called a *Collection.* Returning once more to the traffic signal, look at Figure 16-3. The three different lights are identical except for their color — all their other properties and methods are identical. What is really neat about collections is that, in addition to the standard reference (TrafficLight. Lights.GreenLight), I can also refer to them by their position number in the collection (TrafficLights.Lights(3)). This makes it much easier to do the same thing to every item in the collection, especially if you don't know how many items are in the collection at any given point in time.

Consider, as an example, one of the important collections in MindManager: *Documents.* Every map that you have open in MindManager is a Document, but sometimes you may have only one map open and other times you may have several open. The first "Useful Script" in Appendix C allows you to close all open maps with a single mouse click. I can do this with a very simple program that says, "Close every Document in Documents." Document (without the "s") means the one, single document that I am ready to close; Documents (with the "s") refers to the bucket (Collection) of documents that are currently open. MindManager follows this convention for all items and collections: a Toolbar in Toolbars, a Topic in Topics, and so on.

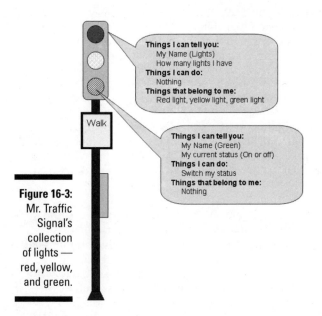

Figure 16-3: Mr. Traffic Signal's collection of lights — red, yellow, and green.

Getting Started with Scripts

MindManager automatically creates a directory for user macros when it is installed on your machine at the following location:

```
Documents and Settings\user\Local Settings\Application
          Data\Mindjet\MindManager\5\Macros
```

If I thought really long and hard about it, I don't think I could have come up with a more obscure and inaccessible place to put such an important directory. What"s more, this directory is only accessible to you, so you can't conveniently share your creations with others. I suggest creating your own macro directory someplace on your hard disk where you can easily find it. You can then name the directory anything you like.

If you want to use some of the macros described in Appendix C and are already familiar with script editors, you can copy the code using the MindManager script editor. Select Tools⇨Macros⇨Macro Editor from the menu bar. The macro editor is shown in Figure 16-4.

Figure 16-4:
The Mind-
Manager
macro
editor with
the "Close
All" macro
loaded.

If you are not familiar with script editors, you can simply use the Windows Notepad program to copy the code from Appendix C that you want to try. Remember, however, to change the normal .txt suffix to .mmbas when you save your file or MindManager will not recognize it as macro code. Notepad also has no error-checking capability, so be careful to copy the code *exactly* as it is given in Appendix C.

The File➪Open command on the macro editor will always looks in the default macro directory rather than remembering the location from which you last opened a macro. Because this is rather inconvenient, I suggest inserting a shortcut to your macro directory in the default directory as follows:

1. **If the macro editor isn't already open, select Tools➪Macros➪Macro Editor from the menu bar.**

   MindManager opens the Macro Editor window.

2. **Select File➪Open from the Macro Editor menu bar.**

   MindManager displays the Open File dialog box. The contents of the default macro directory are displayed but it will most likely be empty.

3. **Right-click anywhere in the Open File dialog box and select New➪Shortcut.**

   Windows displays the Create Shortcut wizard.

4. **Navigate to your macro directory on page 1 of the wizard and then click Next.**

Windows displays the path to your macro directory on the first page of the wizard. It then displays page 2, asking what name you want for your shortcut.

5. **Enter whatever name you like for your shortcut and click Finish.**

A shortcut to your macro directory appears in MindManager's default macro directory.

You can now double-click your shortcut to go directly to your macro directory.

After you have created or downloaded the macro code into your macro directory, you need to tell MindManager a few things about your macro before MindManager can execute your code. Follow these steps for each macro that you want to use:

1. **Select Tools⇨Macro⇨Macros . . . from the menu bar.**

MindManager opens the Macros library management dialog box shown in Figure 16-5. The macros shown are those provided by Mindjet when you installed MindManager on your machine.

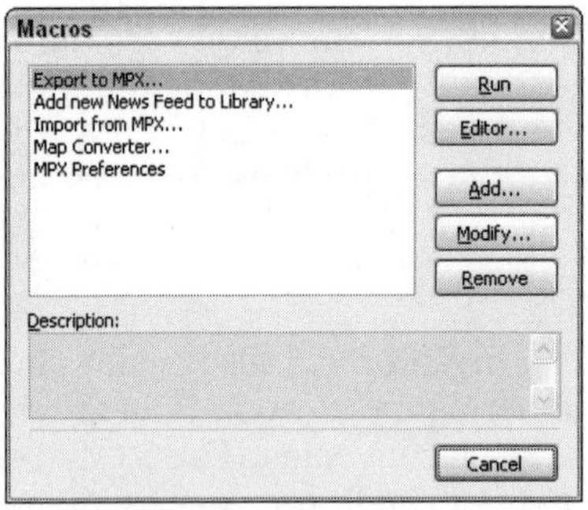

Figure 16-5:
The Macros library management dialog box.

2. **Click the Add. . . button and then complete the Name, Path, and Description fields.**

MindManager opens the Macro dialog box as shown in Figure 16-6. The name you choose should be reasonably descriptive of the macro's action because this is all that will be displayed in the menu. The description is only visible in the Macros library management dialog box (refer to Figure 16-5).

3. **Click the down arrow on the Menu combo box and select the menu where your macro is to appear.**

Your choices are shown in Figure 16-7. Look over the MindManager commands that are on the various menus or submenus and think about the action of your macro. Choose the menu where the action of your macro is most similar to the standard MindManager commands already on that menu. Unfortunately, there is no way to associate your macro with a toolbar button in MindManager. The various context menus are displayed when you right-click an object in MindManager. If your macro is designed to work with only one type of MindManager object (just on topics, for example), the correct context menu may be the best choice. If you write your macro assuming it will be placed on a particular menu, be sure to document this in your macro code.

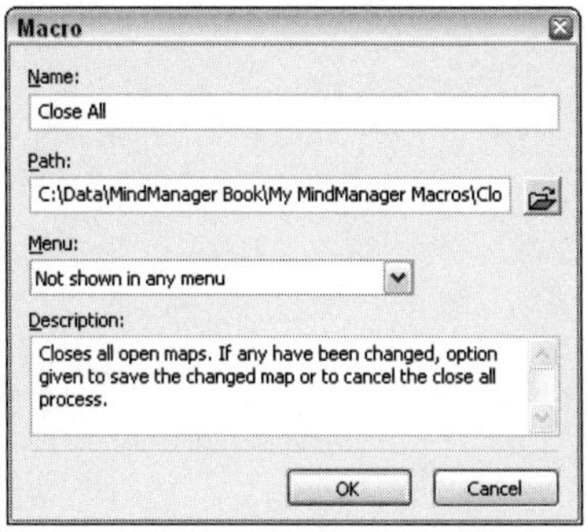

Figure 16-6:
Completed
Macro
dialog box.

4. **Click OK in the New Macro dialog box and then click Close in the Macro Library dialog box.**

   Your macro and its description are displayed in the Macro Library dialog box. After you close the Macro Library dialog box, your macro name will appear on the menu you chose in step 3 and will now function just like any other MindManager command.

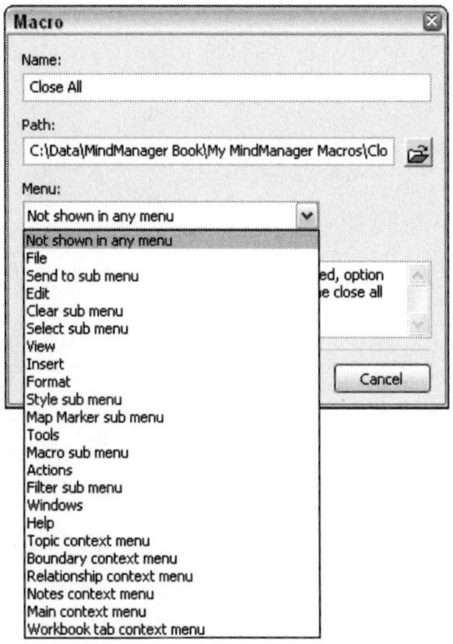

Figure 16-7:
The Macro
dialog box
showing
menu
choices for
the macro.

Part IV
Maps through Webs and Windows

The 5th Wave   By Rich Tennant

"Why, of course. I'd be very interested in seeing this new milestone in Charlie's internet brainstorming project."

In this part . . .

Living in a vacuum isn't very useful, is it? You learn how to share in this part of the book. MindManager gets your ideas out with Microsoft Word, Outlook, Project, and PowerPoint. Creating Web pages is a snap. Remember that sharing thing? You can use MindManager to get other programs to give something useful back to you. MindManager can be a catalyst to getting your ideas across to others, and your visual organization can take on valuable new forms.

Chapter 17

Mining and Managing Information

· ·

In This Chapter

▶ Assembling your maps and hyperlinked documents into .zip or .exe files

▶ Using MindManager's mail function

▶ Managing computer file archives

▶ Structuring large quantities of information

▶ Organizing mail for easy retrieval

▶ Accessing lessons learned while you are working on a new project

· ·

My wife and I love to play games together. One of our favorites is hiding things from ourselves. Maybe you know this game, too: First you have to get ready for the game by putting something important (such as ski gloves, keys to the suitcase, barbeque implements — the really great thing about this game is that you can play it with almost anything) in "a special place" where you will "be sure to know where to find it." (For those of us who are professionals at this game, even the most obvious places will do, but newcomers may need to be more creative in finding that "special place.") Then, go about your normal affairs for a while before beginning the game. Now you can spend hours and days tearing the house apart trying to find that "special place" again!

Information is sort of like this as well. You put a key letter in your filing cabinet, and then you can't remember which file folder it is in; or you save that critical spreadsheet on your computer but can't remember what you named it a few days later.

The problem only gets worse when you have several people on the same team generating and using the information. Some team members get copied on an important e-mail, while others are forgotten. A presentation gets updated, but the presenter uses the old version. A new person joins the team and somehow has to find all the informational bits and pieces in order to become an effective team member.

MindManager offers several tools to help you with this critical information management challenge. You have already seen many of these in prior chapters. In this final chapter of part III, I tell you how to pack up your map and all the hyperlinked documents into one package and send it on its way. In the last sections, I explore ways that you can use MindManager to better handle some common information management problems.

Packaging Everything Together

If you are working with a single map with no hyperlinks to other maps or to other documents of any kind, you really don't need to be concerned about packaging. You write your e-mail, attach your map, and send it off. If, however, you have a huge map like the one discussed in Chapter 10 — with dozens of hyperlinked maps (not to mention PDF documents, spreadsheets, and who knows what else), possibly in multiple directories or even on different servers — assembling the right pieces to send to someone is a daunting task.

Fortunately, MindManager has exactly the tool you need to accomplish this accurately and efficiently — Pack and Go.

When you follow this procedure, you must be using a map containing topic hyperlinks to *all* the other maps or documents that may possibly be included in the packaging process. MindManager will not detect any second-level hyperlinks, nor will it detect any hyperlinks in your text notes.

Follow these steps:

1. **Select File⇨Pack and Go . . . from the menu bar.**

   MindManager displays page 1 of the Pack and Go Wizard dialog box (see Figure 17-1) with the *Add map together with linked documents* option selected.

   Figure 17-1 shows that one of the hyperlinks is broken and that Appendix C cannot be found. If I need to include Appendix C in my package, I must click Cancel and repair the hyperlink before proceeding (see Chapter 12 for details on how to do this).

2. **Uncheck any linked documents that you do not want to include in the package and then click Next.**

   MindManager displays page 2 of the Pack and Go Wizard dialog box (see Figure 17-2).

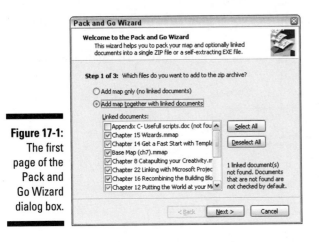

Figure 17-1:
The first page of the Pack and Go Wizard dialog box.

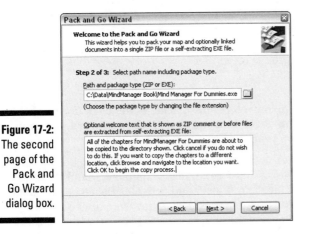

Figure 17-2:
The second page of the Pack and Go Wizard dialog box.

3. **Click the Browse button, navigate to the directory where you want to store the package file, and click OK.**

   MindManager gives the name of your map (with a .zip extension) to the package file and displays the path and file name in the Path and package type field.

   You can edit the name of the package file if you like. If you want MindManager to create a compressed directory (sometimes called a *Zip directory*), leave the .zip extension. If you want MindManager to create a so-called *self-extracting executable*, change the extension to .exe. With a self-extracting executable, the recipient only needs to double-click the .exe file and the compressed files are automatically extracted and saved to the directory specified by the recipient.

4. Add welcome text if desired (only if an .exe file is specified) and then click Next.

MindManager displays page 3 of the Pack and Go Wizard dialog box (see Figure 17-3).

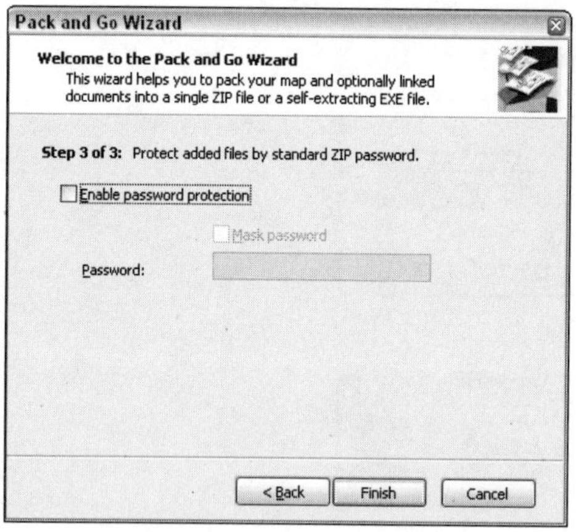

Pack and Go Wizard

Welcome to the Pack and Go Wizard
This wizard helps you to pack your map and optionally linked documents into a single ZIP file or a self-extracting EXE file.

Step 3 of 3: Protect added files by standard ZIP password.

☐ Enable password protection

☐ Mask password

Password:

< Back   Finish   Cancel

Figure 17-3:
The third page of the Pack and Go Wizard dialog box.

5. If you want to password protect your package file, click the *Enable password protection* check box and type in the password you want to use. When you are ready to continue, click Finish.

MindManager displays the Packaging Files progress dialog box (see Figure 17-4). When the .zip (or .exe) file is complete, MindManager changes the word "Cancel" to "Close" and activates the Open and Open Folder buttons. There is seldom any reason, however, to click either of these buttons. Simply close the dialog box and proceed with whatever you want to do next. You will find your package file in the directory you specified on page 2 of the Pack and Go Wizard dialog box.

There is no way to recover your password if you forget it. You will simply have to delete the package file and recreate it from scratch.

Packaging Files...

Copying file: Chapter 8 Catapulting your Creativity.mmap

▓▓▓▓▓▓▓▓▓▓▓▓▓▓▓▓▓▓

Open   Open Folder   Cancel

Figure 17-4:
The Packaging Files progress dialog box.

If you created a self-extracting executable (as specified in Figure 17-2), the recipient will see the dialog box shown in Figure 17-5 when he or she double-clicks the file.

Figure 17-5:
This dialog box is displayed when the recipient double-clicks the self-extracting executable specified in Figure 17-2.

Active Delivery

All of the chapters for MindManager For Dummies are about to be copied to the directory shown. Click cancel if you do not wish to do this. If you want to copy the chapters to a different location, click Browse and navigate to the location you want. Click OK to begin the copy process.

C:\Data\MindManager Book\

[Browse]

[OK]   [Cancel]

If you specified absolute directory addresses in your main map hyperlinks (refer to Chapter 12) and the recipient changes the extraction directory in the dialog box shown in Figure 17-5, none of your hyperlinks will work properly. In general, if you intend to send multimaps to others using a self-extracting executable, always specify relative hyperlink addresses. The recipient can then place the files in any desired directory on his or her computer.

Sending It Off

After creating your package file (as described in the previous section), your next step will usually be to create an e-mail to which you attach this file. You can combine both steps by selecting File⇨Send To from the menu bar and then choosing either Mail Recipient (For Review) . . . or Mail Recipient (As Attachment) . . .

MindManager takes you through the same steps described in the previous section and automatically creates a new mail message and attaches the package file that it has created. The only difference between the two choices ("For Review" or "As Attachment") is that MindManager begins the subject line with "Review" if you chose that option.

This procedure will only work if you are using a MAPI-compliant e-mail program such as Microsoft Outlook or Outlook Express. You cannot create e-mail in any Web-based e-mail program such as AOL or MSN.

The advantages of this approach are as follows:

- ✔ The process is faster because the packaging and e-mail creation process is combined.

- ✔ The package file is created in the e-mail rather than in a specified directory. When the e-mail is sent (assuming you have not specified that your mail application should save a copy of your e-mail), you do not have any files to delete.

- ✔ MindManager automatically appends a message giving the Mindjet Web site address where the recipient can download a free viewer to look at your files if he or she does not have MindManager installed (horrors!).

The disadvantages of this approach are as follows:

- ✔ You do not have the option of creating a self-extracting executable.

- ✔ You may not be ready to create your e-mail immediately. If MindManager starts the e-mail, it won't allow you to do anything else until you at least save the e-mail as a draft.

Knowledge Management Themes

Knowledge Management, or the process of making information available on a timely and relevant basis, has become a very popular topic over the past few years. An Internet search using these keywords will generate several thousand hits. Many consulting organizations now feature this theme as one of their primary areas of business.

I have already explored several areas of Knowledge Management for which MindManager is a particularly good support tool:

- ✔ Chapter 6: Showing relationships between topics and emphasizing certain topics.

- ✔ Chapter 9: Planning and meeting management.

- ✔ Chapter 10: Linking multiple maps together into an overview map.

- ✔ Chapter 12: Using hyperlinks to tie documents of all types together.

I don't introduce any new MindManager functionality in the remaining sections of this chapter. Instead, I combine some things in perhaps unexpected ways to demonstrate a little bit of the enormous power and depth of this marvelous software tool in managing that highly critical resource — information. I hope that these ideas will be a launch pad for your own creativity.

Finding the needle in the haystack

In Chapter 10, I talked about techniques for navigating through a very large map (either a single map or a group of hyperlinked maps) and extracting relevant chunks to build a customized map containing only those parts relevant to a particular need. But what do you do if this big map was created by someone else (or, even worse, several someone elses) and you don't even know where to start looking?

The answer is to combine MindManager's search and multimap capabilities. It is not actually necessary to even open the master map before specifying your search criteria, but since I usually use keywords to do my searching, I want to see where MindManager will find my topic in the information tree. If I open my master map first, it is always the left-most tab in my workspace. This simplifies my exploration a bit.

Figure 17-6 shows the master map for this book. Suppose that I know I have talked about "inserting notes" somewhere, but I just can't remember where. I set up my search parameters as shown (refer to Chapter 25 for details on using the search page if needed) and then click the Search button.

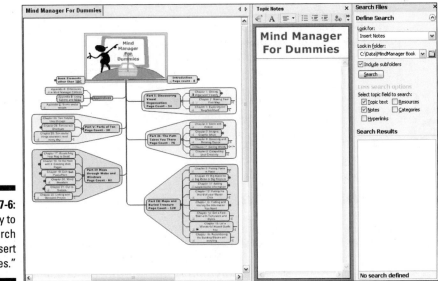

Figure 17-6:
Ready to
do a search
for "Insert
Notes."

After a bit of computer cogitating, MindManager displays the search results in the lower part of the search page. The icons tell you the type of objects where MindManager found your search text. Click any entry, and MindManager opens that map and adjusts the display to show the selected topic. Figure 17-7 shows the result of clicking "Transforming topics into paragraphs."

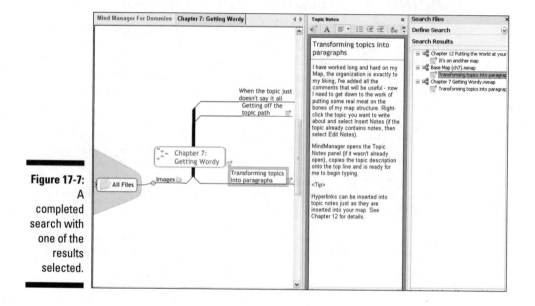

Figure 17-7: A completed search with one of the results selected.

If desired, you can start a new map (leaving the search results still displayed) and then drag one or more of the search icons to your new map. MindManager will copy the selected topic and all of its subtopics to the new map. If you have selected a topic that corresponds to an entire hyperlinked map, the central topic on that map will become a main topic on your new map.

This process searches maps found only in the directories you specify. MindManager will not find any occurrence of your keywords in other types of documents (such as Word or Excel) unless those words are also present in one or more of the map objects that you specified in your search criteria.

Archive reference

It is always difficult to decide which computer files to keep and which to discard, and it seems like whichever choice you make will turn out to be the wrong one. My wife is always afraid she might need something "someday" and so almost never deletes anything. I, on the other hand, am never happier than when I can do some computer housecleaning to get rid of all the "outdated" files. The result is that neither of us can find that particular, older file we are looking for. I can't because I have deleted it, and she can't because it is buried somewhere among thousands of other files.

Cheap CD-R disks have solved the problem for me: I just copy all the outdated files to a CD before I delete them. But — you're already ahead of me, aren't you? — now I have my wife's problem when I need to retrieve a file from the CD.

MindManager to the rescue! Create your archive CD using your favorite CD-burning application and then follow these steps to create a powerful archive index:

1. **Click the New (Standard) button on the Standard toolbar and type the desired description for your archive.**

   Your archive map is ready to be loaded with hyperlinks to your archive files.

2. **Place your archive CD in your reader and then add a hyperlink to the CD to the central topic.**

   Refer to Chapter 12 if you need to review how to do this.

3. **Open the Library page in the Task pane and select Map Parts⇨MindManager⇨File Explorer.**

   The file explorer Smart Map Parts (SMPs) are displayed in the lower half of the Library page.

4. **Drag the All Files and Folders SMP and drop it on your archive central topic.**

   MindManager will "think" for awhile and then display a list of all files and folders on your archive map. If you click the plus sign next to one of the folders, MindManager will display all the files and subfolders that are in that folder.

   This SMP only creates topics corresponding to two levels of folders. If you need to extend your archive index to a greater folder depth, repeat this process (beginning with step 4) for each level 2 directory.

5. **Right-click the All Files and Folders main topic (in your archive map) and select Remove Topic.**

   MindManager makes all your first-level folders and files into main topics in your archive map. You can now do any clean-up and rearranging that you want, such as deleting all the extraneous borders. You can see a portion of my archive CD for this book in Figure 17-8.

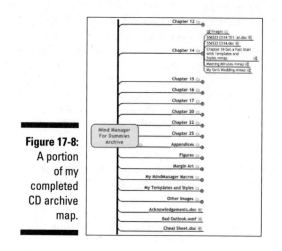

Figure 17-8:
A portion
of my
completed
CD archive
map.

This is one powerful tool! I can open any archive file directly from the CD simply by clicking its hyperlink icon (remember, all of these were created automatically), and I can search my CD using the technique described in the previous section. Lost archive files are a thing of the past!

Mail management

Keeping track of e-mail — who sent something, when it was sent, who it was sent to, what was said, and so on — is another major information management task that you and I must deal with on an ongoing basis.

In order to effectively use MindManager to manage a mail knowledge base, I must first think carefully about a mail *index structure*. In this case, the index structure will reflect the categories of mail that are important to me. Although I can do a keyword search in unstructured mail, I need a well-conceived index structure in order to use many of the knowledge management tools.

There is simply no shortcut here, because there is no "right" index structure — only one that is best suited to my team's (or my company's) particular and unique needs. Of course, I can certainly use the brainstorming tool in MindManager (refer to Chapter 8) to work with others on my team in developing this index and in defining a clear process for additions and modifications.

When you have decided on your index structure, create a map template that captures this structure (templates are covered in Chapter 14). At regular time intervals, depending on your needs, create a new map from this template and link it to your master mail map with a hyperlink. As mail is received, you pick the category that is appropriate and use the Send To MindManager function in Outlook to copy the mail contents into your map (see Chapter 15 for details). If more than one category is relevant, you can repeat this process.

Figure 17-9 shows an example of such a mail map. This map can now be searched using all the tools previously described.

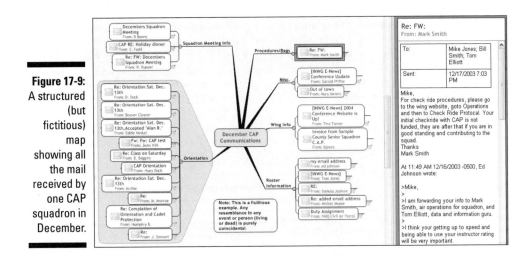

Figure 17-9: A structured (but fictitious) map showing all the mail received by one CAP squadron in December.

Lessons learned

Companies that are involved with project work quickly recognize that mistakes are an inevitable aspect of trying to do something new, but they also become quickly frustrated when they realize that they are making the same mistakes over and over.

When a project is completed, many companies invest some time talking about the mistakes they made on a project (as well as the things they may have done well), and some invest quite a bit of time in formally documenting these *lessons learned*. This is an important and necessary first step. The problem, however, is making this information available in a timely and relevant fashion to the project manager on the *next* project. Most attempts have had only limited success because the project manager has no easy way to extract what is relevant to his or her current project from this mass of documents.

What is needed is a structured way of collecting lessons learned that is organized around the way projects are managed at a particular company. As with the mail management problem discussed in the previous section, the crucial step is the development of the index structure. This will assuredly be far more complex than the index structure needed for mail management and will therefore require thought and input from every team member working for the company. It should be expected that many mistakes will be made and that a means must be defined to allow the index structure to grow, adapt, and mature as the company gains experience with it. The investment, however, can be expected to return significant dividends in terms of more successful projects.

Figure 17-10 shows a very simple first draft of a MindManager template that can be used to collect lessons learned. Each project can have its own master map with links to the individual lessons learned maps. Searching can be done against the index words, the type of project or the description itself. Using the scripting tools (see Chapter 16 and Appendix C), information can also be extracted to databases and Web pages to make it more readily available.

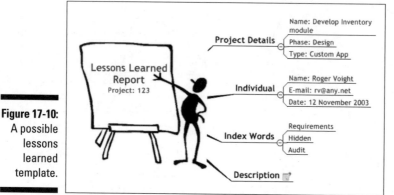

Figure 17-10:
A possible
lessons
learned
template.

There are many other possibilities as well, depending on the particular needs of each organization. Use this as a starting point for your own creative thinking!

Knowledge structuring

I explored knowledge structuring pretty extensively in Chapter 10, using the Civil Air Patrol knowledge base as an example. My next task is to figure out how to make this knowledge management and structuring available to those poor souls who do not yet have MindManager installed on their computers.

In this part (IV), I show you how MindManager enables you to make your map knowledge base available to anyone who has a computer with at least a Web browser installed — in fact, in printed form, even to someone who has no computer at all — with very little additional work. In this section, I just give you a little taste of what is to come!

Figure 17-11 shows the same table of contents map that I discussed in Chapter 10, but now it is dressed up to look like an ordinary table of contents page in a notebook. Using the export tools that I will cover in this part, I can produce this entire knowledge base in the following forms:

- ✔ A series of physical notebooks
- ✔ A linked series of Word documents
- ✔ A series of PDF documents
- ✔ A Web site
- ✔ A series of PowerPoint presentations

It won't matter which form someone uses to access this information — they will always see the same format and the same structure. I manage my information in my MindManager knowledge base. If I need to change something, I change it in MindManager and then re-create all the other forms with a few mouse clicks — seamlessly and effortlessly. Interested? Then check out the rest of the Chapters in Part IV.

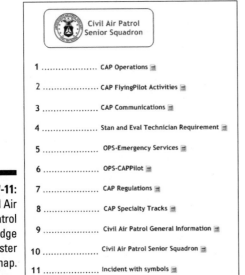

Figure 17-11:
The Civil Air
Patrol
knowledge
base master
map.

The section numbers in Figure 17-11 are all floating topics. The connecting lines from the central topic (Civil Air Patrol Senior Squadron) to the main topics have been hidden. See Chapters 3, 7, and 14 for details on how to do these things. I left the hyperlink icons visible here, but could have hidden them as well by selecting View➪Show/Hide➪Control Strip from the menu bar.

Chapter 18

To the Host with It: Creating Web Pages

Making Web pages and Web sites is an art. The rules seem to be constantly changing. It seems like only months ago that if you had a basic knowledge of HTML, then you had it whipped. In this chapter, you're going to see how MindManager makes Web page generation as easy as pouring Picasso out of a box. The first stop is the creation of a Web page.

Web pages have to be targeted to a user to be effective. Some are interactive, while others contain static information. Fortunately, MindManager has Web templates that take into consideration how people use Web pages. In this chapter, I am going to show you how to select a Web template based on the intended use of the Web page. After creating one Web page, the next step is to create multiple Web pages which will then become an entire Web site.

MindManager can make a full-blown Web site out of a map. You're going to create a Web site with information pulled from multiple MindManager maps. Each map is made up of bits and pieces of Web construction concrete.

I am not an expert on the internal construction of Web pages or Web sites, so I am glad the folks that assembled MindManager are experts on that stuff. MindManager allows you to change the nuts and bolts of a Web page. You hope your car still runs after you have taken the nuts and bolts out of the engine and reinstalled them. I am going to take you right to the edge of being dangerous with the wrench. You're welcome to tread farther. Where did I put that disclaimer?

This chapter uses MindManager maps from the Civil Air Patrol as examples when creating Web pages. The Civil Air Patrol (CAP) is also known as the United States Air Force Auxiliary.

Going from Map to Web Page in Seconds

I am going to show you how to take a MindManager map and create a Web page from it. To create a Web page quickly, first you need a MindManager map. You don't have to have a complicated map at this point. The purpose of this section is to just get a Web page done fast.

Start with the MindManager map shown in Figure 18-1.

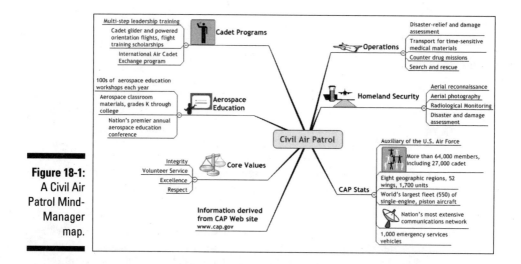

Figure 18-1:
A Civil Air Patrol Mind-Manager map.

MindManager creates numerous files when making a Web page. Create a temporary file folder to hold all the Web page files. Getting rid of Web page files is much easier if the files are in one folder.. Transferring files to the Web is easier, too, if the files are all in one place.

Open your MindManager map completely by showing all the levels. Chapter 2 describes a MindManager map level. The level of detail that the map is opened to is the level of detail used by the template. You may lose information on the Web page if all the levels are not open. On the other hand, if your map is large, then you may want to reduce the level of detail. The Web page may not be able to display all the levels. You have to try it a few times and see what works for your map. Follow these steps:

1. **Select File⇨ Save as Web Pages.**

   The Save as Web Pages dialog box appears, as shown in Figure 18-2.

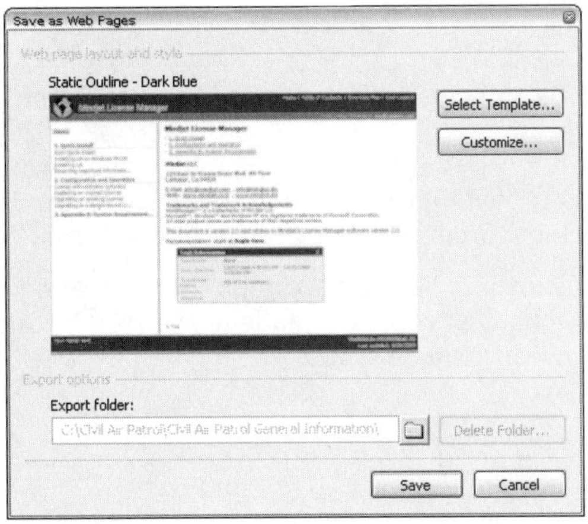

Figure 18-2: The Save as Web Pages dialog box.

2. **In the *Export folder* box, enter the location and folder name that you want to contain the Web files. You can also browse files by clicking the file folder icon.**

3. **Next, click the Select Template button.**

   The Select Web Template dialog box appears, as shown in Figure 18-3.

   The MindManager Web templates are hiding underneath the + signs on the left side of the page.

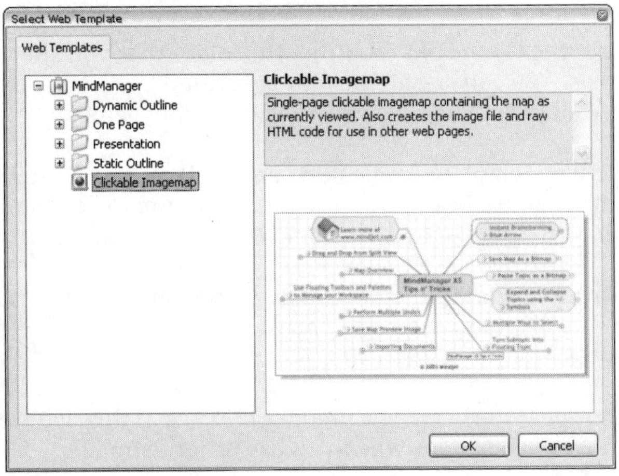

Figure 18-3: The Select Web Template dialog box.

4. Click Clickable Imagemap in the file list.

A brief description of the template is found in the upper right text box. The page is clickable if hyperlinks are attached to the topic. Click a hyperlink and away you go.

5. Click OK.

The Save as Web Pages dialog box (shown in Figure 18-2) returns.

6. Click Save.

The churning starts. A Web page is about to be born. Figure 18-4 shows the I'm Finished screen, or as the dialog box says, Saving as Web Pages.

The Cancel button shown in Figure 18-3 stops the generation of the Web page. However, any changes you have made to the Web layout or in advanced customizations will be saved.

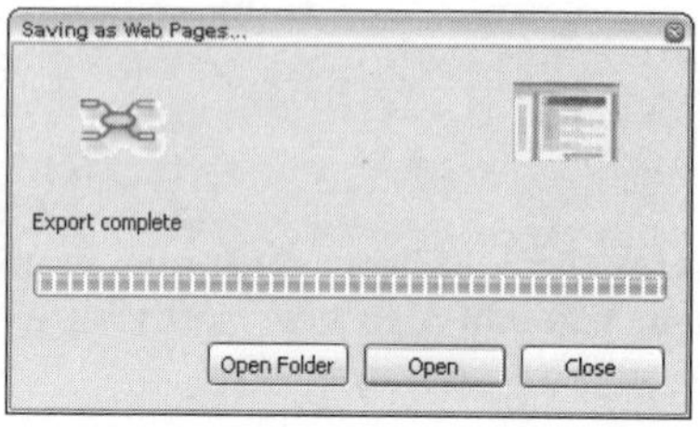

Figure 18-4:
The export is complete, and the Web page is born.

7. Click Open.

Your Web browser opens and your MindManager map appears in a Web page format. Pretty cool. The result is a Web page that looks exactly like the one shown in Figure 18-1, except you're looking at it with your Internet browser.

If you select the Open Folder button, the folder that you specified in Step 2 opens. You can see all the files generated by MindManager to make the Web page. The Close button closes the dialog box.

The most basic Web template creates this type of Web page. The HTML code is automatically generated by MindManager for your map. If you're feeling ambitious, then you can take that code and build it into an existing Web site.

The Clickable Imagemap HTML code can be found in the file index.html.txt. You can paste this file into other Web pages. The index.jpg can also be used in other Web sites.

You're going to repeat these steps a number of times in this chapter. You should follow these same steps when you use other templates.

Finding your Web page from your browser

The Open button shown in Figure 18-4 performs a series of steps that are hidden from you. It automatically closes the dialog box and opens your Web browser. The Web browser is then told which Web file to open. You can instead choose Open Folder or Close in the Saving as Web Pages dialog box (see Figure 18-4) instead of choosing Open. Selecting the Open Folder button or the Close button will not open your browser.

Looking at your Web masterpiece after you exit the Saving as Web Pages dialog box requires a bit of searching with your browser. To look later, open your browser. I am using Internet Explorer, but the idea is the same no matter what browser you use. Search for the index file in the folder that you named in Figure 18-2. To do this, open the folder from the browser. Then open the file named index. Your MindManager map, in its Web format, should appear. I recommend that you practice finding the index file because it will be helpful later, when the Web pages and sites are more complicated and have multiple index files.

Making Template Choices and Taking Credit for Great Web Pages

The Web page templates have certain characteristics in common. In this section, you add information to a template. I will show you how to change a few things in a MindManager template. Don't worry about how complicated your map is. Continue using the map in Figure 18-1 as an example.

The following steps show you how to personalize your map and select a Web layout:

1. **Select File⟹ Save as Web Pages.**

   The Save as Web Pages dialog box appears (refer to Figure 18-2), so that you can start the Web page cooking process.

2. **Click Select Template, because you want to use a different template.**

3. **Open the Static Outline menu by clicking on the + sign, and then click Light Blue.**

4. **Click OK to return to the Save as Web Pages dialog box (refer to Figure 18-2).**

5. **Click the Customize button.**

   The Customize Web Page Layout and Style dialog box appears, as shown in Figure 18-5.

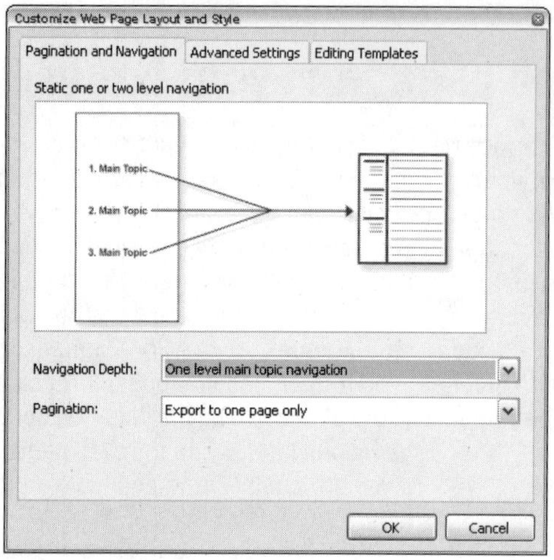

Figure 18-5:
The
Customize
Web Page
Layout and
Style dialog
box gives
you choices
galore.

6. **Click the Navigation Depth drop-down menu.**

   Two selections appear. If you switch back and forth between the selections, then the graphic in the center changes and describes the difference between the two choices. Select *One level main topic navigation.*

7. **Click the Pagination drop-down menu.**

   You have two options. Toggle between the two options and see the result in the graphic box.

8. **Return to the Navigation Depth drop-down menu and select the other choice:** *Two level main and subtopic navigation choice.*

9. **Return to the Pagination drop-down menu.**

   You now have three selections to make. The graphic display changes as you examine each selection. I hope you're beginning to see the flexibility. You have to play with the different selections to get your favorite combination.

10. **At the top of the Customize Web Page Layout and Style dialog box, click the Advanced Settings tab.**

   The dialog box changes to show the Advanced Settings options, as shown in Figure 18-6. Figure 18-6 shows the options scrolled down to the User Information section.

11. **Under the Value column, you can enter your user information to personalize your Web page. Enter text for each item you want to change.**

   The changes you make are not permanent. You have to make the changes for each map you export.

12. **Click OK.**

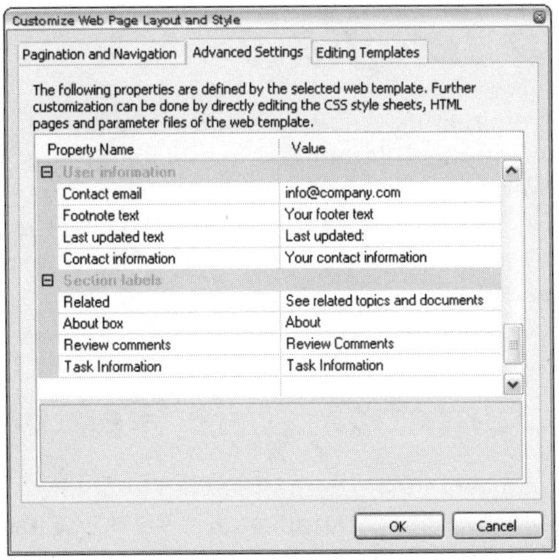

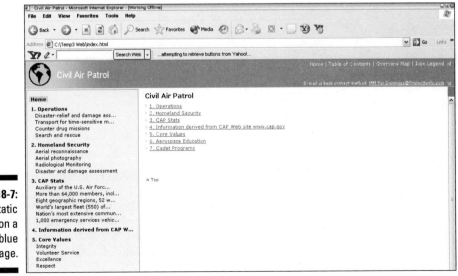

Figure 18-6:
Advanced
Settings to
customize
the Web
pages.

13. **Click Save to generate the Web pages.**

14. **Click Open to view the pages.**

Figure 18-7 shows the home page of the generated Web pages.

If you click on the various options, such as Table of Contents on the upper right side, you notice that the MindManager map is found by selecting Overview Map. The Static Outline template is used for medium-sized maps. The next section shows examples of the other templates and describes when you may want to use them.

Figure 18-7:
A static
outline on a
light blue
home page.

Dishing Up a Web Template

You now know the basics of creating Web pages and changing information in the template. Here I show you the different Web template options. Web templates and the resulting Web pages have different purposes and types of interaction. Refer to Figure 18-1 and note that the MindManager map includes text notes, a floating topic, a callout, and relationships. That map is the basis for the examples in this section.

Creating a presentation style Web page

One template that you can use is the Presentation Web template, which is modeled after the MindManager Presentation mode. (Refer to Chapter 3 for Presentation mode information.) You move around a Web page the same way that you move around in MindManager's Presentation mode. Every time you click on a topic, the subtopics open. Click on another topic, and the first topic closes and the new one opens. Figure 18-8 shows the Customize Web Page Layout and Style dialog box.

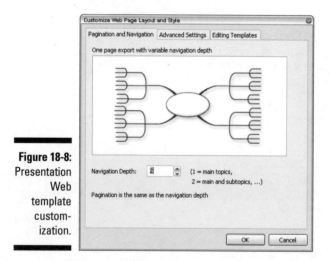

Figure 18-8: Presentation Web template customization.

The Navigation Depth refers to how many topics and subtopics can be opened in the Web page. You want to have the same level of navigation depth as you do levels in your map. I always put the Navigation Depth number very high — for example, 9. That way, I am guaranteed to cover all the topics in my MindManager map. The following list describes which MindManager map elements don't work in the Presentation Web page:

✔ **Floating topics are only visible if the central topic is selected.** Select another topic, and the floating topic disappears.

✔ **URLs don't URL.** Links do not operate in the Web page. The links are shown, but you can click 'til your mouse rolls over without causing anything to happen. This is the same as the Presentation mode in the program.

✔ **Relationships disappear.** A relationship in the map doesn't make it onto the Web page.

✔ **Text notes don't make the trip, either.** The text note symbol is there, but your mouse won't like you if you keep clicking.

Presentation of topics is what this Web page does best. Choose another Web template if you depend on floating topics, URLs, text notes, or relationships to fully explain your map.

The presentation Web page is shown in Figure 18-9.

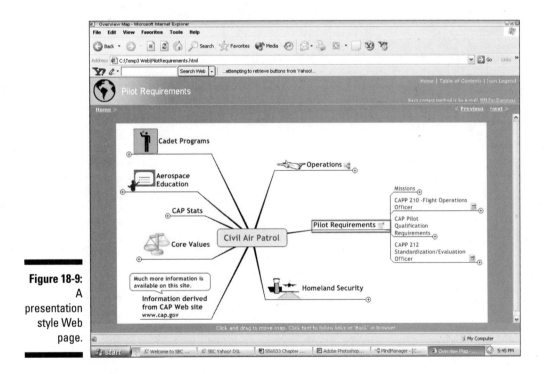

Figure 18-9:
A presentation style Web page.

The One Page template is the next Web template to examine.

Creating a one page Web page with the One Page template

The One Page Web template is a Web page with a standard look and feel. All the topics are listed in outline format. You click on the outline topic to be transported down the page. Select the one page Web template. Figure 18-10 shows the Customize Web Page Layout and Style dialog box.

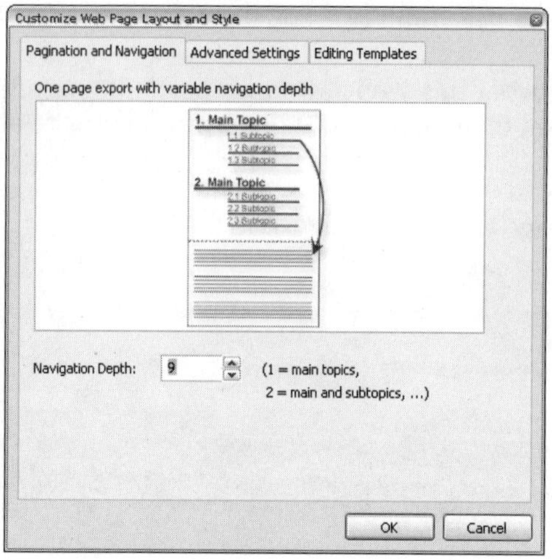

Figure 18-10:
One page template customization.

The only real customization option for this template is the Navigation Depth. Again, you're leaving topics on the table if you use a navigation depth number that is lower than the number of levels in your map. The one page style is a Web page that needs fewer levels to make sense; if you use too many levels, then you can get confused about where you're on the page. Note, too, that in the middle of the page there is no "top" to shoot you back up to the top of the page.

The Advanced Settings of the One Page template contain information similar to the Presentation template, and you can change them the same as in the previous section.

MindManager map elements, such as relationships, make it to the Web page. Relationships are identified on the Web pages as "See Related Topics and Documents." Click on one of these, and you're off to the other end of the relationship. The topic text notes are found underneath the title. Floating topics are not in the outline. The One Page Web template works best for maps with one or two topic levels and a limited number of main topics. Refer to Chapter 2 to understand topic levels.

Figure 18-11 shows the top of the outline. I can't show you the entire one page Web page. The one page Web page is three pages in length (using the CAP map originally shown in Figure 18-1). The first seven lines shown in Figure 18-11 link to information below that on the Web page.

The Dynamic Outline is the final choice for a Web page template. The Dynamic Outline is the Big Daddy, the Whole Enchilada, and the Top Banana. You get the idea. The Dynamic Outline is covered in the next section. I use the Dynamic Outline for big or multifaceted MindManager maps.

I suggest you delete the files in the folder to which you have been saving Web pages. You selected the folder way back in Step 2 of the first section. I checked and I have 330 files. The complexity of your MindManager map determines how many files you have been saving. You don't need these practice files hanging around anymore. Transferring Web pages to the Internet gets confusing if you don't know which files are for which Web page. Get in the habit of cleaning up after yourself.

Figure 18-11:
The top
portion
of the
one-page
Web page.

Using the Tag Team of Multimap Workspace and Dynamic Outline

You access the Dynamic Outline Web template the same way you access the templates in previous sections of this chapter. The Multimap workspace has unique Web page generation characteristics. The combination of the Dynamic Outline template and the Multimap workspace is a good match. The Dynamic Outline is best suited to complex and large maps that have more than two topic levels, while the Multimap workspace (almost by definition) is complex but may contain many simple maps. The Multimap workspace is covered in Chapter 10.

Figure 18-12 shows the linked MindManager maps in the Multimap workspace. I am going to use these linked maps as an example. The files in the Multimap workspace should be linked by a one-to-many relationship. Map A should link to map B, C, D, and so on. A circular link — such as map A links to map B, map B links to map C, and map C links to map D — does not work. Linking is accomplished using the Hyperlink tool. The Hyperlink tool is covered in Chapter 12.

Multimap workspace uses saved files. You can change one of the maps shown in the Multimap workspace, but you have to save the changed file. Use the Refresh command in the Multimap workspace to load (save) the changes.

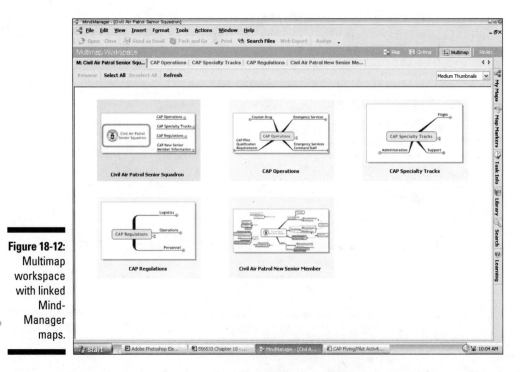

Figure 18-12:
Multimap workspace with linked Mind-Manager maps.

You can only change the Web template before you choose to Select All the maps. The dialog box shown in Figure 18-5 appears only if one map is selected. Change the Web template by selecting Web Export. The dialog box shown in Figure 18-2 appears so that you're able to make changes. A Web page is generated when you click Save. You can also go into the single map view and change the template as described in the "Making Template Choices and Taking Credit for Great Web Pages" section, earlier in this chapter. The *Think ahead* option is also available. You can change Web templates by selecting Tools⇨Template Organizer⇨Web Templates and clicking Modify.

The following steps explain how to prepare the Multimap workspace and create the Dynamic Outline Web pages:

1. **Open your map with the hyperlinks to other maps, and enter the Multimap workspace.**

   You should be looking at a screen similar to the one shown in Figure 18-12.

2. **Click the Select All button.**

3. **Select Open.**

   All the linked maps are opened.

4. **Return to the Multimap workspace map by looking for M:*filename* in the list of open MindManager files. Select that map.**

   Your screen should still look similar to the one shown in Figure 18-12, but all the maps should be open and blue boxes should surround each map. You're now set to perform the Web Export.

5. **Click Assign⇨Web Template.**

   The Select Web Template dialog box appears (refer to Figure 18-3).

6. **Select the Dynamic Outline template, and choose your color (for example, Light Blue).**

7. **Click OK.**

   The Dynamic Outline in Light Blue is attached to each map.

8. **Select Web Export.**

   The Multimap Web Export Settings dialog box appears, as shown in Figure 18-13.

   Selecting the top button causes all the linked maps to adopt the style and layout of the map with the shaded or bluish background. The bottom button keeps the maps the same. I usually choose the top button.

You should save the individual map styles under different style template names. MindManager has been known to save a new style on top of a map, and you can't undo the damage. Create a backup of the map's layout and style by saving the layout and style with a unique name. You can then resurrect it as necessary.

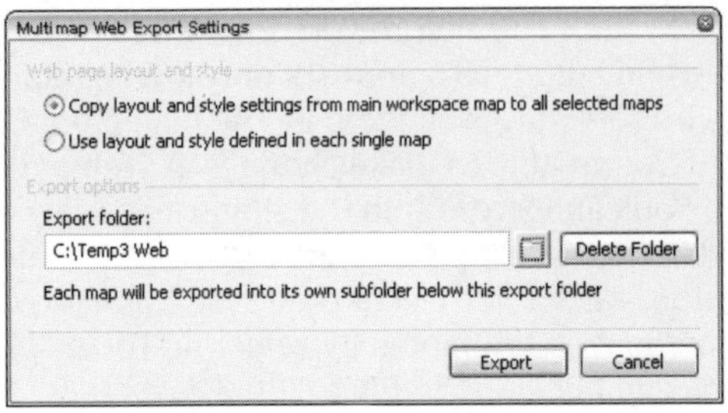

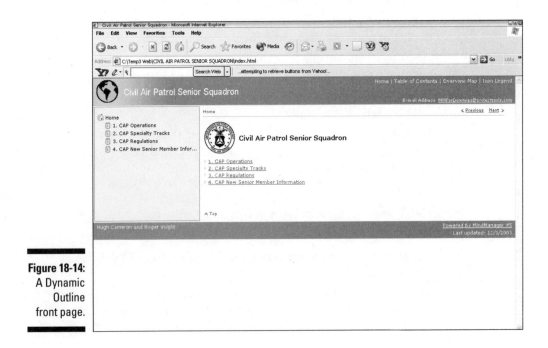

Figure 18-13:
The
Multimap
Web Export
Settings
dialog box.

9. **Point your finger toward the screen and say "Engage." Click the Export button if nothing happens.**

10. **Click Open when the exporting is done.**

Each map is transformed into Web pages. The Web pages are contained in subfolders. The subfolder's name is the same name as the MindManager map. All the subfolders are located under the folder you originally specified. All this happens because you clicked a button. Figure 18-14 shows the front page of the generated Web pages.

Figure 18-14:
A Dynamic
Outline
front page.

Opening the Web pages at this point is easy; going back and opening the pages later is more difficult. View the Web pages later by looking for the file folder with the name of the main Multimap file. The main Multimap file is highlighted in blue in the Multimap view. Open the file folder and select the Index file. There may be index files with additional letters, but look for just the word *index*. Open the index file in your browser and your Web pages appear.

Don't forget to choose the Select All the maps option in the Multimap view. Omitting this step will prevent your Web pages from generating. I have omitted this step on many occasions, and it always produces a loud groan.

The Dynamic Outline contains all the elements of the MindManager Map except floating topics. Each of the maps is shown in the Overview Map section. Links operate and can pull up other Web sites or document pages. The outline format is quite effective for moving through lots of information.

Floating topics are not transferred to Web pages. You can get floating topics to look like they are floating though. Let the red tractor beam grab the topic and place it. Then turn the color of the line to the same color as the background. You're not able to place the topic anywhere you want on the map using this technique, however. The red tractor beam emanating from the central topic is covered in Chapter 11.

Performing Web Page Template Surgery

You may have noticed that I strategically omitted one of the menu choices on the Web Page Customize Layout and Style dialog box shown in Figure 18-5. The Editing Template selection is the subject of this section of the chapter.

I will show you the safe way to do surgery on your Web template. Please realize that I am not a Web template surgeon. You may be an expert who is fully prepared to do brain surgery. But I am going to take you only to the level of splinter removal.

This section shows you how to replace a graphic in the Web template. Unlike real surgery, you will clone the Web template patient first. It's a nice option for safety.

Refer to Figure 18-14, and you see a small logo in the top left corner. Let's replace the logo with the Civil Air Patrol seal. The old logo and the new seal are shown in Figure 18-15. Follow these steps to make the replacement:

Figure 18-15:
Replace the
Web page
logo graphic
with the
CAP seal.

1. **Select Tools⇨Template Organizer⇨Web Template.**

   Figure 18-16 shows the Template Organizer dialog box with a Web template open.

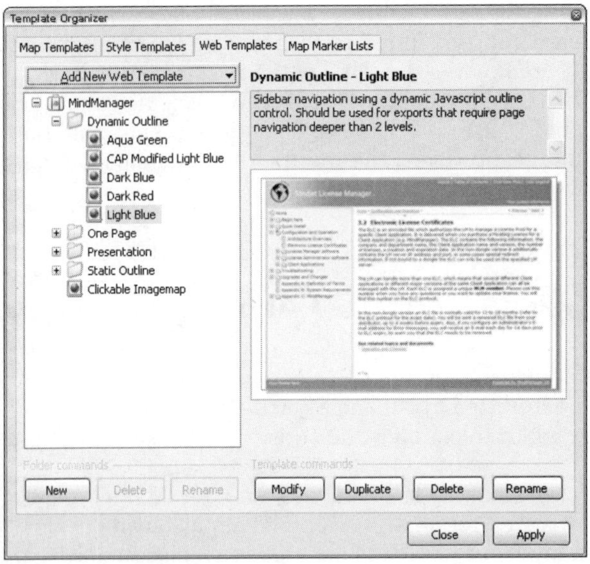

Figure 18-16:
The
Template
Organizer
displaying
Web
templates.

2. **Click the Duplicate button.**

   This is the safety step. A copy of the template appears in the folder list.

3. **Select the copied Web template.**

   I have forgotten this step a few times and wondered why the copy didn't have any changes. Imagine my surprise when I try to use the original and my changes appear.

4. **Click Modify.**

   Figure 18-17 shows the Editing Templates tab of the customization dialog box. Click at your own risk.

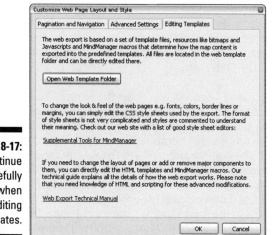

The Web Export Technical Manual is an excellent source of information. The manual has in-depth material on how MindManager translates maps to Web pages. The Web Export Technical Manual is found on the Customize Web Page Layout and Style dialog box shown in Figure 18-17.

5. Click Open Web Template Folder.

The multitude of files that make up a Web template appear. Figure 18-18 shows a partial list of the files.

Figure 18-18:
The Web
page jungle.

As I said, I am not a Web site developer or a Web page designer. I am impressed at the magnitude of pieces that go into a Web template. Have a blast if you know what all this stuff is. I am comfortable with images. I am going to search out and replace the Logo image with the Civil Air Patrol seal — hopefully, without disturbing the integrity of the Web page.

I begin my search for the elusive Logo. As you enter the plain of Web parts, take note of the folder named Res. Res is another hiding spot where Web parts take refuge. I opened the Res folder and found another lair called Images. The Images folder contains a treasure of graphics — the prize being the Logo graphic. I quietly cut the Logo graphic and paste in the CAP graphic. No other Web piece notices. I am careful, though. The size of the Logo graphic is small, only 52 x 52 pixels. The replacement graphic is sized to match perfectly so that it will not upset the Web page. I move cleverly away from all the folders by closing each folder window. I close the final window (shown in Figure 18-18). My final act is to click OK (shown in Figure 18-17). Although tired from my ordeal, I am excited to see the fruits of my labor. Don't forget to use the same image type. A gif is the right one. Stick in a .jpg picture and MindManager chokes.

I create the Web pages using the copied template. The new Dynamic Outline looks like the one shown in Figure 18-19. The CAP seal is now in the upper left corner of the Web page.

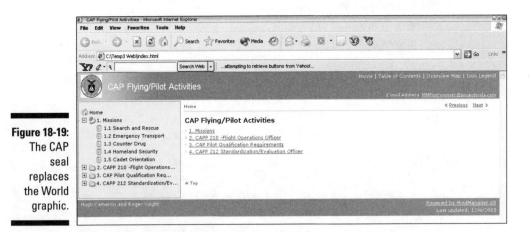

Figure 18-19:
The CAP seal replaces the World graphic.

You're ready to transfer the Web page files to the Web. I look forward to seeing your masterpieces on the Internet.

Chapter 19

Presenting Your Maps with PowerPoint

*D*o you get cold chills when someone says, "Can you give us an informal presentation of your ideas, say . . . by lunchtime?" Perhaps you remember the trauma of making stick figures on overhead slides. But programs like PowerPoint can make even the artistically challenged look good. Snazzy presentations are possible, but it seems to take forever to get one right.

The MindManager link to PowerPoint takes your ideas straight from your map and — miraculously — transforms your ideas into a presentation. Amazingly, the presentation is organized and even makes sense.

This chapter uses maps as examples but does not go into detail on how to create the map. If you need to polish up on creating topics or other map basics, check out Chapter 2. There is one other small caveat. You have to have PowerPoint on your computer.

This chapter shows you how to send a MindManager map to PowerPoint. It identifies some gotchas to look for in the presentation and shows you how to fine-tune the map based on the presentation's purpose and the information to be displayed. Finally, this chapter explains how all the pieces are assembled and how the final presentation is made.

Introducing Your Map to PowerPoint Transformation

A photograph (a single image) and a movie (a moving collection of images) are different entities. In the MindManager world, there's a difference between a fully developed MindManager map (which looks cool and has tons of information, but doesn't move) and a presentation that leads the viewer through the information in a particular order. Sure, the colors and symbols in a map may stimulate both sides of your brain, but a large map requires using a mouse to see everything. As a result, your audience may look at a map and perceive only a fraction of what is there. PowerPoint to the rescue!

MindManager has the ability to break the map into PowerPoint slide elements. The elements include map images, headings, and text. MindManager then transfers the elements to PowerPoint. You determine what information appears in the resulting PowerPoint slides and the order of the slides.

Transforming a MindManager map into a PowerPoint presentation happens with one click on the PowerPoint icon in MindManager. If you want to fine-tune the output, you can use MindManager's global and topic PowerPoint settings. I show you how to change these settings in the sections "Adjusting the Global and Topic Settings in Your Presentation" and "Setting the Topic Defaults in PowerPoint," later in this chapter.

Transferring the MindManager map to PowerPoint is a good way to send someone the essence of your map. Some folks may not be familiar with MindManager and therefore wouldn't know how to navigate around a map like the one shown in Figure 19-1. This particular map is for planning a high school reunion. PowerPoint takes out the guesswork by leading them through the map slide by slide. However, after you send your masterpiece, be prepared to answer the question, "How did you make that incredible presentation?"

Figure 19-1: Start with a Mind-Manager map to transform into a PowerPoint slide presentation.

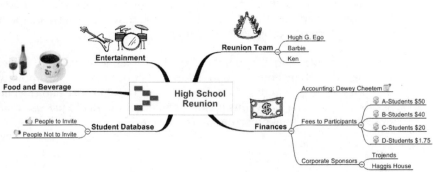

Creating a Presentation Using the Default Settings

MindManager can *almost* read your mind about a presentation. But tweaking is sometimes required to get the right information transformed in just the right way. Before you start tweaking, first send the map to PowerPoint. (By the way, *tweaking* is a technical term used by biomedical electronic technicians. It is accomplished by using a 16-oz ball peen alignment tool.)

Any MindManager map can be sent to PowerPoint. You can send a map as many times as you like without causing a problem. You can use the initial defaults in MindManager and PowerPoint as a starting point the first time you create a PowerPoint presentation from any map. Create the map; then send it to PowerPoint. Next, look at the PowerPoint presentation to find glaring problems with any of the paths and review the organization of the presentation. The goal is to ensure that the presentation says what you want it to say. Refer to Chapter 2 if you need to brush up on how to create a MindManager map. The next section describes the mechanics of sending the MindManager map to PowerPoint.

Sending your map to PowerPoint

Follow these steps to send a MindManager map (using the default settings) to PowerPoint:

1. **Click the PowerPoint icon on the toolbar.**

   The first dialog box requests a file name for the PowerPoint file. Enter a name or just Click OK for the default. The PowerPoint Export Format Settings dialog box opens with initial defaults checked, as shown in Figure 19-2.

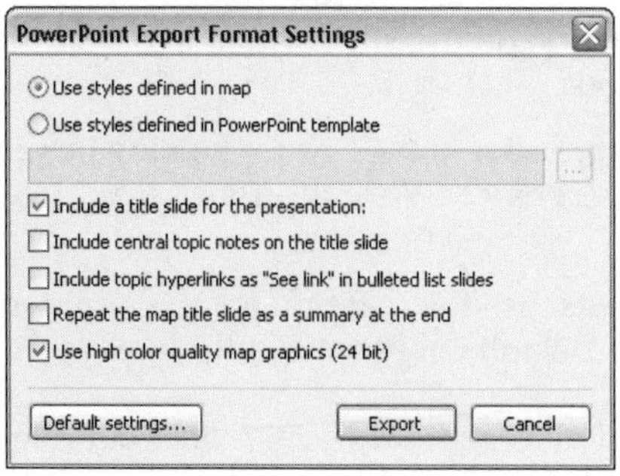

Figure 19-2:
The
PowerPoint
Export
Format
Settings
dialog box.

PowerPoint Export Format Settings

- ◉ Use styles defined in map
- ◯ Use styles defined in PowerPoint template

- ☑ Include a title slide for the presentation:
- ☐ Include central topic notes on the title slide
- ☐ Include topic hyperlinks as "See link" in bulleted list slides
- ☐ Repeat the map title slide as a summary at the end
- ☑ Use high color quality map graphics (24 bit)

[Default settings...]   [Export]   [Cancel]

2. **Add a check mark to all unchecked boxes.**

   You can see the effect of all the settings by checking the boxes and sending it to PowerPoint.

3. **Select the *Use Styles Defined In Map* radio button, if it is not selected already.**

   The other radio button (*Use Styles Defined in PowerPoint Template*) enhances the map using the PowerPoint styles and is covered in the section "Going to PowerPoint to View the Templates," later in this chapter.

4. **Click OK.**

   The magic begins. Sit back and watch.

The first slide — after a title slide if you choose to add one — consists of the topics closest to the center of the map. Main Topics connect to the map center and are described as first-level topics. MindManager transforms the topic text, symbols, and codes to the PowerPoint slide. The next slide comes from the topics in the upper-right corner of the map. The following slides detail the information on the connected topics. The pattern repeats in a clockwise fashion around the map. The first slide is shown in Figure 19-3.

Reviewing your presentation

The presentation may be a bit bland, so it is a good idea to go through the presentation slowly and see if the layout of each slide is right. Particularly, keep an eye out for text running over other text or continuing onto a second slide.

After you have created and sent your map to PowerPoint, you need to look for the following glaring problems:

✔ **Too much text:** The topic text or text notes are too long and run onto the next slide.

   Keep the length of the topic text under 15 to 20 words. PowerPoint fits the topic text into a default size text box, and topic text that is too long will overrun other information on the slide. When in doubt, send it to PowerPoint and check it out.

✔ **Presentation is too boring:** I offer some tips for solving this problem in the section "Going to PowerPoint to View the Templates," later in this chapter.

✔ **Too much information:** I discuss the solution for this problem in the section "Setting the Topic Defaults in PowerPoint," later in this chapter.

Some sprucing up may be needed to get to the full "Ooh...Aah" effect. This sprucing starts with the global and topic settings, which I discuss in the following sections.

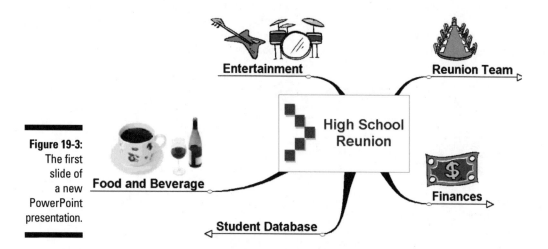

Figure 19-3:
The first slide of a new PowerPoint presentation.

Adjusting the Global and Topic Settings in Your Presentation

The three ingredients to cook up the best PowerPoint presentation are the MindManager map, the PowerPoint export settings in MindManager, and the PowerPoint program. The MindManager export settings, both global and topic settings, create the transfer characteristics between MindManager and PowerPoint. The global settings determine how the MindManager map transforms the map information to PowerPoint. The topic settings tell MindManager what information is to be taken from the topic and how to format the information in the PowerPoint presentation. Where are the global settings? Follow these steps to find and alter the default global settings:

1. **Click the PowerPoint toolbar icon.**

   An "Export Map As" pop-up appears. Click Save. The same PowerPoint Export Format Settings dialog box shown in Figure 19-2 appears. Each time this dialog box appears, the previous settings appear. There is no way to preserve the original defaults.

2. **Select the *Use Styles Defined in PowerPoint Template* radio button.**

   The text field underneath the radio button is now active. The small box on the right lets you browse to find the PowerPoint templates.

3. Click the browse button that is next to the text field.

The Select PowerPoint Template dialog box appears, as shown in Figure 19-4. If you don't see any files listed in the dialog box, you may have browsed to the wrong location to find your PowerPoint templates. You should at least see the templates shipped with PowerPoint. The PowerPoint template is the background of the PowerPoint slide. The template affects where the text is located on the slide.

Figure 19-4:
The Select PowerPoint Template dialog box.

Select PowerPoint Template
Look in: Presentation Designs

Artsy.pot	Dad's Tie.pot	Nature.pot	Soaring.p
Blends.pot	Expedition.pot	Network Blitz.pot	Straight E
Blueprint.pot	Factory.pot	Notebook.pot	Strategic.
Bold Stripes.pot	Lock And Key.pot	Ribbons.pot	Sumi Pair
CAP Template.pot	Marble.pot	Ricepaper.pot	
Capsules.pot	Mountain.pot	Sandstone.pot	

File name: _____ Open

Files of type: PowerPoint Template Files (*.pot) Cancel

☐ Open as read-only

4. Highlight a template, and click the Open button.

I know . . . It doesn't open it, but it does add it to the selection box. The PowerPoint template specified in the selection box is used to create the PowerPoint presentation.

The selection of a template is an important step toward creating an impressive presentation. Experiment with a number of the templates. My favorites include Blends, Dads Tie, Straight Edge, and Strategic. I also like anchovies on my pizza.

5. Refer to Figure 19-2. Select whether to include a topic hyperlink.

A topic with a hyperlink confuses PowerPoint. The audience for your presentation can't move to your hyperlink. You have the option of including the hyperlink in the presentation or just displaying the topic text. Check the box if you want to include the hyperlink in the presentation. I prefer to leave it unchecked because the hyperlink is separated from the topic text and becomes a separate page in the PowerPoint presentation.

The inclusion of the hyperlink in the presentation only occurs if the topic is exported as a bulleted list. The hyperlink selection in Figure 19-2 refers to topic hyperlinks. Hyperlinks in the text notes don't count.

6. Select the *Use high color quality map graphics* (24 bit) in the PowerPoint Export Format Settings dialog box.

7. **Click on the *default settings* box that is hiding on the lower-left corner of this same dialog box, as shown in Figure 19-2.**

   The box is used to set the double deep dark secret topic defaults. Clicking on the *default settings* box brings up the PowerPoint Export Default Topic Settings dialog box, as shown in Figure 19-5.

8. **Select *Automatic* from the drop-down box for all settings.**

9. **Click OK twice, and you're done entering the global defaults.**

PowerPoint Export Default Topic Settings

Export status: Automatic

Slide layout: Automatic

Heading: Automatic alignment

☐ Use transparent background for map images

☐ Use border for map images

☑ Create speaker notes from topic notes

OK   Cancel

The next section discusses the map topics. You can specify precise ways to export each topic to PowerPoint. You do not — I repeat, *do not* — need to adjust each topic. That would be way too much trouble. Besides, the automatic settings work quite well.

Going to PowerPoint to View the Templates

The list of template names shown in MindManager does not explain what the related PowerPoint template looks like. And you may want to know this to choose the best template for presenting your map's information. To view a sample of the PowerPoint templates, follow these steps:

1. **Open the PowerPoint program.**

   The Create a New Presentation Using dialog box appears.

2. **Select Design Template and click OK.**

   The list of templates appears.

   Your PowerPoint program may already be open because you have already created your first presentation. In that case, go to the template list by choosing Format⇨Design templates from the PowerPoint main menu.

3. **Select a template from the list.**

   The view box on the right shows a sample of the selected template.

   When you find one you like, remember the name and select the template in MindManager.

Setting the Topic Defaults in PowerPoint

Click the PowerPoint toolbar icon, and all the topics are transferred to PowerPoint when the topic default settings (refer to Figure 19-5) are set to automatic. However, you may not want to transform all the topics, so you can make a presentation out of selected topics. For example, you may use MindManager to take meeting notes. Within the meeting, a status report is given on the project. The status report information is on one series of topics in your Map. The status report information is important to the stakeholder with the big stake (your boss), but the boss wasn't at the meeting. The other topics contain the gossipy details of the meeting which your boss doesn't want to see. You can select just the status report series of topics and create a PowerPoint presentation specifically for your boss.

The MindManager PowerPoint Export Topic settings have to be changed if you want to export only one topic.

The following steps describe how to export one topic by changing the PowerPoint export characteristics:

1. **Click on one of the topics that contains the information you want to include in the PowerPoint presentation.**

2. **Select File➪Send To➪Microsoft PowerPoint.**

   The PowerPoint Send To Settings dialog box, shown in Figure 19-6, appears.

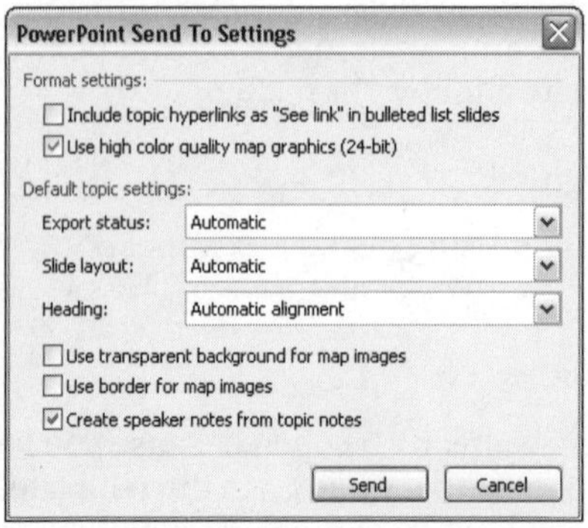

Figure 19-6:
The
PowerPoint
Send To
Settings
dialog box.

PowerPoint Send To Settings

Format settings:
- ☐ Include topic hyperlinks as "See link" in bulleted list slides
- ☑ Use high color quality map graphics (24-bit)

Default topic settings:
- Export status: Automatic
- Slide layout: Automatic
- Heading: Automatic alignment
- ☐ Use transparent background for map images
- ☐ Use border for map images
- ☑ Create speaker notes from topic notes

[Send] [Cancel]

3. **Select the Export This Topic option from the Export status drop-down list.**

4. **Click Send.**

Now the PowerPoint presentation contains only the status information topics. The other topics didn't make the jump.

Select the first topic to send to PowerPoint and then use the Ctrl+Shift Click technique to select more than one topic at a time. You can also leave the PowerPoint Export Settings dialog box open and select other topics.

Choosing a Slide Layout in PowerPoint

The Slide Layout drop-down list of the PowerPoint Send To Settings dialog box (refer to Figure 19-6) offers a multitude of slide layouts.

The slide layout choices are useful in determining how the topic will be presented in PowerPoint. The Automatic setting is still the choice du jour, but other selections can add some sizzle. In particular, I want to point out the following layout options:

- ✔ **Text Notes Only or Title Over Text Notes:** *Text notes* are important in MindManager maps. Text notes normally become PowerPoint speaker notes and are not shown on any slides. Select Text Notes Only or Title Over Text Notes to include the text notes in a presentation. MindManager transfers approximately the first 20 text note words to one slide and the remaining words are put on the next slide. The title of the text overrun slide includes the word *continue* placed after it. (The word should be *continued* but MindManager is allowed one error.) Try to keep your text notes short to fit on one slide; the overrun slide just doesn't look good.

- ✔ **Picture + Bullets or Bullets + Picture:** I like to add picture files to slides. You can use pictures to convey subliminal messages in your presentation. Pictures of money may even enhance the potential of getting a raise. You can add a picture and keep the bullets that would normally be on the slide. My preference is to use the Picture + Bullets option. The picture you choose is placed to the right of the bullets on the slide. The Bullets + Picture option just places the picture on the other side of the bullets.

Adjusting the topics is the final part of assembling your presentation. It is now time to look at the product.

Engaging with PowerPoint

This section visually shows the output of transforming a MindManager map to PowerPoint — just in case you've been only reading along and not actually making a map and sending it to PowerPoint.

The MindManager map from Figure 19-1, shown earlier in this chapter, is ready to send to PowerPoint, as shown in Figure 19-7.

The selected PowerPoint Template is Blends.pot. The Default settings are set to Automatic, as shown in Figure 19-8.

The topic with Dewey Cheetem has the settings shown in Figure 19-8.

The time for transforming your map is at hand. Click on the PowerPoint icon. The PowerPoint icon is located in the toolbar below the map.

Click OK and you should see the slides shown in Figures 19-9 to 19-14. This is a high school reunion side slow that I started in MindManager and exported to PowerPoint. There were two more but I ran out of space.

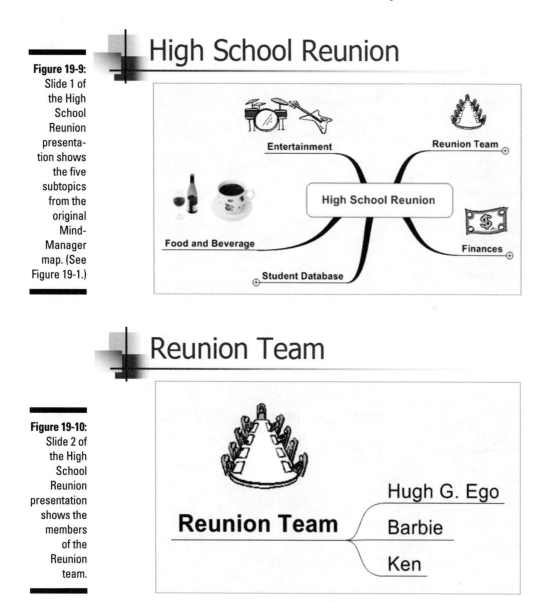

Figure 19-9:
Slide 1 of the High School Reunion presentation shows the five subtopics from the original Mind-Manager map. (See Figure 19-1.)

Figure 19-10:
Slide 2 of the High School Reunion presentation shows the members of the Reunion team.

Finances

Accounting: Dewey Cheetem

Dewey is the cousin of a friend of the class president. The reunion accounting activity will help him get back on his feet after his ethics issues of the past.

Figure 19-13:
Slide 5 of
the High
School
Reunion
presentation
shows the
various fees
extorted
from
reunion
participants.

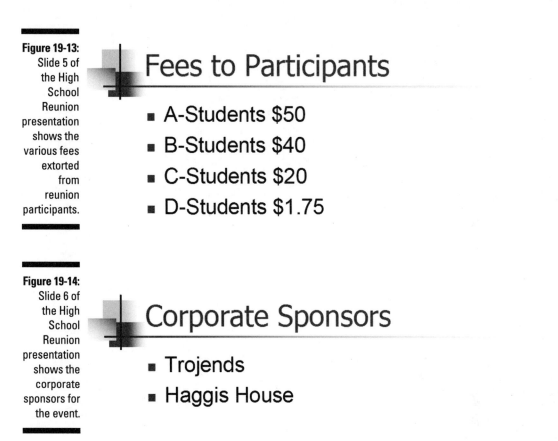

Figure 19-13:
Slide 5 of
the High
School
Reunion
presentation
shows the
various fees
extorted
from
reunion
participants.

Fees to Participants

- A-Students $50
- B-Students $40
- C-Students $20
- D-Students $1.75

Figure 19-14:
Slide 6 of
the High
School
Reunion
presentation
shows the
corporate
sponsors for
the event.

Corporate Sponsors

- Trojends
- Haggis House

The High School Reunion slide show is a basic example of a presentation made by MindManager and PowerPoint. My latest project map has over 250 topics. You can make fantastic presentations with as few as 20 topics, as in this example, or a more complex project with 250 topics.

Don't forget the subliminal messages and go get that raise!

Chapter 20

Word Wonders

In This Chapter

▶ Setting up your map template in Word

▶ Getting your map ready for export

▶ Going out to Word and back again

*E*ven when you intend to ultimately produce a Word document, MindManager is a fantastic tool for gathering and organizing your thoughts and ideas. It is so easy to jump from one place to another in your map, add new ideas, put in reminders (Callouts are great for this), and see connections between ideas that you may have missed at first.

This entire book was initially written in MindManager (as you may have gathered from the numerous examples). The master map was our table of contents as well as our project management tool. We used it to assign responsibility for writing each chapter, monitor the status of the writing, and capture open notes and questions with colors, icons, Callouts, and Topic Notes.

Each topic on the Table of Contents map also had a hyperlink to the detailed chapter map where the chapter introduction and section headings were laid out as topics. I used Callouts to remind myself of the points I wanted to cover in each section and used relationships to show where a topic mentioned in one place was explained in detail in another. I typed the actual text of the initial draft of each section directly into the topic notes.

When I was satisfied with the chapter, I exported everything to a Word document and did my final polishing there. In this chapter, I explore the export of maps to Word.

Getting Ready for the Export to Word

If you're planning to use the Word export functionality only rarely and are not doing anything fancy in your topic notes (no pictures or tables), you can probably just skim this section or even skip it entirely.

If, however, you will be exporting frequently to Word, then you will save time in the long run if you first create a special template in Word that you can specify during the export process. You can complete the template in 15 minutes or less by following these steps:

1. **Start MindManager and open a new map. Create topics and Callouts, as shown in Figure 20-1.**

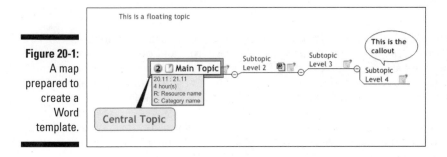

Figure 20-1:
A map prepared to create a Word template.

It doesn't matter what you type in the notes for each topic. If you will be working with pictures and tables, create one or two that will be typical for your use so you can see how they will export. The document, spreadsheet, or other file that you hyperlink to is also unimportant — you just need a hyperlink. If you need help doing any of these things, here is where you can find more details:

- Adding topics and subtopics: Chapter 2

- Adding Callouts, notes, pictures, and tables: Chapter 7

- Adding task information (only if you're using X5 Pro): Chapter 9

- Adding hyperlinks: Chapter 12

2. **Click Modes and select Review from the View bar.**

MindManager shifts into Review mode.

3. **Select Main Topic and add a review comment.**

Review Chapter 11 if you need help doing this. It doesn't matter what comment you actually enter.

4. Click Finish Review on the View bar.

MindManager closes down the Review mode display and re-opens the Map view.

5. Click the Word icon on the Export toolbar.

MindManager opens the Word Export Settings dialog box (as shown in Figure 20-2).

If you haven't already saved your map, MindManager will prompt you to save it before showing you the Word Export Settings dialog box. Enter a name for your map and click OK.

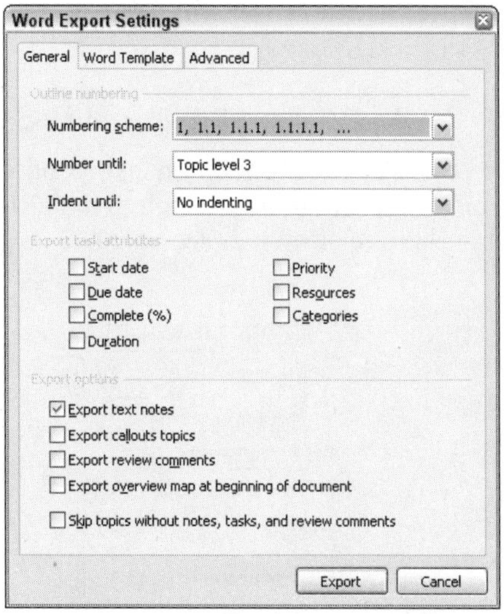

Figure 20-2:
The General tab of the Word Export Settings dialog box.

6. Click each checkbox on this page except the last one (*Skip topics without notes . . .*) and then click Export.

MindManager opens the File Save dialog box and requests a name for the document to be created. The default name will be the text of your map's central topic.

7. Choose a name and file location and then click OK.

MindManager displays a series of progress messages ending with a dialog box stating that it has successfully exported the document, followed by the name you gave to your file.

Depending on the other programs running on your computer, you may see the Server Busy dialog box shown in Figure 20-3. The message does not refer to your network server but rather to the Microsoft Word program, which is "serving" MindManager while MindManager is creating your document. Wait a few seconds until the disk activity stops, and then click Retry.

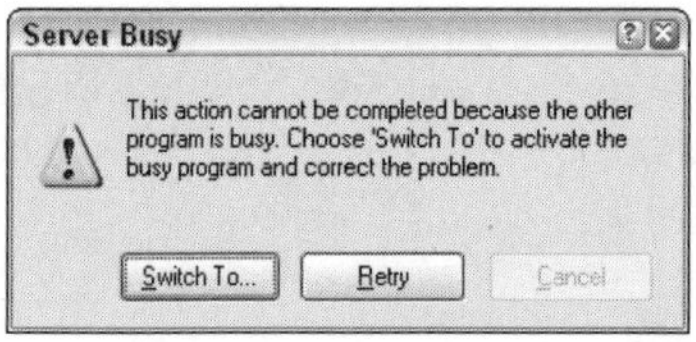

Figure 20-3:
The Server
Busy dialog
box.

8. Click the Open button on the Word Export Progress dialog box.

Word opens and displays your exported document. The content will depend on what you actually entered on your original map, but your document should resemble the one shown in Figure 20-4.

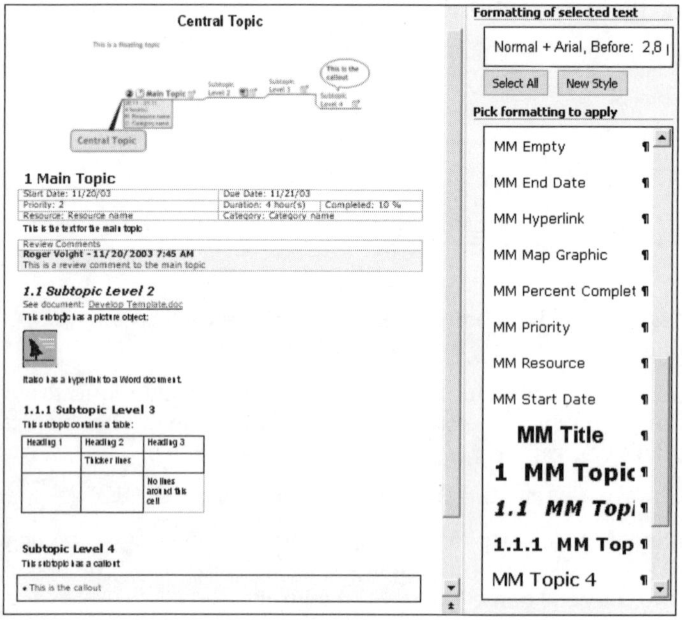

Figure 20-4:
The Mind-
Manager
map
exported
into Word.

9. **Modify the MindManager styles (everything beginning with MM) to suit your needs.**

Look at Figure 20-5 for some ideas.

To display the style page, select Format⇨Styles and Formatting from the Word menu bar. If you need help with defining styles, check out *Word 2003 For Dummies* by Dan Gookin, published by Wiley, Inc.

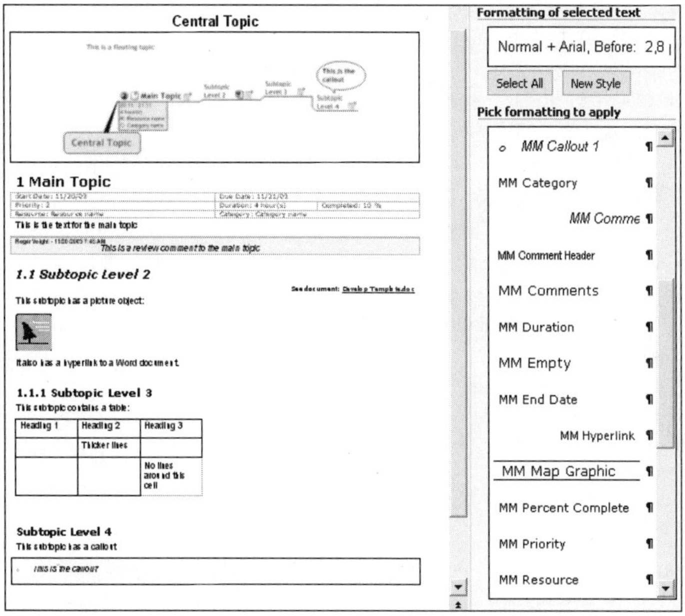

Figure 20-5: Mind-Manager styles changed to the way I want them.

10. **Delete the entire contents of the Word document.**

All your style changes remain in the document. If you want a standard header and/or footer, add those now.

11. **Save the document as a template in your personal or workgroup's template folder.**

Change the Save as Type field on the Save As dialog box to Document Template (*.dot). Word will automatically change to your templates directory when you make this selection. Give the template a distinctive name such as MMap.dot or something similar.

You have successfully created your MindManager Word export template.

Do's and don'ts with MindManager styles

MindManager creates the topic level styles (MM Topic 1, MM Topic 2, and so on) each time you export a Word document, so there is no point in making any changes to these styles in your template. By default, MindManager bases each topic-level style on the corresponding Heading-level style in the template (for example, MM Topic 1 is based on the style Heading 1), so you can effectively control what MindManager creates in the Topic styles by changing the corresponding Heading styles.

So far, so good. Unfortunately, for reasons known only by the people at Mindjet, MindManager ignores all margin information and tab settings in the Heading styles and substitutes its own — and you have no access to or control over the size of the indent. Furthermore, all the MM styles and Heading styles are based on the so-called Normal style — and MindManager uses the Normal style for all text notes (again, you can't change this). The net result is that you just can't do anything that will reliably give you any kind of acceptable indented style directly out of the export.

If you want indents by topic level with the topic text also appropriately indented, you will need to do a bit of style reapplication after the export. I use the Body Style for the indented notes (but be careful — by default, Body style is also based on Normal) and then use the style replace function on the Styles and Formatting page of the Task pane to quickly make the changes.

If you will mostly be using the export function to Word, you can fully exploit all the style possibilities available in Word. If, however, you're planning to re-import your document back into MindManager, remember that most of the style characteristics are not supported in MindManager and will be lost.

Task information, callouts, and comments are exported as tables configured for the full width of the page. You cannot control this on the export but can, of course, modify them afterwards in the Word document itself.

Exporting Your Map to Word

If you know you're going to export your map to Word, remember that graphics and tables are handled a bit differently in the MindManager Notes pane than they are in Word. In MindManager, if you have a large picture or table, you simply use the slider bar to scroll to the left or right to see the entire picture or table. With Word, of course, the page is fixed in size, so you need to ensure that your graphics and tables do not exceed the page width.

 A general guide to use for tables or graphics is the width of the expanded Topic Notes pane (click the Expand button on the Notes toolbar). A table or graphic that is not wider than approximately 80 percent of the width of this expanded pane will usually fit within the standard margins of your Word document.

When you're ready to export your map, follow these steps:

1. **Click the Word icon on the Export toolbar.**

   MindManager opens the Word Export Settings dialog box (refer to Figure 20-2).

2. **Click the checkbox next to each type of item you want to export, select the desired outline numbering scheme, and then click the Word Template tab.**

   MindManager displays the Word Template page of the dialog box (as shown in Figure 20-6).

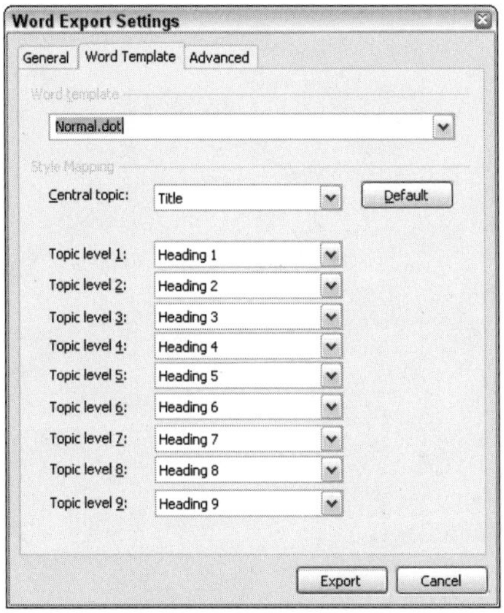

Figure 20-6: The Word Template page of the Word Export Settings dialog box.

Word Export Settings

General | Word Template | Advanced

Word template

Normal.dot

Style Mapping

Central topic: Title   Default

Topic level 1: Heading 1
Topic level 2: Heading 2
Topic level 3: Heading 3
Topic level 4: Heading 4
Topic level 5: Heading 5
Topic level 6: Heading 6
Topic level 7: Heading 7
Topic level 8: Heading 8
Topic level 9: Heading 9

Export | Cancel

3. **If you created a Word template to use for map exports, select that template from the Word Template combo box.**

   MindManager will redisplay the style names from the new template in the other combo boxes.

   This Word Template page allows you to map topic levels to some style other than the Heading styles but, as of this writing, there is no point to changing any of the topic-level style mappings as MindManager always uses Heading 1 through Heading 9. The style changes you made in your template will, however, be used.

4. **Click the Advanced tab and make any desired changes to the defaults and then click Export.**

MindManager displays the Advanced page of the Word Export Settings dialog box (as shown in Figure 20-7). Uncheck the types of hyperlinks you do not want to export to Word. If hyperlinks are exported, they will be prefixed by the words shown in the Prefix fields. You can change this to any text you like. The Map graphics section will be enabled only if you checked *Export overview map at the beginning of the document* on the General tab. The *Level of detail* combo box lets you specify how many topic levels will be displayed in the exported graphic.

After you click Export, MindManager opens the File Save dialog box and requests a name for the document to be created. The default name will be the text of your map's central topic.

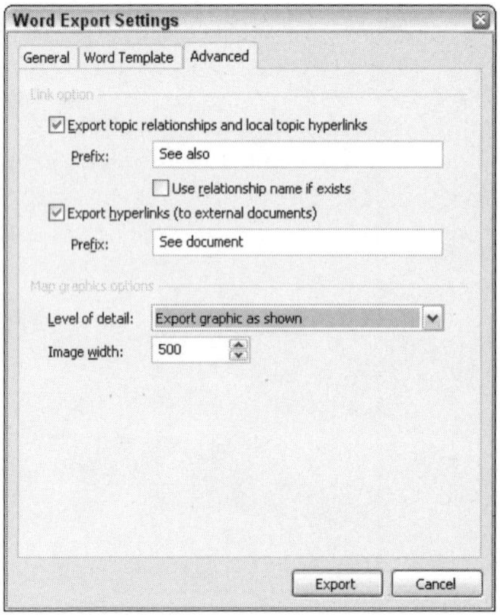

Figure 20-7:
The
Advanced
page of the
Word Export
Settings
dialog box.

5. **Choose a name and file location and then click OK.**

   MindManager displays a series of progress messages ending with a dialog box stating that it has successfully exported the document, followed by the name you gave to your file.

6. **Click the Open button on the Word Export Progress dialog box.**

   Word opens and displays your exported document.

Importing Your Word Document to a Map

You can also import a Word document into MindManager, but you may need to do a bit of work on your document first before it will import correctly. Every paragraph that uses one of the heading styles will become a topic in the imported map. All text following a paragraph with a heading style is treated as a topic note to that heading style until another paragraph is reached that has one of the heading styles. Remember these heading sequence rules:

- ✔ If the new heading style has a higher number (for example, "Heading 3" when the prior heading style was "Heading 2"), then that text becomes a subtopic.

- ✔ If the new heading style has the same level number, then that text becomes a sibling of the prior topic.

- ✔ If the new heading style has a lower number, then MindManager will make that text a sibling of the topic created the last time (reading your document from top to bottom) it encountered that heading level.

- ✔ If you skip a heading level (going to higher numbers; for example, Heading 2 and then Heading 4), your document will probably not import correctly.

If your document was not created with heading styles, you will need to go through the document (in Word) and add your topic headings according to these rules before beginning the import. See Figure 20-8 for an example.

Heading 1	**This is my first main topic**
Normal	This text will appear in the notes for my first main topic
Heading 2	*This is a subheading 1 to main topic 1*
Heading 3	**1. This belongs to subheading 1**
Heading 3	**2. This belongs to subheading 1**
Heading 2	*This is subheading 2 to main topic 1*
Heading 3	**1. This belongs to subheading 2**
Heading 3	**2. This belongs to subheading 2**
Heading 1	**This is the second main topic**
Normal	Notice that I went from Heading 3 to Heading 1. This is OK.
Normal	If I went directly from Heading 1 to Heading 3, however, I would have an import error.
Heading 2	*This is subheading 1 to main topic 2*
Heading 2	*This is subheading 2 to main topic 2/*

Figure 20-8: Headings created in Word in preparation for import into Mind-Manager.

To import a Word document into MindManager, select File➪Open from the menu bar, change the *Files of Type* combo box to Microsoft Word Documents (*.doc), select the desired file, and click OK. MindManager will then complete the import process without further input. The resulting import of the document shown in Figure 20-8 is shown in Figure 20-9.

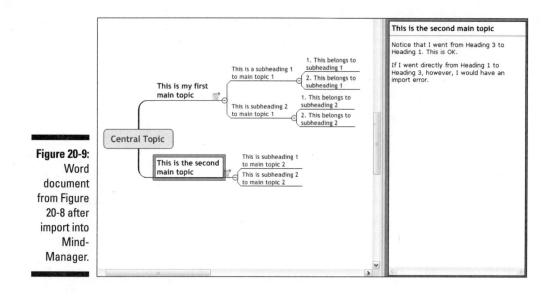

This is the second main topic

Notice that I went from Heading 3 to Heading 1. This is OK.

If I went directly from Heading 1 to Heading 3, however, I would have an import error.

Figure 20-9:
Word
document
from Figure
20-8 after
import into
Mind-
Manager.

You also have the option of exporting only a portion of your Word document into your map. To do this, open your Word document and select the text you want to export. You can only export one block of text at a time, and you should be sure that the first line of text that you select has one of the heading styles. After you have selected your text block, then select File⇨Send To⇨ MindManager to complete the export.

If there is no map open, MindManager will create an entirely new map. If, however, there is an open map, the selected headings will be appended to the selected topic in the map. This means that you can export multiple blocks of text from your Word document to a single map by repeating the process described in the previous paragraph.

The guidelines previously given about heading styles still applies to the block of text you are exporting.

Chapter 21

Out to Outlook

1 use the link between MindManager and Outlook all the time. Fast forward to the last section of this chapter, "Using the MindManager-Outlook Mind Meld," to see how I use the connection, or link, between MindManager and Outlook. Come back though. You're going to use many more features of the program in the other sections of this chapter. Very likely, you're going to find your own way to use this powerful MindManager feature.

A MindManager map can be complex to use. Imagine looking at a 350-topic MindManager map and trying to quickly see what should be done today. MindManager becomes a more powerful tool when you export and link to other software products to manage complexity and enhance usefulness. Microsoft Outlook is one such software product that you can link to. MindManager exports task data so Outlook can suck it up and use it. Outlook may also contain information that belongs in a map. MindManager grabs this Outlook data and makes a map out of it. The two programs can then dance in synchronized harmony. Outlook adds new tasks based upon changes in the MindManager data, and MindManager brings new Outlook tasks to the MindManager map. The dance can be fast and a bit head-spinning. Controlling the two partners is one of the goals of this chapter.

Outlook is an excellent program. The most basic Outlook settings are discussed in this chapter. For more detailed information, see *Outlook 2003 For Dummies,* by Bill Dyszel. That book explains how to use and view MindManager information after it is in an Outlook task format.

Connecting the MindManager map and Outlook together takes visual organization to a new level. First, you're going to add tasks to Outlook to get one half of the duo ready.

Getting a New Outlook on Life with Tasks

Time to get out the data raincoat for protection. Your Outlook task list may be filled with cool important stuff. I would hate to send you into the Matrix wondering which tasks are real and which aren't. To add some unreal tasks to Outlook simply open Outlook, choose Tasks from the File list, and add a few tasks with dates one year from today. Make sure that some of the tasks have a start date and a due date, and then sprinkle in some priorities.

I am a pilot and own a small airplane. I have used Outlook to create a list of the typical tasks required to keep the airplane flying. I want to combine aircraft maintenance tasks from Outlook with the flight activities that I keep in MindManager. The goal is to keep my flying dates coordinated with the maintenance activities.

Figure 21-1 shows the Outlook task list that I created for the airplane. Due Date is the normal default heading, but I added a Start Date heading and Priority column so I can see all the data that is sent to MindManager. The Priority column is indicated by the exclamation point in the heading line. Outlook uses exclamation points and arrows to indicate task priority.

The Outlook task list is now ready. Adding MindManager topics is next.

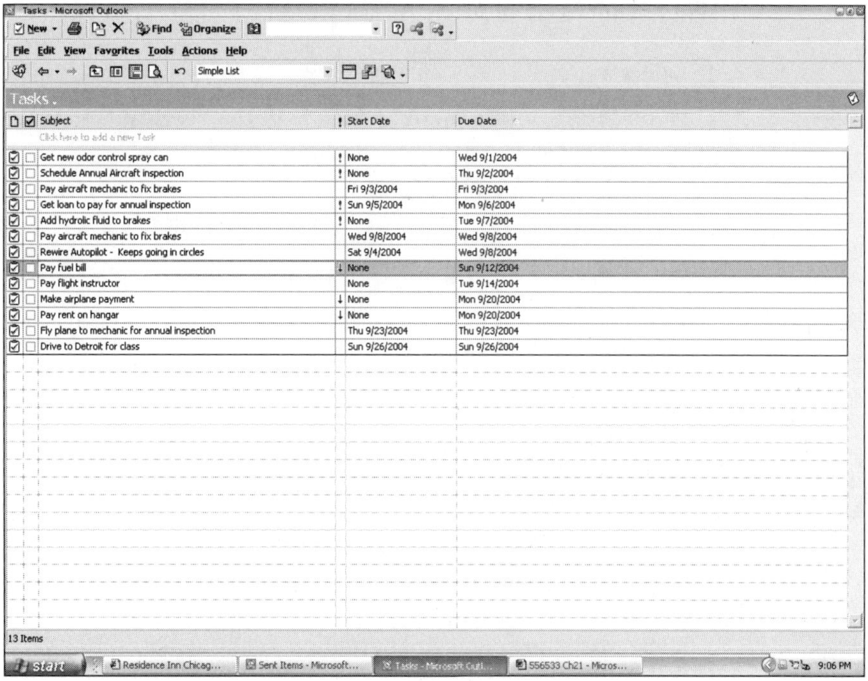

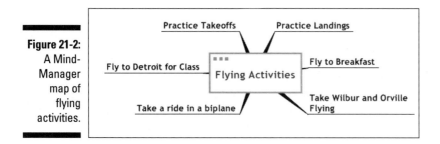

Figure 21-1:
An Outlook
task list.

Combining Topics with Tasks on Your MindManager Map

Next, create a small MindManager map with a few topics. The topics should be action-oriented things — in other words, *tasks*. Refer to Chapter 2 for information on making a map, and refer to Chapter 9 for details on MindManager task information. You're now going to add task information to the topics. Use the map shown in Figure 21-2.

Figure 21-2:
A Mind-
Manager
map of
flying
activities.

The following steps show you how to add task information to a topic:

1. **Select a topic.**

2. **Open the Task Info menu, which is in the vertical list on the right side of the screen.**

   The Task Info dialog box appears.

3. **Click the drop-down arrow next to the Priority box.**

4. **Select Priority 1, Priority 2, or Priority 3.**

   Priority 1, Priority 2, and Priority 3 are translated in Outlook as High, Medium, and Low priority.

5. **Enter a start date or use the drop-down arrow to use a calendar.**

   Choose a date that is far removed from the dates of your real Outlook tasks. Erasing practice tasks is easier if they are grouped separately from real tasks.

6. **Enter a Due Date or use the calendar by selecting the drop-down arrow.**

   Unfortunately for me, the due date can't be before the start date. I keep trying — unsuccessfully — to use the Procrastinator Law of Time, which states that start dates are permitted *after* due dates. But MindManager won't allow it.

7. **Next, click the Complete % drop-down arrow.**

8. **Select a percent complete.**

   The percentage you select gets exported to Outlook. In MindManager, an icon is placed next to the Topic. This percent complete icon looks like a gold star you may have received in third grade, but with some of the points missing.

You can also enter a category that transfers to Outlook.

The remaining task entries, duration, and resources are not transferred to Outlook. Continue to add task information for most of your topics.

Topics with task information are now set up in MindManager, and tasks are set up in Outlook. Now it is time to start the music. Figure 21-3 shows my planned flying activities for one month. Combining this information with the tasks in Outlook is the next step.

Figure 21-3:
Topics
with task
information
in Mind-
Manager.

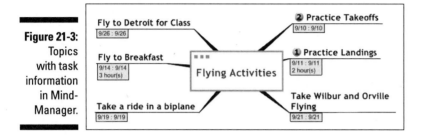

Fly to Detroit for Class
9/26 : 9/26

Fly to Breakfast
9/14 : 9/14
3 hour(s)

Take a ride in a biplane
9/19 : 9/19

Flying Activities

❷ Practice Takeoffs
9/10 : 9/10

❶ Practice Landings
9/11 : 9/11
2 hour(s)

Take Wilbur and Orville
Flying
9/21 : 9/21

Getting, Sending, and Synching Task Data

MindManager is pretty flexible when you first start the synchronization process. But options quickly dry up after the initial export or import is performed. In the beginning, you have only two choices. You can export from MindManager to Outlook, or you can import from Outlook to MindManager. Of these two choices, you have a tool bar selection for only one of them. The margin art shows the button for Export Tasks to Outlook. Don't click it yet. The other way to initiate the sequence of events is to click Select➪Actions. The menu shown in Figure 21-4 appears.

Another option appears in this menu. You can now *Import Outlook Tasks*. Don't do anything yet though. If you don't see the menu selections shown in Figure 21-4, then you probably already tried to export/import tasks. If you see "*Synchronize Outlook tasks*" then you have already exported or imported to Outlook.

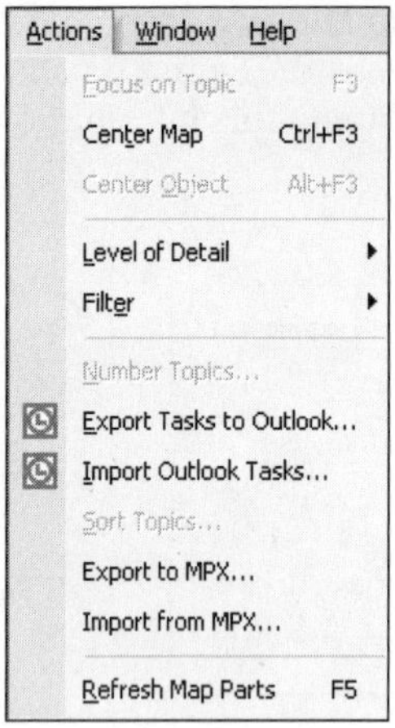

Actions Window Help

Focus on Topic   F3
Center Map   Ctrl+F3
Center Object   Alt+F3

Level of Detail   ▶
Filter   ▶

Number Topics...
🕐 Export Tasks to Outlook...
🕐 Import Outlook Tasks...
Sort Topics...

Export to MPX...
Import from MPX...

Refresh Map Parts   F5

Figure 21-4:
The initial
Import
Export menu
between
Mind-
Manager
and Outlook.

Unfortunately, you can't start over again after you initially selected Export Tasks to Outlook or Import Outlook Tasks. You can only synchronize tasks between the two programs. Use the MindManager Undo command to retreat.

Getting Outlook tasks into MindManager

The setup is now complete. The MindManager map shown in Figure 21-2 contains the MindManager tasks. The Outlook task list shown in Figure 21-1 is the other half.

The following steps show you how to import tasks from Outlook into MindManager:

1. **Click Actions⇨Import Outlook Tasks.**

   The Import Outlook Tasks Wizard dialog box appears, as shown in Figure 21-5, enabling you to choose how the added task will appear in the MindManager map. The first selection adds the task to the central topic of the map. The second selection adds a new topic to the map that says *Imported from Outlook at* followed by the date of the import. All the imported tasks are attached to this new topic. I use the default, which is the first selection.

2. **Click Next to proceed.**

   The second page of five appears, as shown in Figure 21-6.

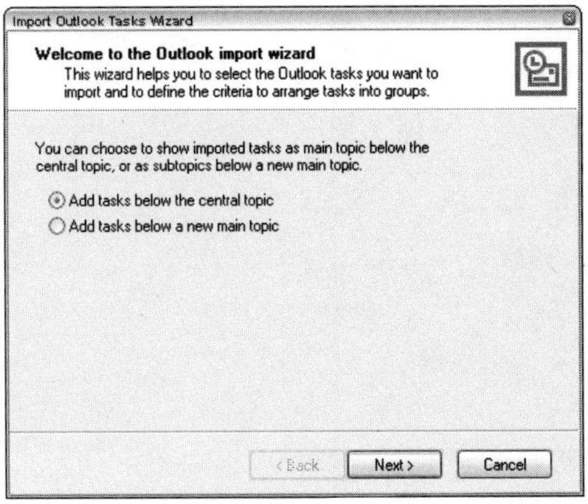

Figure 21-5:
The first
page of the
Import
Outlook
Tasks
Wizard.

Import Outlook Tasks Wizard

Welcome to the Outlook import wizard
This wizard helps you to select the Outlook tasks you want to import and to define the criteria to arrange tasks into groups.

You can choose to show imported tasks as main topic below the central topic, or as subtopics below a new main topic.

⦿ Add tasks below the central topic
◯ Add tasks below a new main topic

[< Back] [Next >] [Cancel]

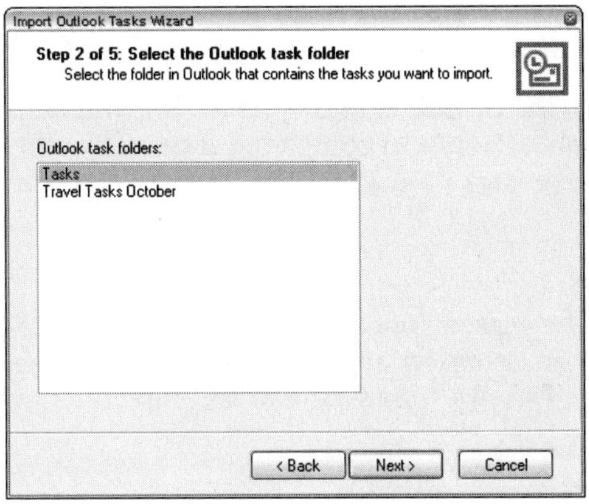

Figure 21-6:
Step 2 of
importing
tasks from
Outlook.

Import Outlook Tasks Wizard

Step 2 of 5: Select the Outlook task folder
Select the folder in Outlook that contains the tasks you want to import.

Outlook task folders:

Tasks
Travel Tasks October

[< Back] [Next >] [Cancel]

3. Select Tasks.

The other selections are the subfiles found under the heading of Task in Outlook. You can import the subfiles (such as Travel Tasks October) into MindManager, but the synchronization does not work.

Outlook Task subfiles can be imported into MindManager, but the synchronization does not work with the imported tasks. Error messages result. Only the Tasks level file is synchronized.

4. Click Next to look at the third page of the Import Outlook Tasks Wizard, as shown in Figure 21-7.

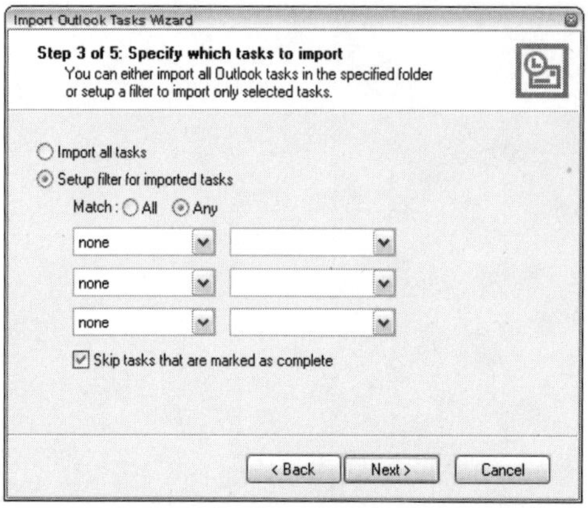

Figure 21-7: Step 3 of importing tasks from Outlook.

5. **Click the *Setup filter for imported tasks* button, and check the box for *Skip tasks that are marked as complete.***

   You may want to use the default of *Import all tasks* if you're using MindManager to analyze trends of completed tasks. The other filters that you can select are Start Date, Due Date, Priority, Category, and %Complete.

6. **Click Next.**

   The fourth page of the wizard appears, as shown in Figure 21-8. The attributes that you can Group By are the same as the previous filters: Start Date, Due Date, Priority, Category, and %Complete.

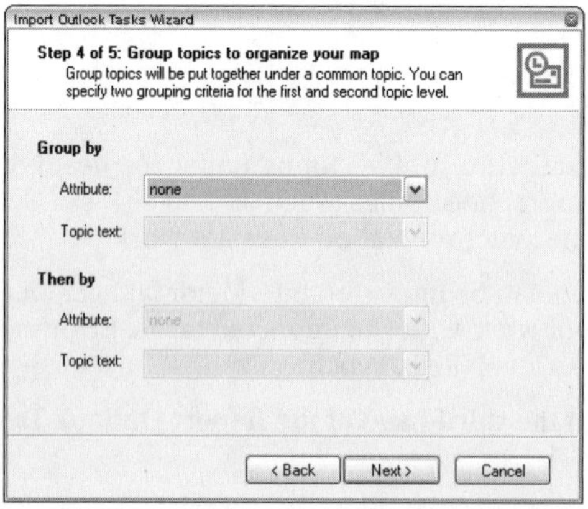

Figure 21-8: Step 4 of importing tasks from Outlook.

7. **Click Next.**

   The final page of the wizard appears, as shown in Figure 21-9.

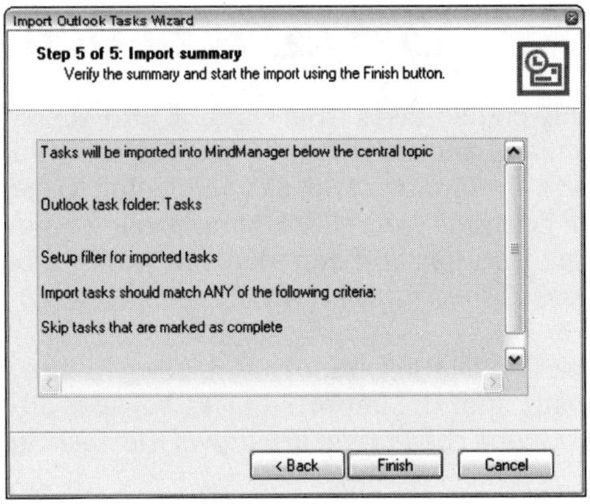

Import Outlook Tasks Wizard

Step 5 of 5: Import summary
Verify the summary and start the import using the Finish button.

Tasks will be imported into MindManager below the central topic

Outlook task folder: Tasks

Setup filter for imported tasks

Import tasks should match ANY of the following criteria:

Skip tasks that are marked as complete

< Back   Finish   Cancel

Figure 21-9:
Step 5 of
importing
tasks from
Outlook.

8. **Click Finish.**

No choices are given on this one. The selections you made on the previous slides are shown. Click the Back button if you see something amiss and want to change your selections

The Outlook tasks now appear in the MindManager map. I have rearranged the topics a bit. The resulting map is shown in Figure 21-10. The map is a combination of the Outlook tasks shown in Figure 21-1 and the MindManager topics shown in Figure 21-2.

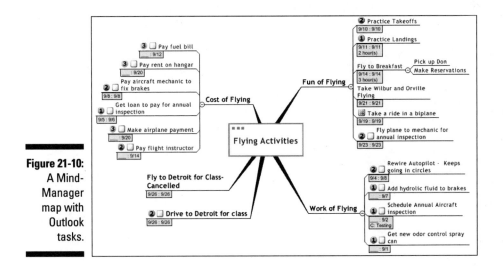

Figure 21-10:
A Mind-
Manager
map with
Outlook
tasks.

Sending MindManager tasks to Outlook

At this point, you have only copied tasks from Outlook into MindManager. The Outlook task list has not changed. Now I am going to show you how to copy MindManager tasks to the Outlook task list. I am going to use the map shown in Figure 21-10 and continue from there. MindManager knows which tasks have been taken from Outlook. You don't have to worry about sending over a duplicate list of tasks.

The Task Start icon is added to all the Outlook tasks brought into the Mind-Manager map. You can easily spot the imported tasks because all other tasks do not have the Task Start icon. The margin art shows the Task Start icon.

You have now imported tasks from Outlook. Now it's time to export Mind-Manager tasks to Outlook. The button to Export to Outlook (shown in the margin art) has changed. It is no longer highlighted. The Export to Outlook option (refer to Figure 21-4) has even disappeared from the Actions menu. Oh what to do?

Not to worry. Selecting *Export Tasks to Outlook* brings up the same menu as when you select *Synchronize Outlook Tasks*. Now you're ready to export MindManager tasks to Outlook.

Follow these steps to export MindManager tasks to Outlook:

1. **Click the Synchronize Outlook Tasks tool button.**

   The button is shown in the margin art. The Export and Synchronize Tasks with Outlook dialog box appears, as shown in Figure 21-11. (You may have different check boxes shown when the pop up first appears.)

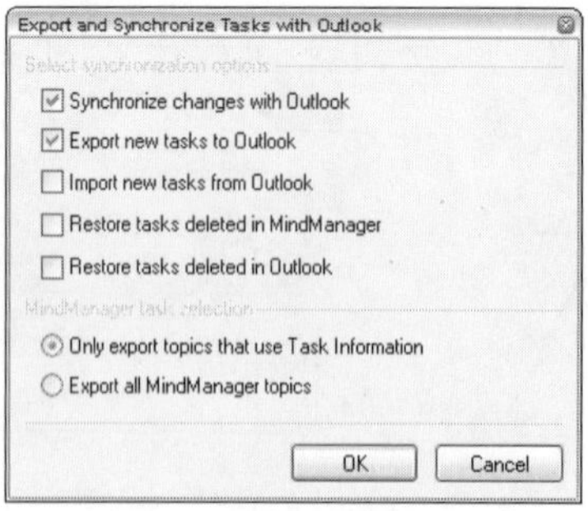

Figure 21-11:
The Export and Synchronize Tasks with Outlook dialog box.

Export and Synchronize Tasks with Outlook

Select synchronization options

☑ Synchronize changes with Outlook
☑ Export new tasks to Outlook
☐ Import new tasks from Outlook
☐ Restore tasks deleted in MindManager
☐ Restore tasks deleted in Outlook

MindManager task selection

◉ Only export topics that use Task Information
○ Export all MindManager topics

[OK] [Cancel]

2. **Click the two check boxes and one button as shown in Figure 21-11.**

   The *Synchronize changes with Outlook* check box exports changes in the Outlook task list into the MindManager map. The *Export new tasks to Outlook* selection is the important one.

3. Click OK.

Figure 21-12 shows the resulting Outlook task list. Now all the MindManager tasks are in the task list.

Wait a minute. Something is wrong. What happened to the task Fly to Breakfast? It is shown in the MindManager map in Figure 21-10 as a subtopic of Fun of Flying. Why isn't Fly to Breakfast in the Outlook task list? MindManager tells a bit of a fib. The buttons *Only export topics that use Task Information* and *Export all MindManager topics* refer only to topics (or subtopics) at the very end of the map. The reason Fly to Breakfast didn't make the leap is because the subtopics Pick up Don and Make Reservations prevented Fly to Breakfast from being transferred to the Outlook Task list, as shown in Figure 21-13.

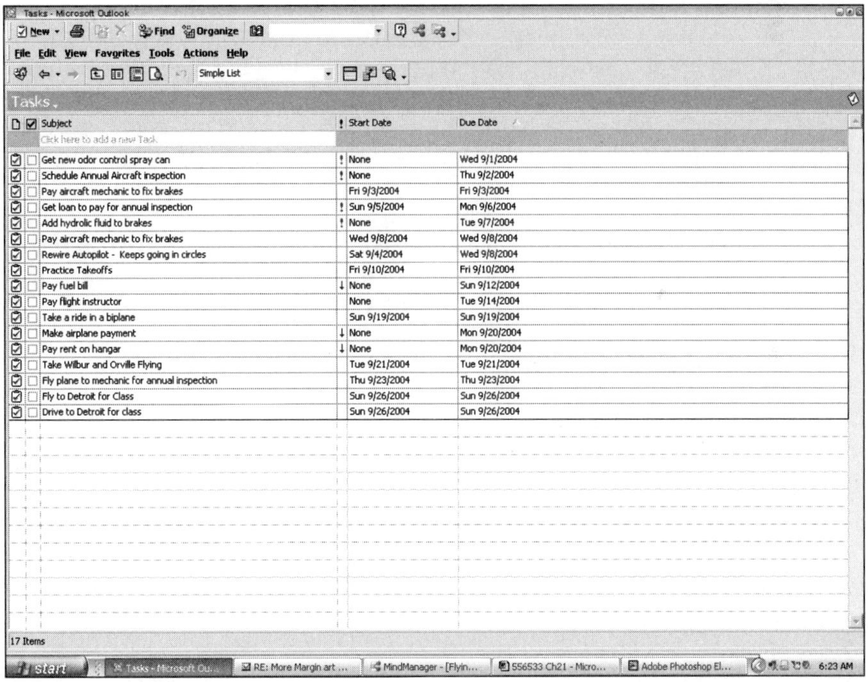

Figure 21-12:
An Outlook task list with Mind- Manager tasks.

Only topics at the very end of the MindManager map can be exported to the Outlook Task list.

The dance partners are set. Outlook has received tasks from MindManager and vice versa. Let the synching dance begin.

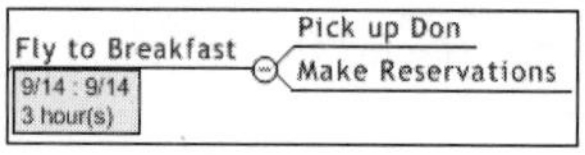

Figure 21-13:
Topics with
subtopics
are not
transferred
to the
Outlook
task list.

Synching MindManager and Outlook

You don't have much to do after the MindManager map and the Outlook task list are set. Synchronization permits changes in either MindManager or Outlook to affect the other. Complete a task, enter the completion into MindManager, and the same task in the Outlook list is crossed out signifying completion. Change a priority in the Outlook task list, and the priority icon in MindManager changes, too.

Let's change a few items in the map shown in Figure 21-10 and the task list shown in Figure 21-12. Let's pretend that half of the month has gone by and you want to alter the MindManager map and the Outlook tasks. This list is what you're changing.

In MindManager, make the following changes:

- ✔ Flight with Wilbur and Orville. Complete with a date change. It was a short but historical flight.
- ✔ Ride in a Biplane cancelled. Biplane hit cumulus granite. Everyone OK.

In the Outlook task list, make the following changes:

- ✔ Change airplane payment from low to high priority. The bank called.
- ✔ Pay flight instructor. Payment date moved up before Practice Landing date.

To cancel the Ride in a Biplane, mark the task as complete rather than removing it from the MindManager map. Deleting a task in the MindManager map does not delete the task in the Outlook task list.

You can synchronize your map by clicking Actions⇨Synchronize Outlook Tasks or by using the Synchronize Outlook Tasks tool that is found on the lower toolbar.

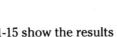

Figure 21-14 and Figure 21-15 show the results of making the changes. I have added arrows to make the changes easy to find.

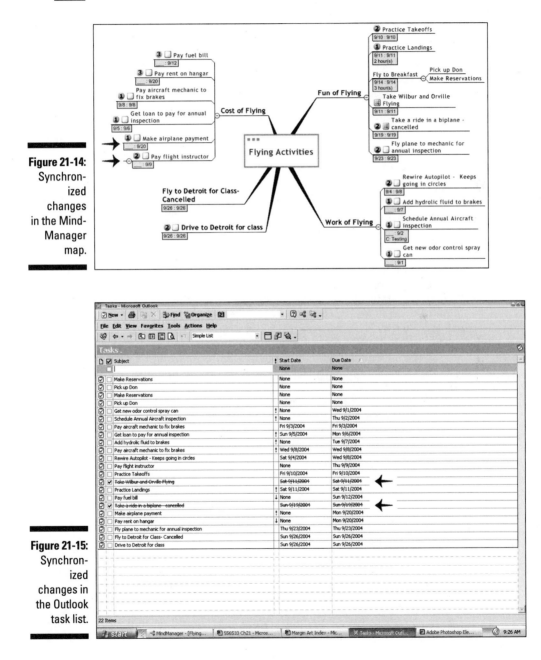

Figure 21-14: Synchron-ized changes in the Mind-Manager map.

Figure 21-15: Synchron-ized changes in the Outlook task list.

Using The MindManager-Outlook Mind Meld

Now that you know how to link Outlook and MindManager, you may wonder what kind of scenarios would lead you try this software mind meld. I use the link between MindManager and Outlook every month. I've become hooked. This section leads you through a specific example that we can all use regularly — paying bills.

I pay bills every month, every quarter, annually on a constant basis, ad infinitum. I use the Internet for just about everything. I use it for direct deposit, banking, paying bills, linking into Web sites to find what I owe, direct withdrawals, and everything else. Most snail-mail bills never get opened because they are already paid and processed. Keeping track of all the stuff associated with paying bills is the problem. For example, you used to get a bill in the mail. You would get your checkbook out, write a check, and send it back. You were done. Not any more. Now you have many, many choices.

And this is where the MindManager-Outlook link becomes so handy. Outlook is designed to remind you to take care of a task — in this case, pay a bill. Sometimes, I take care of it right away, and other times I don't. With MindManager linked to Outlook, I can take a quick look at MindManager and see exactly which bills are on track and which ones have suffered because of procrastinitis. When I do pay attention to the task notice, it is easy to pay the bill. All the information is right there in MindManager. I just click on the link, enter the connection information that is shown, do my business, and I am done. Completion of the bill-paying task is transferred to Outlook. The old task is shown as completed, and the next task and due date based on the reoccurrence schedule appears. The updated date information is transferred to MindManager. The next month is ready in a snap. (Now all I need is the money to pay the bills. If you're just browsing in this book. Stop. Buy it.)

The following two sets of steps show you how to create your own bill-paying and tracking system. First, set up MindManager:

1. **Make a MindManager map showing all the bills you have to pay.**

   Mine are shown in Figure 21-16. Arrange them any way you like.

2. **Add in the URLs of any Web sites you use.**

   I get most of my billing information from the supplier's Web sites. Chapter 12 discusses adding URLs.

3. **Insert text notes of any paperwork that should be sent with the bill if it goes by snail mail.**

   I send a cover letter to the Hangar #1 payee, so I include the form letter in text notes. Chapter 7 can help with text notes.

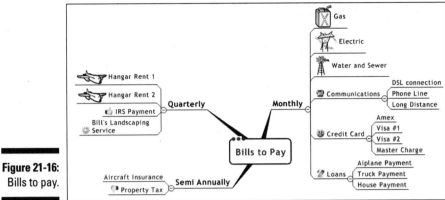

Figure 21-16:
Bills to pay.

4. **Add a callout topic that has password and connection information. Make up memory tools for passwords unless you have an incredible trust factor or you live in Ida Grove, Iowa.**

   You can copy the callout topic and apply it to any of the topics. Be sure to use the Paste as a Callout option, or MindManager pastes it as a subtopic. Inserting Callout Topics is discussed in Chapter 11.

   Do not use a subtopic. A subtopic will prevent proper synchronization. A callout topic is the way to go.

5. **Click the Export Tasks to Outlook tool.**

   The Outlook task list is shown in Figure 21-17.

Now you have to set up the Outlook tasks with the appropriate billing cycle. The following steps give you some basic instructions for Outlook (refer to *Outlook 2003 For Dummies* for more in-depth information about Outlook):

1. **Enter the date you need to take care of a bill.**

   Don't enter the due date of a bill. You'll always wonder why you have late charges if you do.

2. **If the bills are reoccurring, enter the frequency of the reoccurrence.**

3. **Enter priorities, if you choose.**

That's all it takes. You are ready to do the first synchronization. Return to the MindManager map and click the Synchronize Outlook Tasks tool. All the due date information comes back to the MindManager map. The MindManager map loaded with everything is shown in Figure 21-18.

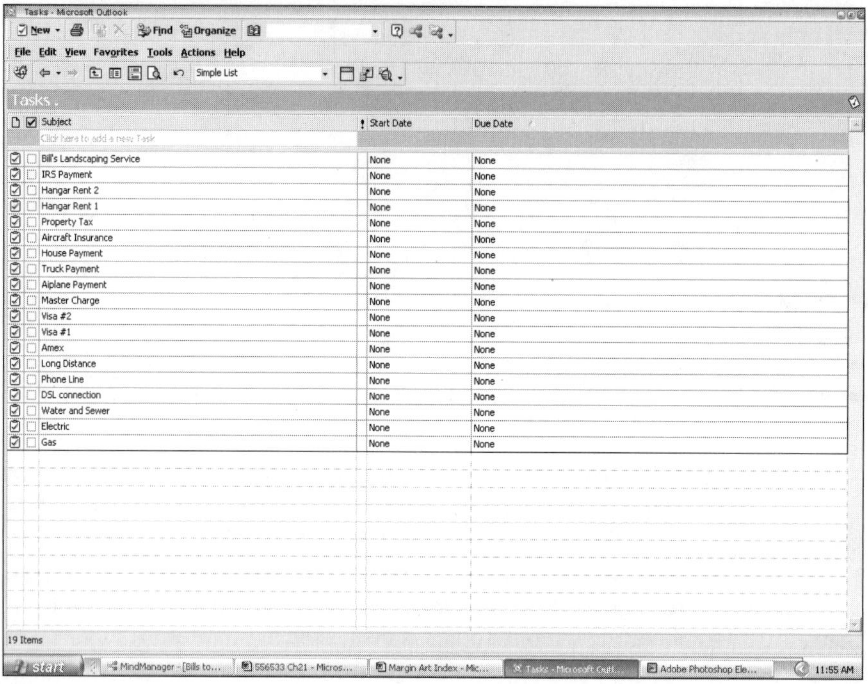

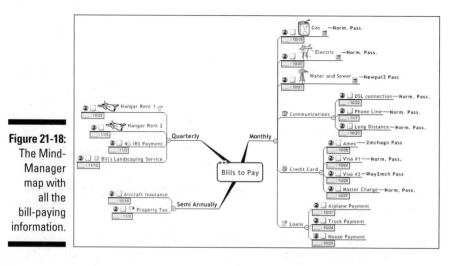

Figure 21-17:
The Outlook task list filled with bills to pay from Mind-Manager.

Figure 21-18:
The Mind-Manager map with all the bill-paying information.

Using this setup is easy. Follow these steps:

1. **Open your bill-paying MindManager map every time Outlook triggers you to pay a bill.**

2. **Go to that bill and click on the Web site or open the text notes. Pay the bill.**

3. **Click on the task icon until the red X appears.**

   The red X icon signifies that the task has been completed. See the margin art.

4. **Now you have to make a choice. Do you want to update information every time you pay a bill or wait until the end of the month?**

   I recommend waiting until the end of the month. All the bills that are due in the month should have the Task Complete icon next to them. Click the Synchronize Outlook Tasks tool. All the competed information goes to Outlook. Each of the completed tasks has a red line through the task in the Outlook task list. Reoccurring tasks are then regenerated with the next due date.

5. **Click the Synchronize Outlook Tasks tool again to bring the new due dates back into MindManager.**

   This step is very important. Each bill is updated with the new due date information. Now you're ready to go again.

MindManager stores the information you need to pay your bills, and the updated information from Outlook tells you when they are due. The icons make it easy to see your bill-paying status at a glance.

Listing out all your bills and identifying when they are due can be very depressing. Take a break. Breathe deeply.

Chapter 22

Linking with Microsoft Project

• •

• •

*I*n Chapter 9, I tell you how to use MindManager maps and the Task Info page to define action items, assign responsibility and due dates, and track the completion of those action items.

In Chapter 10, I explain how to use Smart Map Parts to link and synchronize tasks, contacts, and appointments with Outlook. In Chapter 21, I explore the integration with Outlook and how you can use its integration with Exchange Server to carry out a wide variety of group management tasks.

These tools are sufficient if the number of tasks is relatively small and the relationships and dependencies between the tasks are simple. MindManager is a superb tool for planning small projects because of its focus on "what" is to be accomplished.

Unfortunately, few projects have these characteristics. Most projects involve dozens, hundreds, or even thousands of tasks with many complex dependencies. The questions of "how" the tasks should be organized and how long the project will take to complete go beyond the scope of an application like MindManager. The optimal solution is to work out as much of the "what" is to be done (and to some extent the "who" is to do it) in MindManager and then export the map to a scheduling program to complete the time planning.

In the first two sections of this chapter, I show you how to export directly to Microsoft Project and import from Project back into MindManager. In the last section, I tell you about exporting and importing using the standard MPX format. Almost all major scheduling software applications have the ability to read MPX files, so you can probably use MindManager with your favorite package.

Exporting your map directly to Project is essentially a one-way street. It's true that you can also import a Microsoft Project file, but you do this only when you want a "snapshot" of your project at a given point in time. This snapshot cannot be used to re-export back to Project again because of the way in which task start and end dates are imported from Project. Therefore, if you want to do some work in Project and then do additional planning in MindManager, you *must* use the MPX export/import method, which is described in the last section of this chapter.

Sending Your Map to Microsoft Project

Figure 22-1 shows a completed map for my team's meeting minutes. We discussed a new project and came up with a high-level list of tasks to complete. Because we didn't know exactly when the project would start, nor when particular skills would be needed for the individual tasks in the project, we were unable to do more than structure the tasks into some semblance of order and to estimate how long each one would take to complete.

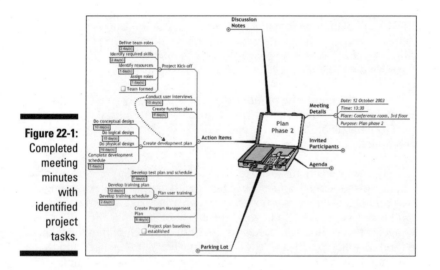

Figure 22-1: Completed meeting minutes with identified project tasks.

There was some rather extended discussion about whether the team could begin creating the development plan before the interviews were finished. We concluded that this would not be a good idea, so I noted this particular *dependency* with a relationship arrow. This means that the development plan work could not start until the interviews were finished (so it is called a *finish-to-start* dependency).

I am now ready to export this plan data to Microsoft Project where I will complete the remainder of the project-planning work. There are four ways that I can do this:

1. Create a separate map from the Action Items topic (see Chapter 12) and then select File⇨Save As from the menu bar to save that map as a new Project file.

2. Create a filter to hide all topics that are not tasks (see Chapter 13) and then save this map as a new Project file (only visible tasks are exported).

3. Use the Only Export Topics that Use Task Information filter that is built into the Export tool. Because this method automatically includes every higher-level topic in the tree down to the central topic, I choose this method for my example.

    Because milestones have no duration (and MindManager can't distinguish an intentional zero from a default zero), I add a zero percent completion icon to ensure that milestone tasks are exported when I use option 3. (As an example, look at the milestone task *Team Formed* in Figure 22-1. And refer back to Chapter 4 for details on adding icons.)

    Select all the desired task topics using Ctrl+click and then select File⇨Send To from the menu bar.

If a project file is currently open, the last method in the preceding list will add the selected topics on to the end of the plan rather than creating a new file. Therefore, I use this method when I want to update an existing project plan with new tasks.

Regardless of which method I choose, MindManager displays the dialog box shown in Figure 22-2. With the third method from the list, I click the Only Export Topics that Use Task Information radio button; with the other methods, I leave the Export All MindManager Topics button selected.

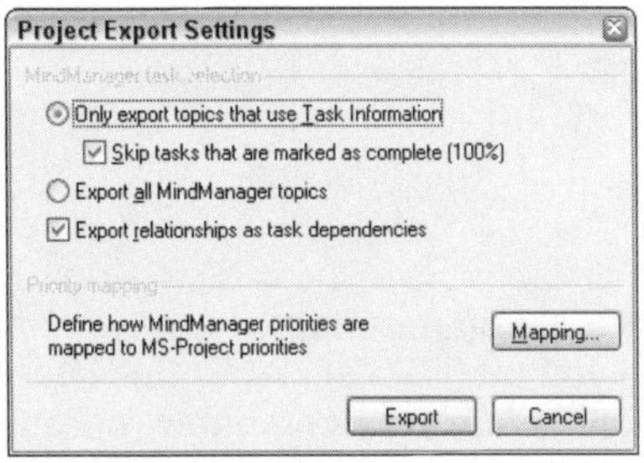

Figure 22-2:
The Project
Export
Settings
dialog box.

> **Project Export Settings**
>
> MindManager task selection
> ⦿ Only export topics that use Task Information
>   ☑ Skip tasks that are marked as complete (100%)
> ○ Export all MindManager topics
> ☑ Export relationships as task dependencies
>
> Priority mapping
> Define how MindManager priorities are
> mapped to MS-Project priorities   [Mapping...]
>
>   [Export] [Cancel]

MindManager has nine priority levels, while Project has 1,000. If you want to use priorities in your project plan, click the Mapping button on the Project Export Settings dialog box and indicate the ranges of Project priorities that correspond to MindManager priorities (see Figure 22-3).

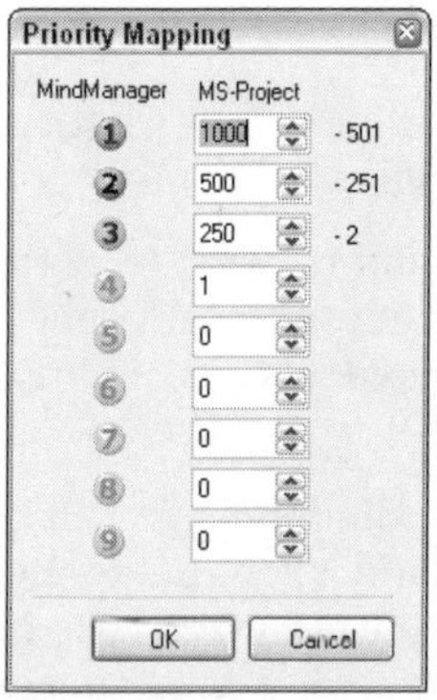

Priority Mapping

MindManager	MS-Project	
①	1000 ⇕	- 501
②	500 ⇕	- 251
③	250 ⇕	- 2
④	1 ⇕	
⑤	0 ⇕	
⑥	0 ⇕	
⑦	0 ⇕	
⑧	0 ⇕	
⑨	0 ⇕	

OK   Cancel

Figure 22-3:
The Priority
Mapping
dialog box.

You only need to enter the maximum value for each range in the MS-Project column. MindManager automatically completes the minimum value for you. As this example shows, you do not need to use all nine priority levels.

After completing the export settings, click the Export button on the Project Export Settings dialog box. MindManager will display the Export Progress dialog box (as shown in Figure 22-4), adding little green bars as it exports the topics. When the export is completed, you can open the file directly by clicking Open or open the folder containing the file by clicking the Open Folder button.

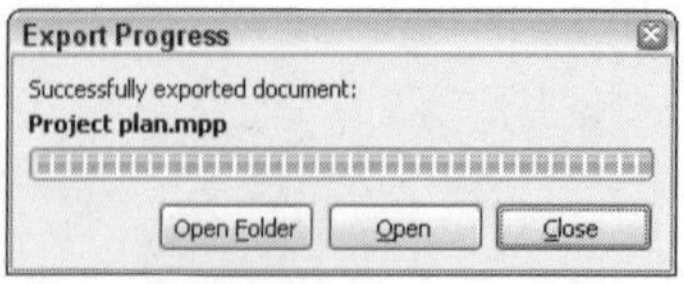

Export Progress

Successfully exported document:
Project plan.mpp

Open Folder   Open   Close

Figure 22-4:
The Export
Progress
dialog box.

Depending upon what other programs you're running on your computer, you may see a dialog box that informs you that the "server is busy." The "server" in this case is Microsoft Project running on your computer (because it is "serving" MindManager commands) rather than your network server. If this happens, wait a few moments until the disk activity on your computer stops, and then click Retry.

Figure 22-5 shows my exported map as a Project file. The critical dependency my team identified (development planning cannot start until the interviews are completed) has been exported to the plan, but I still have quite a bit of additional work to do before I have a usable project plan.

Notice that the exported dependency was to the header topic (Create Development Plan). This forced all the tasks (that were subtopics on the original map) to not be scheduled until after the interviews are completed. Use this technique to capture and export high-level dependencies in your map. It will make things a little easier when you have to start working on the exported Project file.

Figure 22-6 shows my completed work in MS Project. I have entered all the lower-level dependencies and have assigned people to do the various tasks.

MS Project can both read and update MPX files, but it cannot create a new MPX file from an existing Project file. If you plan to do *any* further planning work in MindManager that you want to re-export to Project, you must use the MPX method described in the last section. However, you *can* reimport the Project file into MindManager with the calculated dates and resources and then use MindManager's Outlook linker function to manage the project. See the next section for more details.

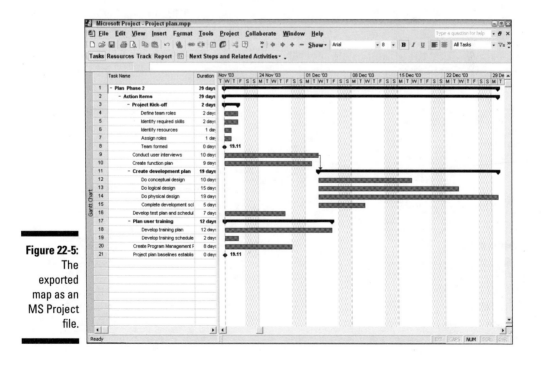

Figure 22-5: The exported map as an MS Project file.

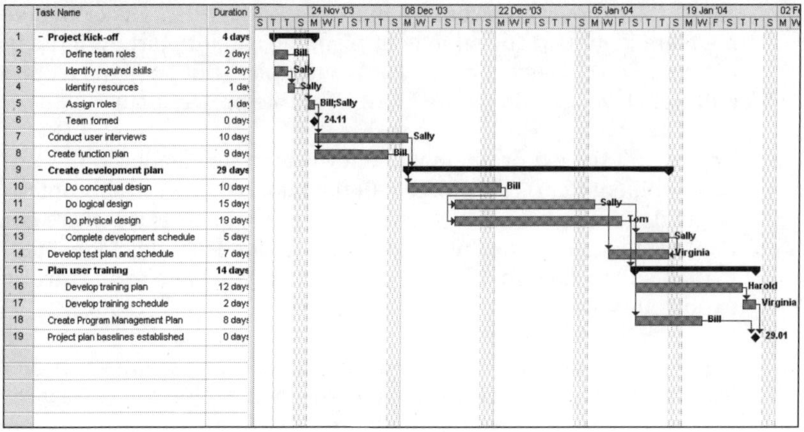

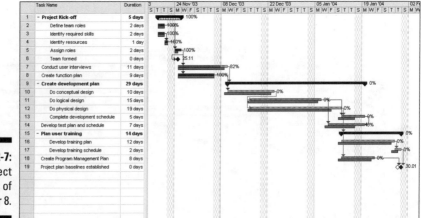

Figure 22-6:
The completed project plan.

Bringing Your Project Back to MindManager

Figure 22-7 shows my project plan in Tracking mode (an option in Microsoft Project that displays both planning and actual data) after a couple of weeks of work. Things got off to a reasonably good start although the task "Assigning roles" took two days instead of one. My most pressing concern, however, is that the all-important interviews are still not finished and it is making the entire project late.

Figure 22-7:
My project plan as of December 8.

I could use this presentation as it is to talk about the status of my project with my boss, but I don't want to focus too much on this problem and I do want to include other material as well — and MindManager is the tool I want to use to do this. So, I begin by taking a MindManager "snapshot" of my project by importing the plan.

Start MindManager and select File➪Open from the menu bar. In the Open File dialog box, select *Files of Type Project Files* from the *File Type* combo box, click your project file, and then click OK.

MindManager displays the Project Import Settings dialog box (shown in Figure 22-8). Choose the settings that you want and click Import.

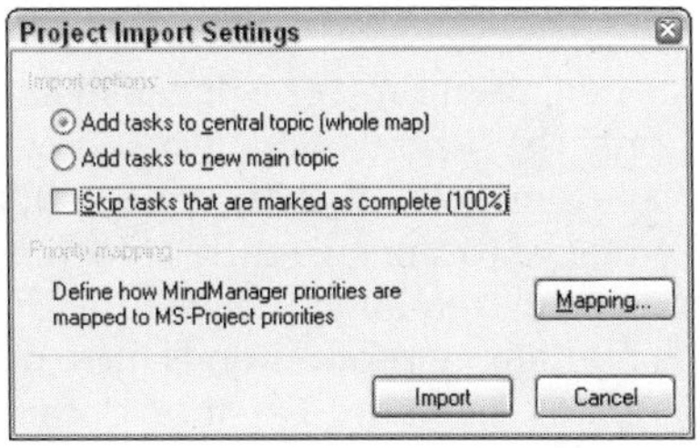

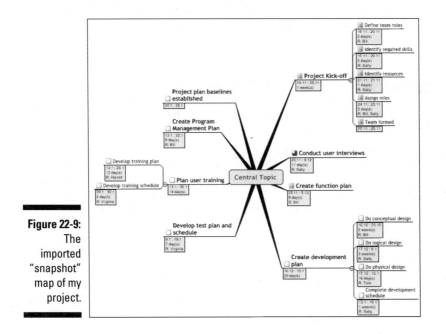

Figure 22-8:
The Project
Import
Settings
dialog box.

MindManager creates a map from the project file, as shown in Figure 22-9.

Figure 22-9:
The
imported
"snapshot"
map of my
project.

I can now use this map to create a slide show (see Chapter 19), a Word document (see Chapter 20), a Web page (see Chapter 18), or some other presentation type that seems most appropriate.

If you're working with a large plan, this approach may create far more information in your map than you may be interested in because it imports the *entire* plan (including tasks that may have been completed weeks ago and which have already been reported, as well as tasks scheduled weeks in the future). If you're interested only in certain tasks, you can select them in Microsoft Project (either by using the Ctrl+click approach or using Project's filtering tools) and then selecting File⇨Send to . . .⇨MindManager in Project. Project will display a dialog box with the same choices as the one illustrated in Figure 22-8 except that you will see an "Export" rather than an "Import" button.

If you do not have a map currently open, then Project will cause MindManager to create a new map that contains only the tasks you have selected when you click the Export button. If you *do* have a map open, then Project will cause MindManager to add all the selected tasks to the currently selected topic in the open map. This feature is particularly useful if you have already started a project status report map (perhaps containing reports on issues, newly identified risks, and key communications) and you want to include detailed information on tasks in progress or tasks completed since the last reporting period.

Regardless of which method you use to create a map from an existing Project file, you only have a *snapshot* of your project at a particular moment in time. You cannot re-export the resulting map back to Project and have a useable file because of the way that MindManager handles the start and finish dates.

Importing and Exporting Maps with Microsoft Project Exchange, er MPX

MPX (Microsoft Project Exchange) is a plain-text file format that can be used to exchange project information between Microsoft Project and most other project-planning software vendors. Ironically, Microsoft no longer provides the capability of generating MPX files from its own Microsoft Project application, although it still has the ability to read and update MPX files.

MindManager's ability to generate MPX files is therefore primarily useful in providing an interface to other scheduling software applications such as Sure Track, P3, Microsoft Visio, and others. (Of course, if you do not have Microsoft Project installed on your computer, then creating an MPX file to transfer data to a computer that *does* have project is the only way you can create a project file.) It also provides the means for re-importing task data from Project back into MindManager for further planning work that can again be exported back to Project. I tell you how to do these things in this section.

Setting your MPX preferences

To set preferences for both import and export using an MPX file, select Format⇨MPX Preferences from the menu bar. MindManager displays the dialog box shown in Figure 22-10.

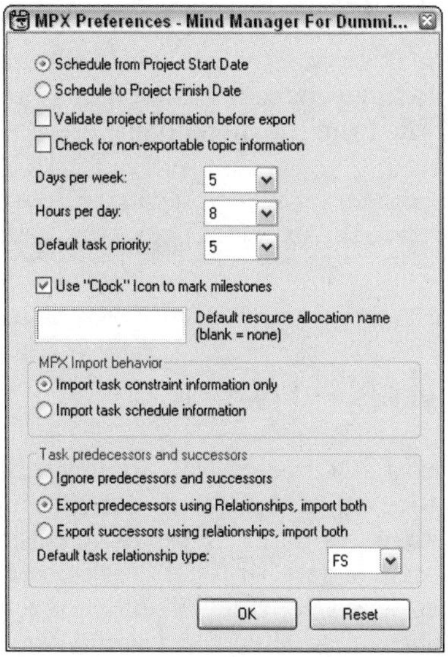

Figure 22-10:
The MPX
Preferences
dialog box.

Most of the default settings will work just as they are. However, a few of the settings require you to take additional steps to prepare your map:

✓ **Schedule from Project Start Date/ Schedule to Project Finish Date:** These options tell the receiving software (the application that opens the MPX file exported from MindManager) whether to schedule the project from the Start date or to the Finish (due) date. You need to enter a start date or a due date in either the central topic (if you're exporting the whole map) or the root topic (if you're only exporting part of the map). Schedule from Project Start will be automatically selected. Be sure to click Schedule to Project Finish Date if this is appropriate.

✔ **Use "Clock" Icon to mark Milestones:** Most project management packages use zero duration for a Task to indicate a "Milestone" (the end or
beginning of a significant event in the project) for reporting purposes, but
MindManager has no way of knowing whether a zero duration means it
really is a milestone or simply that the proper duration was not entered.
Add a clock icon (click the Library tab on the Task pane and select the
clock) to all topics that are intended to be milestones.

Any lowest-level topic that does not have a duration other than zero or the
Clock icon will be ignored during the export.

Exporting to an MPX file

You can export either your entire map or exactly one selected topic and all
its subtopics. In Figure 22-1, I would have clicked "Action Items" before
selecting Actions⇨Export to MPX File from the menu bar.

The export function exports only visible topics, so you can use filtering to hide
(and therefore exclude) any topics from the export. Check out Chapter 13 if
you need details on how to do this.

Importing from an MPX file

The start and end dates of most tasks in a project plan are never directly
determined by the user but are rather calculated by the scheduling software.
The key word here is *most*. There are a few dates that may be entered when a
task must start no later than a particular date, or must finish on or before a
specified date (for example, the day when the chief executive is flying in from
New York to see a presentation). These are called *constraint dates*.

MindManager has no way of distinguishing calculated dates from constraint
dates, so you must specify which dates should be imported from the MPX
file. You do this in the MPX Import Behavior section of the MPX Preferences
dialog box (refer to Figure 22-10):

✔ **Import task constraint information only:** Selecting this option will
result in task dates being imported only if they are constraint dates, the
beginning date of the project (if scheduled as soon as possible), or the
ending date of the project (if scheduled as late as possible). You must
choose this option if you intend to re-export the map back to MS Project.

✔ **Import task schedule information:** Selecting this option will result in all task information being imported into MindManager. This will be useful in preparing project status reports but will make the map unsuitable for re-export to Project.

The other key decision you must make is whether or not you want to import task dependencies.

✔ If you're interested in only a project snapshot (in other words, you have selected Import task schedule information), then the relationship information is probably of little interest and will definitely clutter up your map. The appropriate choice is to click Ignore Predecessors and Successors.

✔ If you're planning to re-export your map back to Project, the dependency information is critical and you should click Export Predecessors Using Relationships, Import Both.

✔ If you're working with a different scheduling software package, then review that package's documentation to determine whether you should export predecessors or successors.

If you will be working very much with your imported map before re-export, you may find the numerous relationships on your map to be a bit distracting. Use the style sheet to make the relationship lines and text thin and pale so that they blend somewhat into the background. Refer back to Chapter 14 for details on how to do this.

After you have set the preferences appropriately, select Actions➪Import from MPX File from the menu bar. If you have a map open, the MPX file will be imported as a new main topic. If there is no map open, MindManager will create a new map.

Part V
The Part of Tens

The 5th Wave   By Rich Tennant

"Okay, Darryl. I think it's time to admit we shouldn't have mapped out this trip on the back of a cocktail napkin."

In this part . . .

All kinds of helpful information can be found in this part. Good advice, interesting tidbits, and useful facts are gathered together in short vignettes. We have even put in some jewels of wisdom that you may never need, but then again, you might. If you find yourself scratching your head and wondering what might be next on the MindManager horizon, look here. On the other hand, if you're short on time, like the fast lane, or are searching for shortcuts, then take a look at this section — we've got it covered.

Chapter 23

Ten Helpful Add-Ins and User Groups

. . . .

In This Chapter

▶ Trying add-ins for extra features

▶ Sharing with other MindManager users

. . . .

I am amazed at how fast the MindManager software program has spread around the globe. The marketing of MindManager is nontraditional. You can find support, development assistance, and training in all corners of the world. Look on the Mindjet Web site if you want to find someone in your backyard. All of the add-in providers mentioned can provide specialized service. Give them a call for any MindManager need you might have. Look at www.mindjet.com under Mindjet Partners for additional listings.

The chapter title says Ten. Wrong. You get Eleven today! An added bonus at the back of the book. Enjoy!

Add-Ins

Numerous companies around the world are making add-ins for MindManager. Add-ins focus on specific uses or links that expand the effectiveness of MindManager. Now where is that lawyer for the small print disclaimer? I have not used many of these add-ins. You can find more info on the companies on the Mindjet Web site.

MindManuals.com, Ltd (Coventry, United Kingdom)

You can find information about MindManuals.com at www.mindmanuals.com. MindManuals.com has been producing MindManager add-ins for many years. The product set includes MiniProject, MindManuals, and Decision Mill.

MiniProject

MiniProject schedules, tracks, and controls small projects within MindManager. You don't need to export task information to an external project management program. MiniProject is targeted at projects with up to 60 tasks. MiniProject calculates a resource-level schedule using the task information in MindManager. Answer those ever-present project management questions such as "Which tasks should start today?" or "How far ahead is the project?"

MindManuals

Another product from MindManuals.com is MindManuals, which is a collection of templates, resources, and guides used with MindManager. Here are some of the available MindManuals collections:

- ✔ **Successful Projects with MindManager:** Resource tools for Project Managers who use MindManager.
- ✔ **Defining Small IT Projects:** Create specifications and documentation for small IT projects.
- ✔ **BizSmart LLC Small Business Planner:** BizSmart LLC is an innovative visual business planner for small businesses.
- ✔ **Presentations with MindManager:** Resource tools for planning and creating convincing presentations with MindManager.
- ✔ **Teleworking for Organizations:** Comprehensive planning and strategy guide for successful telecommuting and distance working.

DecisionMill

DecisionMill is the link between brainstorming in MindManager and the creation of actionable tasking. Decisions are analyzed in DecisionMill with a weighted scoring system. A record is created to track your decision-making process. The resulting task lists are prioritized using due dates. New ideas and information are worked through the process to review decisions and update the task list.

Gyronix (Kent, United Kingdom)

Information about Gyronix and ResultsManager is found at www.gyronix.com. Gyronix creates MindManager add-ins to enhance business team communication and task management.

ResultsManager

The ResultsManager add-in creates a map that acts as a dashboard. Project or program managers use the dashboard map to drive multiple projects. Project plans are viewed in the dashboard map by resource activity and task lists. The question "What comes next and by whom?" is easier to answer in a complex, multiproject environment using ResultManager.

1 and A Research (Saint Sauveur, QC, Canada)

Information about I and A Research is found at www.iaresearch.com. Specific information about MindPlugs Export-to-Excel for MindManager information is found at www.mindplugs.com.

Mindplugs Export-to-Excel

Mindplugs Export-to-Excel installs a Microsoft Excel icon on the toolbar adjacent to the other Microsoft product icons.

Click the new Microsoft Excel icon to convert a MindManager map into a spreadsheet grouped by hierarchy. MindManager map task information — containing project start, duration, and resources — is transferred to Microsoft Excel cells.

MindPlugs Export-to-Excel can answer many questions, such as "How much does a brainstormed project cost?" You can answer this question using the add-in by following these steps:

1. **Use MindManager to brainstorm all the project tasks.**

2. **Put the price per hour of each task in the task info resources column.**

3. **Click the Microsoft Excel icon installed by the add-in.**

   The MindManager map information is transferred to Microsoft Excel.

4. **In Microsoft Excel, use Find and Replace to remove the word "hour(s)."**

5. **Multiply the duration column by the resource column and place the result in another column.**

6. **Sum the additional column to get the cost of the project.**

The product enables MindManager to be used as an effective "cost estimate brainstorming" system.

Mindplugs Real-Time Calculator

The Mindplugs Real-time Calculator add-in creates the ability in MindManager to process mathematical expressions. In fact, the Real-time Calculator has a Visual Basic base, and any Visual Basic function can be executed from a topic in a MindManager map.

JCVGantt

I & A Research (as a result of a contract with JCV Management, Inc.) produces and distributes JCVGantt for MindManager.

JCVGantt creates a *Gantt chart* that links to MindManager task information. (A Gantt chart is a horizontal bar chart that identifies the start, stop, and duration of tasks in a project plan.) Changes made to MindManager task information immediately change the Gantt chart display. Conversely, changing the Gantt chart information also changes the MindManager map task information.

You change the task information in the Gantt chart by manipulating the bars on the graph. Project complete percentage is represented on the Gantt chart and is changed in the same way.

Most project managers use the Gantt chart as a preferred method of presenting project information. This add-in is a valuable tool to increase the usefulness of MindManager.

You can obtain purchasing information from JCV Management at (450) 653-3365 or from I & A Research, Inc. at (450) 227-7250.

ThinkQuick

ThinkQuick is a service of I & A Research, Inc. ThinkQuick is not exactly an add-in to MindManager. ThinkQuick is a way to share and communicate with people interested in visual organization, brainstorming, and advanced thinking and management techniques. MindManager users are frequent participants.

A special browser delivers content in a format that resembles a television set. Change channels to view the 18 channels of information, videos, and eLearning information.

Common features on the ThinkQuick Network include video tutorials on using MindManager, video eLearning workshops, chat rooms, and a discussion board.

I & A Research is offering a special gift to *MindManager For Dummies* readers: A free one year subscription to the ThinkQuick Network is available at www.iaresearch.com/readergift.htm.

Mindsystems/Teamlink (Mt. Eliza, Victoria, Australia)

Knowledge Link

You can find information on Teamlink Australia and Knowledge Link at `www.mindsystems.com.au`.

Knowledge Link is a companion software product to MindManager. Knowledge Link organizes MindManager map information into a knowledge base. Single or multiple MindManager maps are imported, and one or more knowledge bases are created. Other data from ODBC databases such as Microsoft Access can be added to the knowledge base. Knowledge Link is a pathway from multiple databases to MindManager.

The knowledge base is displayed in a tree format to easily comprehend complex information. The information is rearranged and reorganized easily.

Knowledge Link contains templates to organize the knowledge base information depending on intended use or application.

The output from Knowledge Link encompasses many forms. New MindManager maps are possible. The program also exports the knowledge base information to Microsoft Excel and Microsoft Word.

Knowledge Link is available as a standalone product or as a fully integrated add-in to MindManager.

User Groups

User groups represent a place to go to find other people that share your interest. The common link in this case is MindManager. I hope you decide to participate in the user groups mentioned below. Companies do listen to the issues presented in the forums and discussion areas. Join in. Get ideas and add your comments.

Yahoo MindManager user group

The Yahoo MindManager user group started in 1999. Martin Silcock in the UK is the founder and moderator. The objective of the MindManager user group is to share ideas, uses, and techniques of — you guessed it — the MindManager program. The group is not sponsored by Mindjet LLC, but many MindManager groupies find a home within this user group. You can find a link to the Yahoo MindManager user group on the Mindjet Web site. Some of the techies hang out in this user group, so if you want to get into the nuts and bolts, you have found a source. Don't worry, because you'll find some basic users, too.

Find the Yahoo MindManager user group at: groups.yahoo.com/group/mindmanager.

MindManager User to User Forum

Another source for discourse among users of MindManager is found on the Mindjet Web site (www.mindjet.com). Go to the support section and look for the User to User Forum under Community. A healthy chunk of knowledge exists in this forum.

Chapter 24

Ten (Or So) Shortcuts

Shortcuts are a matter of personal preference. You may be a shortcut freak. Your fingers are lightning on the keyboard. You don't need no stinking mouse! You do the multiple finger placements and sequences with guitar-playing precision. On the other hand, there are the plodders like me. I deliberate between each mouse click, and a shortcut only speeds the trauma.

I am a process shortcut user. I like to figure out how to make a program behave the way I want. I may spend an hour creating a shortcut that I use once to save myself 30 seconds. Somehow it still qualifies as a shortcut in my book. This chapter addresses both preferences. Get your fingers ready if you're a keyboard shortcutterist. Get your process scissors out if you're an intuitiverist.

You may have a multitude of your own shortcuts. Feel free to jot them down in the blank spaces, and don't forget to share.

Keyboard Shortcuts: Fast, Fun, and Fastidious

Table 24-1 shows basic Windows shortcuts. No big surprises here.

Table 24-1	General Windows Command Shortcuts
Close a window or dialog box	Esc
Terminate a process	Esc
End MindManager	Alt+F4
Help	F1

MindManager map documents

You know the routine if you have dogs. Open the door to let dogs out, open the door to let dogs in, open the door to let dogs out, open the door to let dogs in, repeat over and over... Wouldn't a door shortcut be nice? Files are kind of the same way. Table 24-2 gives a few shortcuts for working with files.

Table 24-2		Map Document Shortcuts
New Map		Ctrl+N
Open a Map		Ctrl+O
Saving	Save current Map	Ctrl+S
	Save as	F12
Close current Map		Ctrl+W
Print current Map		Ctrl+P
Define Hyperlink		Ctrl+K
Create Bookmark		Ctrl+Shift+F5

MindManager screen management

I can get lost in a MindManager map. Zooming back to the center is quite useful. My map levels are never at the right level. Table 24-3 shows ways to minimize mouse malfunction by using the keyboard instead of smacking the mouse in the left or right ear.

Table 24-3		Display Shortcuts
Next Map		Ctrl+F6
Show/Hide topic notes		F11
Center/Focus	Current Map	Ctrl+F3
	Current Object	Alt+F3
	Current Topic	F3
Detail level	None	Alt+Shift+0
	1 Level	Shift+Alt+1
	2 Levels	Shift+Alt+2
	3 Levels	Shift+Alt+3
Remove Filter		Ctrl+Shift+A
Enlarge		Ctrl +
Reduce		Ctrl -
Show entire map		Ctrl+F5

MindManager objects

I swear there are a jillion ways to add objects. Table 24-4 gives a few. The table also includes map part shortcuts. Don't forget the map part update shortcut. Even I use that one.

Table 24-4	Adding an Object Shortcuts
Topic	Enter
Subtopic	Insert
Topic Note	Ctrl+T
Callout	Ctrl+Shift+Enter
Border	Ctrl+Shift+B
Open Library Map Part	Ctrl+Shift+N
Update all Map Parts	F5

Editing the MindManager map

Table 24-5 contains the edit speed shortcuts. I have one that I use all the time, but it doesn't fit with any of the tables, so I'll mention it here: Moving a topic near the central topic evokes the red tractor beam. The red tractor beam jumps out and grabs your topic. Turn off the red tractor beam by holding down the Shift key as you move a topic. Now back to the table.

Table 24-5		Editing Command Shortcuts
Select all		Ctrl+A
Select all topics at same level		Ctrl+Shift+A
Copy		Ctrl+C
Cut		Ctrl+X
Paste		Ctrl+V
Paste as callout		Ctrl+Shift+V
Edit topic text		F2
Deleting	Remove topic (keep subtopics)	Ctrl+Del
	Delete Topic	Del

Formatting the text

Not much introduction is needed for shortcuts listed in Table 24-6. Select the text and these shortcuts work great.

Table 24-6	Text Formatting Shortcuts
Bold	Ctrl+B
Italic	Ctrl+I
Underline	Ctrl+U
Remove all formatting	Ctrl+ Space Bar

Strategic Shortcuts

Strategic shortcuts use MindManager in a specific way to speed up work or make your life easier. I am going to give you two examples of ones that I use. Be creative and share your strategic shortcuts with others.

Opening and closing files en masse

I like to use the Multimap view to open and close files. Many of my uses for MindManager require complex, large, and multiple-linked maps. Open and closing linked maps can be a bit of a chore if you don't use this shortcut. I used this method while writing this book.

I create a Table of Contents (TOC) map. The TOC map contains a list of all the maps that I use. Each entry in the TOC map has a link to a corresponding map. I always open my TOC map first. I then enter the Multimap view. All the maps linked in the TOC are shown. I can use Ctrl+Click to select the various maps that I want to work with. I then use the Open command in the Multimap view. The files I selected are opened. I can then go and work on each map individually. Periodically, I go back to the TOC map, which is still in Multimap view, and the files are still selected. I use the Close command, and the files are saved. Just open them again if you need to keep working.

Creating the TOC has a shortcut. Create a map with lots of topics. Select a topic and add a hyperlink. Search for the MindManager map file and create the hyperlink. Now the TOC map has a topic with a hyperlink, but the name of the topic is still *main topic*. Place the cursor over the hyperlink. Use Ctrl+K, Ctrl+C, Esc, F2, and finally Ctrl+V. These five quick steps go into the hyperlink, copy the name of the hyperlink, close the hyperlink menu, select the topic name for editing, and paste the name of the hyperlink into the topic. Very fast. You can create a TOC map in minutes even if you have a bunch of maps. This technique calls out for a script.

Naming images

I work with many different kinds of images. I recently set up an inventory with digital picture records, and I used this shortcut. MindManager has search functions for images that work quite well. The drawback is the need to add keywords to get the searching to find your images. And there is a twist. Searching also looks at the *original* filename. The word *original* is key. You cannot rename the file inside the program and use the search command to find the new name.

I always create unique and descriptive filenames when I change from the digital camera filename at the time I download the pictures. In the MindManager library, adding the image maintains these faux keywords. You can always look at the filename by selecting Rename. You can even rename the image and it won't change the effectiveness of this shortcut.

Scripting is the shortcut shortcut

I won't go through how to create a shortcut or even show any scripted shortcuts in this section. I want to call your attention to Chapter 16 and Appendix C. Chapter 16 shows you how to build scripts, and Appendix C contains some examples of script shortcuts. Using macros and scripting is the next leap in creating shortcuts. Develop your shortcuts in a step-by-step way and then turn to scripting to make them automatic.

Chapter 25

Ten Useful Things You Won't Need Every Day

MindManager is an extraordinarily rich-featured product. Even after working with it almost daily for a year, I am still discovering new things. The features I explore in this chapter are ones that are fun and interesting, but not ones that I use very often. Your style is probably different than mine, and you may well find something here that makes you go, "Wow, fantastic!"

Happy exploring!

Searching for a Map

You can use the Search Files feature to find all maps that contain a word or phrase in the topic text, topic notes, hyperlinks, resources, or categories. You can base your search either on a specified directory (and, optionally, all of its subdirectories), or on a set of linked maps (multimaps). All maps satisfying your search criteria are then displayed in the Search Results window. You can simply click on the topic and MindManager will open the map and position the topic containing the desired word or phrase in the center of the workspace.

Follow these steps to search through maps in a folder:

1. **Click the Search tab on the Task Pane.**

   The Search Task pane opens.

2. **Complete the Look For and Look In Folder fields and choose the topic fields that you want MindManager to search.**

   Figure 25-1 shows the search parameters to use when looking for all maps containing the word "Harold" in the topic text.

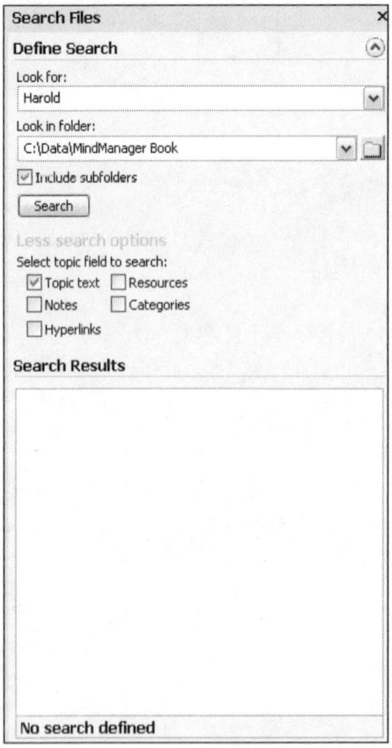

Figure 25-1:
Completed search parameter fields.

If you see only Define Search and then Search Results immediately below it, click the down arrow next to the words Define Search to display the search definition fields. If you don't see the Select Topic Field to Search check boxes, click More Search Options.

3. **Click Search.**

   MindManager displays the Search dialog box (as shown in Figure 25-2). When the search finishes, the search results are displayed in the lower half of the Search Files task pane.

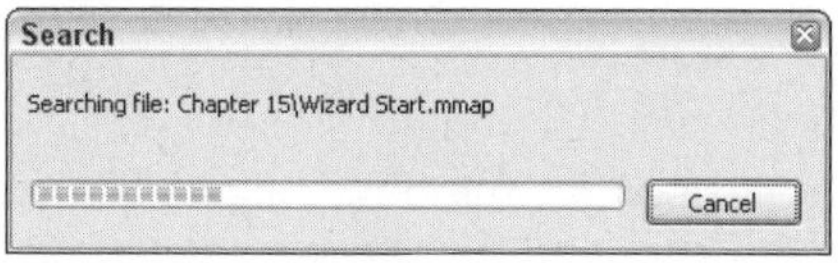

Figure 25-2:
The Search
dialog box.

Figure 25-2:
The Search
dialog box.

> **Search** ⊗
> Searching file: Chapter 15\Wizard Start.mmap
>
> [▓▓▓▓▓▓▓▓▓▓   ]   Cancel

4. **Click the map of interest.**

   MindManager will open the map and select the topic where the search
   text was found.

Select Special

Map objects can be selected by simply holding down the left mouse button
and dragging the cursor across the objects of interest. If the map is large,
however, or the objects of interest are intermixed with others, selecting each
one individually (with Ctrl+Click) can be a bit tedious.

With the Select Special command, you can select all map elements of a given
type, regardless of where they are located on the map. Click the background
first if you want to select objects from the entire map or click a specific topic
if you want to select objects only on that topic's tree.

Select Edit➪Select➪Select Special from the menu bar, check the types of elements you want to select, and then click OK (see Figure 25-3).

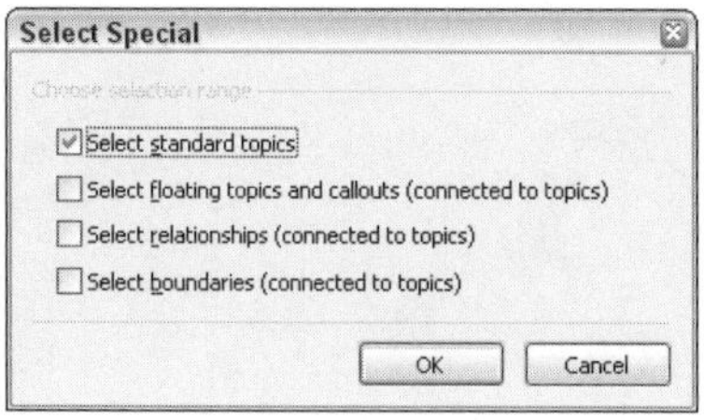

Figure 25-3:
The Select
Special
dialog box.

> **Select Special** ⊗
> ┌ Choose selection range ──────────────┐
> │ ☑ Select standard topics │
> │ ☐ Select floating topics and callouts (connected to topics) │
> │ ☐ Select relationships (connected to topics) │
> │ ☐ Select boundaries (connected to topics) │
> │   OK   Cancel │

After the elements have been selected, you can modify their style, copy them,
filter them, or remove them entirely from your map.

Autocorrect

The Autocorrect feature is a great boon for fumbling fingers like mine. I seem to always type "teh" when I mean "the" and there are some words that I never seem to be able to spell correctly.

MindManager comes with an extensive list of Autocorrect data already loaded, so I normally don't have to concern myself with it. If there is a particular word, however, that I just "know" is spelled one way when the rest of the world spells it differently, I can enter my spelling and the rest of the world's spelling in the table and MindManager will thereafter correct my spelling without my having to worry about it further.

I do this by selecting Tools⇨AutoCorrect Options from the menu bar, entering my spelling on the left-hand side, entering the correct spelling on the right-hand side, clicking Add, and then clicking Close (see Figure 25-4). I can also change existing entries by selecting a pair, making my changes, and clicking Replace, or I can delete them completely by selecting a pair and then clicking Delete.

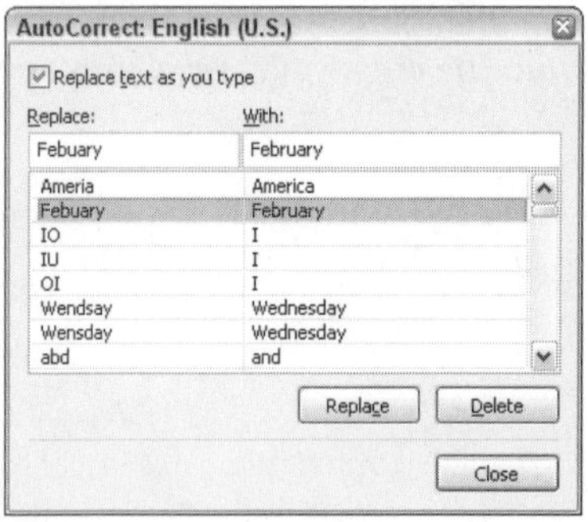

Figure 25-4:
The
AutoCorrect
dialog box.

Number Topics

You can automatically add a numbering scheme to the topics on your map, or to a portion of your map, using the Number Topics command. Select the main topic if you want to add numbers to every topic on the map, or select one topic if you want to just number all the subtopics of that topic.

Select Actions⇨Number Topics from the menu bar, choose the options you want to use, and then click OK (see Figure 25-5).

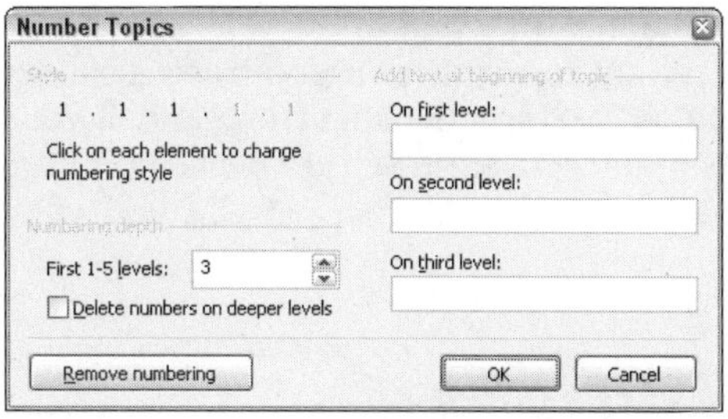

Figure 25-5:
The Number
Topics
dialog box.

Number Topics

Style
1 . 1 . 1 . 1 . 1

Click on each element to change
numbering style

Numbering depth

First 1-5 levels: 3

☐ Delete numbers on deeper levels

[Remove numbering]

Add text at beginning of topic
On first level:

On second level:

On third level:

[OK]   [Cancel]

MindManager records additional information (invisibly) to each topic that it has numbered using this command so that it has the ability to remove the numbering again. If you edit any of the numbers (you can still edit the rest of the topic text), MindManager will lose the ability to remove or further modify the numbering — meaning that from that point on you will have to do *all* number editing by hand!

MindManager is aware of what topic you have selected when you use this command, and it executes your choices relative to that selection. This means, for example, that you can select a numbered topic, click Remove numbering, and only the numbering on that topic and its subtopics will be removed.

If you have numbered your topics, remember to select No numbering if you print from Outline view, export your map to Word, or export your map to the Web.

Sort Topics

You may, from time to time, want to sort subtopics in alphabetical or numerical order, or to sort tasks according to priority or percent complete. Remember to select the topic or topics before beginning the sorting process; otherwise you will sort all topics on the map.

Select Actions⇨Sort Topics from the menu bar, choose the sorting options you want to use, and then click OK (see Figure 25-6).

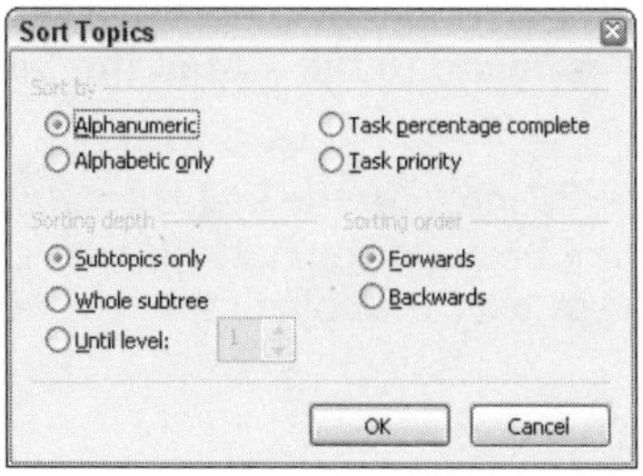

Figure 25-6:
The Sort
Topics
dialog box.

Sort Topics

Sort by
⦿ Alphanumeric   ◯ Task percentage complete
◯ Alphabetic only   ◯ Task priority

Sorting depth   Sorting order
⦿ Subtopics only   ⦿ Forwards
◯ Whole subtree   ◯ Backwards
◯ Until level: 1

[OK]   [Cancel]

Callouts and relationships that are attached to the selected topics are not automatically sorted. If you want to sort the subtopics on a callout, you must first select the callout and then perform the sort command. If you want to sort all topics and callouts at once, use the Select Special command previously described in this chapter.

Creating Custom Buttons

With context menus and all the toolbars, it may be some time before you discover that you don't have a convenient button or mouse-click to run a specific command. But the time may come. For me, it was not having the Macro menu where I could get at it with one mouse-click. To create your own button on one of the MindManager toolbars, follow these steps:

1. **Right-click any toolbar, select Customize, and then click the Commands tab.**

   MindManager displays the toolbar's Customize dialog box with all command categories on the left and the individual commands on the right (as shown in Figure 25-7).

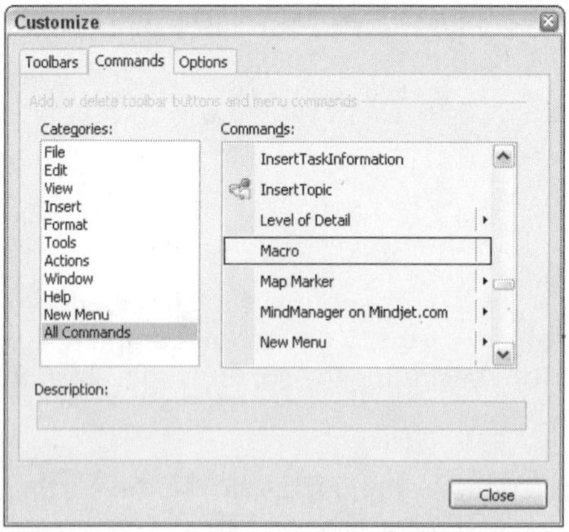

Figure 25-7: The toolbar's Customize dialog box.

2. **Select All Commands in the Categories list box, scroll to the Macro command, and then drag the command to the end of the Insert toolbar.**

   MindManager displays the word "Macro" on the Insert toolbar. I could simply close the Customize dialog box and the button (with the text "Macro") would be ready for me to use. To replace the text with a custom image, continue on.

3. **Right-click the Macro button that you just placed on the toolbar and select Image.**

   MindManager displays the Button Appearance dialog box (as shown in Figure 25-8).

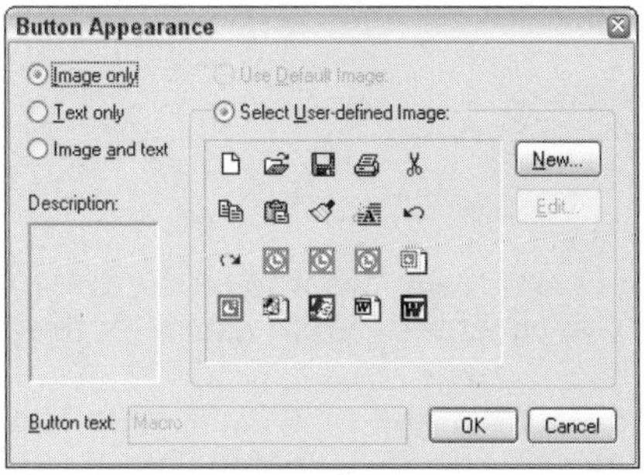

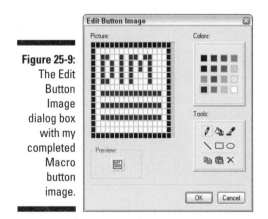

Figure 25-8:
The Button
Appearance
dialog box.

4. **Click New and create the button image you want to use.**

   My example is shown in Figure 25-9.

Figure 25-9:
The Edit
Button
Image
dialog box
with my
completed
Macro
button
image.

5. **Click OK twice to close both Button dialog boxes and then click Close on the toolbar's Customize dialog box.**

   The finished button is now ready to go on the Insert toolbar (as shown in Figure 25-10).

As of this writing, MindManager has the highly annoying habit of discarding all custom button images when it is closed. I am assuming this behavior will be corrected by the time you read this.

Figure 25-10:
Using the
completed
Macro
button.

Macros...	Alt+F8
Macro Editor	Umschalt+Alt+F11

News Service

If you're connected to the Internet and really "want to be the first to know," you can use MindManager to keep you constantly up to date with the latest news.

Open a new map, click the Library tab on the Task pane, go to Map Parts⇨ News Feeds⇨Cnet News.Com, and drag the Smart Map Part of your choice to the central topic. After a few seconds of connecting and inquiring, the latest headlines will be displayed on your map and details in the topic notes. (See Figure 25-11.) You can also press F5 any time you want to get the *latest* latest headlines.

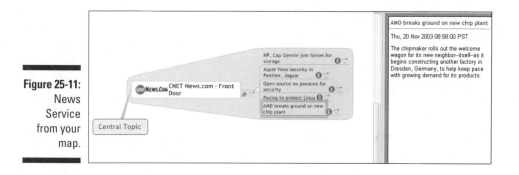

Figure 25-11:
News
Service
from your
map.

Google Searching

Google service works very similarly to News service. The only difference is that you need to attach the Google Smart Map Part (which is in the Samples folder) to a topic with the key word or phrase that you want to search on. Oh yes, there is one more difference: It isn't free (see Figure 25-12), although you can apparently get a limited key for small searches at no cost.

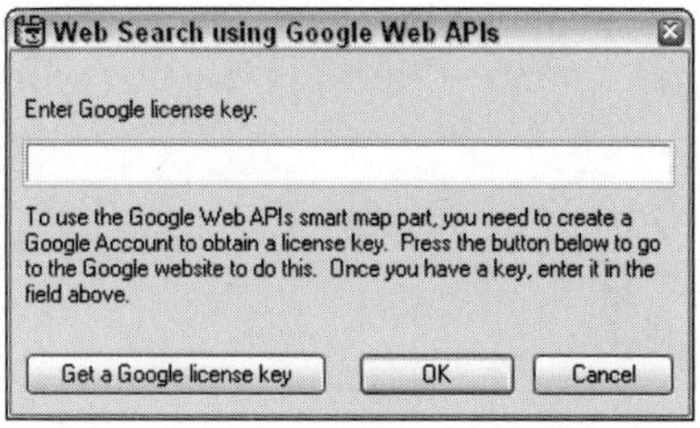

Figure 25-12:
You have to
register and
pay a fee to
use Google
search.

Protecting Your Document

If your map contains sensitive information, you can password protect it so
that only authorized people can open your map. To access this dialog box,
select Tools➪Protect Document. . . from the menu bar (see Figure 25-13). If
you password protect your map, be very sure you remember the password.
No one can help you recover your map if you forget it and have not written it
down someplace.

Figure 25-13:
The Protect
Document
dialog box.

Add-ins

MindManager comes with several pre-installed add-ins, or modular program
units, that provide additional functionality while remaining completely insu-
lated from the basic MindManager engine. For example, all of the MS Office
interfaces are provided by Add-ins.

With time, other developers will offer their own Add-ins, which you can install
with your MindManager application. The Add-Ins dialog box is primarily useful
in seeing what modules have been installed and which company created them.
See Figure 25-14.

You can, however, temporarily disable an Add-in without uninstalling it by simply unchecking the box next to its name. Checking the box will enable the Add-in functionality once more.

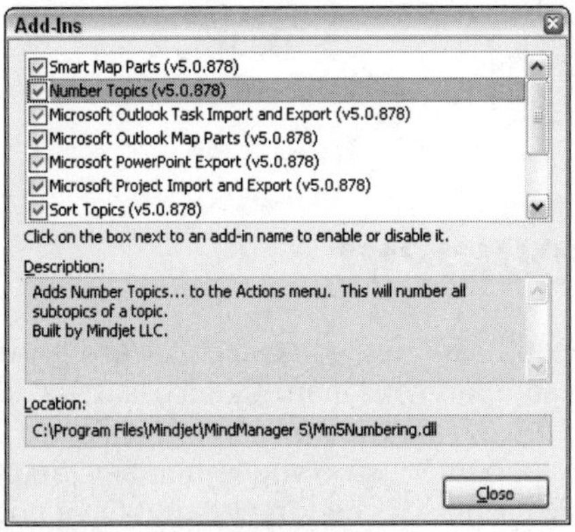

Figure 25-14: The Add-Ins dialog box.

Part VI
Appendixes

The 5th Wave   By Rich Tennant

How to use MindManager

"Can't I just give you riches or something?"

In this part . . .

MindManager is a creation from the folks at Mindjet LLC and comes in more flavors than described in this book. Other versions of MindManager are floating around in the user community. The appendixes in this part provide supplemental information about Mindjet products and past MindManager versions. You'll also find examples of MindManager.

Appendix A

Differences in MindManager Editions

• •

*M*indjet released two new versions of MindManager in October of 2002, MindManager X5 and MindManager X5 Pro. In this appendix, I first describe the changes made to MindManager 2002 and then I compare the features of the two current versions of the product.

Changes from MindManager 2002

Terminology

1. A Branch is now a Topic. There are main topics and subtopics.
2. The Map title is now called the Central Topic.
3. Attached Floating Text is now called a Callout Topic.
4. Detached Floating Text is now called Floating Text.
5. Text Notes are now called Topic Notes or just Notes.
6. A Symbol is now called an Image and the Symbol Gallery is now called the Library.
7. Codes are now called Icons.
8. Highlight color is now called Fill color.
9. Find in Files is referred to as Search Files.
10. Document Properties are now just called Properties.
11. The Standard Mind Map template is now called the Blank Map template.
12. HTML Export is now called Save As Web Pages.
13. Task Planning is now called Task Information.

Branches to objects

MindManager has just one map object, now called a Topic. The topic object is divided into three subtypes:

- ✔ Topic: The map title is also a regular topic now.
- ✔ Callout Topics: These can have subtopics now.
- ✔ Floating Topics: Floating Text and Floating Images are now Floating Topics, and can also have subtopics.

You have different choices for the shapes of these Topic subtypes, but they are otherwise identical in their functionality. You can have different colors for the Topic lines and the Topic text. Subtopics will inherit the color of the lines of the parent Topic but will not inherit the color of the text.

Boundaries are also treated as objects. The boundary fill color is inherited from the Topic fill color of the parent Topic. All objects can be selected, copied, pasted, dragged and dropped, and deleted.

Dropped commands (with replacements)

1. The Power Select task pane has been dropped, and the functionality is distributed to other commands. Filtering has been optimized and always works on the current selection. Selecting a topic can be done iteratively or using other commands such as Find&Replace (Find All), Review Mode (all comments), and Map Marker quick selection. Other Filter options have been dropped.

2. The Toolkit feature has been dropped. The Number and Sort commands still exist under the Actions menu.

3. The Pack and Delivery command has been dropped and replaced by the Pack and Go and Send To commands.

4. Map Info has been dropped completely. Instead, use the Comments field in File⇨Properties for the same purpose.

5. The Map Organizer has been dropped and replaced by the My Maps task pane.

Dropped commands (without replacements)

1. The Sync feature in the Project add-in has been removed.
2. The Save All command has been dropped.

3. The Import and Export to MindManager Smart has been dropped.

4. The Branch Length command has been dropped.

5. The Order of Main Branches command has been dropped. Outline order is now always the clockwise order.

6. The Quick Export command has been dropped.

7. The storing of named filter selections is no longer supported.

8. The Conference feature has been dropped.

Mouse and keyboard

1. Double-clicking to insert new main topics is disabled by default but can be switched on again in Tools⇨Options. Single-click insertion of floating topics makes the double-click not really necessary anymore.

2. Double-clicking a topic no longer opens a hyperlink. You need to single-click on the hyperlink icon.

3. Dragging and dropping of topics using a right-click has been eliminated. All drop functions can now be achieved using different drop zones. Press the Shift key to prevent dropping in an unwanted zone.

4. Transferring topic formats using the Alt key is replaced with the Format Painter command.

5. Right-clicking in empty map space pans the map immediately without delay.

6. The Enter key now adds a new sibling Topic directly below the selected topic and not at the end of the sibling list, as was previously the case.

Command changes

✔ **Multimap features are completely redesigned.** This feature is not spread among different commands (for example, Print or Web Export) but is now combined into the Multimap View. Multimaps now only follow one level of hyperlinks in order to simplify the whole feature. You can select the maps on which a Multimap command is executed. The Multimap main menu has been dropped and replaced by the Multimap toolbar, which is visible when working in Multimap mode.

✔ **Brainstorming mode has been redesigned to reflect a more real-world brainstorming model.** Since you can enter Floating Topics by simply clicking anywhere on your map and typing, this also provides an "Instant Brainstorming" mode.

✔ **The Dynamic Legend pane has been redesigned.** It is now a more powerful pane called Map Markers.

- ✔ **The Branch Template feature has been redesigned to support Smart Map Parts.** Smart Map Parts add active links to data sources using XML, XSL, and Web Services. The term Branch Template has been dropped and replaced with Map Parts.

- ✔ **The Language field from Document Properties has been moved.** It now has its own command: Tools⇨Language.

- ✔ **The Outlook Sync command has been split into an Import command and an Export command.** You can now find those commands on the Tools menu.

- ✔ **All Export commands have been moved.** They are now in the File⇨Save As dialog box and on the File⇨Send To menu.

- ✔ **All Import commands have been moved.** They are now in the File⇨Open dialog box and in the Office applications.

- ✔ **Customizing Add-ins, Macros, and Package Folders has been moved from the Customize dialog box.** They now have their own commands and dialog boxes, and they are still on the Tools menu.

- ✔ **Validate Hyperlinks is now called Repair Broken File Links.** The functionality remains the same.

Keyboard shortcuts

The following keyboard shortcuts have changed:

- ✔ F12 for Notes has changed to F11 or Ctrl+T to open/close topic notes.

- ✔ F5 for Fit to Screen has changed to Ctrl+F5. F5 is now used to Refresh Smart Map parts.

- ✔ Ctrl+H for Edit Hyperlink has changed to Ctrl+K to be Office compliant.

- ✔ F6 for Center Object has changed to Alt+F3.

The following keyboard shortcuts have been dropped:

- ✔ Ctrl+J to Open Hyperlink.

- ✔ F11 for Full Screen.

- ✔ Ctrl+M for Highlight.

Toolbars, windows, and dialog boxes

1. The Workbook tabs for multiple documents have been moved from the bottom to the top.

2. The Formatting toolbar has been moved to the bottom of the screen.

3. The Status Bar has been dropped with no replacement.

4. The Notes window is now always docked (on the right side) and no longer floats.

5. The Full Screen command has been dropped, because it overlapped too much with Presentation mode.

6. The Topic Property dialog box doesn't exist anymore and has been replaced by a separate hyperlink dialog box, a separate font dialog box, and a separate shape/color and layout dialog box.

7. The Office export toolbar is now shown at the bottom.

8. The Icon (code) toolbar has been dropped. It is replaced by the Library, the Map Marker pane, and a special Map Marker picker.

9. The Priority command and drop-down menu have been dropped and replaced by the Task Information pane and Map Markers.

Wizards

Wizards are no longer supported for the former branch templates, now called Map Parts.

New features

1. Improved look and handling of boundaries.

2. Relationships can now be used to link to all Topic types.

3. More Topic formatting options, more control over the look of a map, and a right-click context menu for topics.

4. Added a new Topic type: the Callout.

5. Map Markers can be saved and applied to multiple maps across a project. You can add your own Icons or customize the existing Icons.

6. Formatting control is enhanced with the Format painter, Select all, and Rubberband select commands.

7. Styles sheets can be quickly applied to change the look and feel of a map. They are customizable and can be saved and used in the same way as templates.

8. Export to Bitmaps.

9. Hyperlink icons represent linked document.

10. Static Task Pane toolbar with dynamic expand/collapse.

11. PDF export.

12. Outline view.

13. Review mode.

14. Rich-text capability in both topics and notes.

15. Improved Web Page Export capabilities using CSS Style Sheets, which are completely customizable. Templates are extensively redesigned.

16. Improved integration with Microsoft Office. Here are some examples:

✔ File Save as and Send to commands are redesigned to function like Office.

✔ PowerPoint features an improved user interface and higher quality of exported map images.

✔ Word now supports the export of callouts, subtopic callouts, and review Comments.

✔ Outlook features an improved and extended integration with both synchronization of tasks and Smart Map Part links to contacts, notes, folders, and the calendar.

✔ Several changes to the Microsoft Project interface, including the following:

   • Show % complete icon in MindManager.

   • Searchable resources and categories field.

   • Export Relationships as dependencies.

   • Input duration in hours, days, weeks, or months.

   • Only export topics that hold Task Info.

   • Export unfinished tasks only.

   • Synchronization dropped.

   • MPX 4.0 file format.

X5 Pro Features Not Found in X5

Visual elements and formatting options

✔ Customizable packages for individual elements (images, templates, icons, and map parts).

✔ Business map templates.

✔ Wizard framework for map creation.

✔ Wizard customization to create your own wizard from any map.

Microsoft Office integration

- ✔ Outlook advanced import/export of calendar, contacts, tasks, and notes data.

- ✔ PDF export.

- ✔ Project import/export, MPX import/export, and map templates for the project manager.

Miscellaneous

- ✔ Multimap view.

- ✔ Review mode.

- ✔ Task information for assigning task properties (deadlines, priorities, and responsibilities).

- ✔ Smart Map Parts.

- ✔ Object model for customization using the built-in Macro script editor.

- ✔ You cannot create or edit macros on X5, although you can run any macro developed on X5 Pro that does not use XML-related methods and properties.

Appendix B

Using Tablets and PDAs

*M*indManager has made the leap to mobility and ease of use. This book is about MindManager for the desktop, but other MindManager versions are available. The tablet and PDA version of MindManager 2002 has been out for a little over a year. By the time this book hits the shelf, a new version of the tablet and PDA MindManager should be available.

I would like to introduce Hobie Swan. Hobie is an information fountain at Mindjet. He assisted in keeping the authors synchronized with Mindjet as the new version of MindManager unfolded. I requested that he write a short epistle about this subject. He has responded in wonderful style. Rather than rewrite the perfect pontification, here are Hobie's own words.

Using MindManager for Tablet PCs

A fully pen-enabled note-taking application, Mindjet's first Tablet PC software was released in April, 2003, and it gained the immediate support of Microsoft and major Tablet PC manufacturers. Featuring 18 pen gestures and seamless integration with Microsoft Office, MindManager 2002 for Tablet PC let users easily capture, organize, and communicate unstructured information typical of meetings, planning sessions, and brainstorming. Maps made on MindManager 2002 for Tablet PC can be exported to Microsoft Word, PowerPoint, Project, and Web pages.

The real promise of integrating personal notes into team collaboration and corporate business processes comes with MindManager 5.1 Service Pack 2 (SP2), released in the first quarter of 2004. This service pack extends the XML-enabled functionality of MindManager X5 Pro and X5 (released in October 2003) to the Tablet PC. As a result, users can now take advantage of XML technology to push notes captured on the Tablet PC directly into corporate information systems, scheduling applications, and data sets.

The new XML-enabled MindManager will also give users access to "Smart Map Parts" that enable users to reach into specific databases and bring data into the map interface. The first such Smart Map Part will provide access to data stored in proprietary CRM databases. Users will be able to gain a better view of complex CRM information and instantly use that data to plan sales strategies and assign specific tasks and actions — all within the MindManager framework.

Tablet PCs equipped with SP2 have access to all the improvements offered in MindManager X5 Pro and X5 and to MindManager's natural, pen-based "Ink and Gesture Control" features. MindManager X5 Pro and X5 for Tablet PC enable information workers to do the following:

- Create concise and searchable handwritten notes that can be saved as handwriting or recognized and converted into type.
- Use drag-and-drop functionality to quickly organize note entries.
- Employ a visual structure that clearly communicates relationships among note entries.
- Create sketches and insert them into meeting notes.
- Attach graphics, codes, documents, and Web links to notes.
- Export notes to Microsoft Word, PowerPoint, Outlook, and Project, as well as to HTML, XML, and MPX to integrate content into broader business activities and decision-making processes.
- Use MindManager Smart Map Parts, based on XML technology and Web Services, to reach into a growing number of databases.
- Improve team collaboration with the combination of digital ink and MindManager's classic productivity features, in order to increase productivity, enable more effective meetings, and speed decision-making.

Mindjet will continue to introduce new Smart Map Parts that will improve the ability of information workers to pull together a broad range of information needed to make good decisions quickly.

Mobile MindManager

Imagine sitting on an airplane, equipped with nothing but a PDA, and planning a concise, well-reasoned, professional-looking PowerPoint presentation, project status report, or fully functional Web site. Mindjet's MindManager Mobile for Pocket PC, first released in June 2002, gives mobile workers a way to access the full range of power of their desktop PC edition of MindManager.

With the first quarter 2004 release of MindManager 5.1 Service Pack 2 (SP2), Pocket PC users will have access to MindManager X5 Mobile, which has many of the XML-based features available in the desktop and Tablet PC versions of MindManager X5 and X5 Pro (released in October, 2003).

By synchronizing MindManager Mobile with their desktop or Tablet PC, users can get a full copy (in outline form) of MindManager maps. Users can also build from scratch on MindManager Mobile. But the more common usage scenario is to make a travel copy of a map made on a desktop or Tablet PC. Users then have access to mapped information and can also edit the maps to refine presentations or reports while in transit. When users return to the office, MindManager Mobile maps can be exported to Microsoft Project, Outlook, Word, and PowerPoint to instantly create reports and presentations; they can be exported to HTML to create fully functional Web sites; they can be converted to PDF documents; and they can be exported as XML to populate corporate information systems, scheduling applications, and databases.

The XML capability of SP2 gives Pocket PC users access to such information as RSS News Feeds accessed via their desktop PC or Tablet PC. After the Pocket PC is synchronized with the desktop or Tablet PC, users will be able to access XML-based content (but not XML functionality) from their Pocket PC.

Key MindManager Mobile features include the following:

- ✔ Insert text notes to each topic to add supporting detail.
- ✔ Add icons to visually represent an idea or meaning.
- ✔ Drag and drop topics within an easy-to-use interface.
- ✔ Search maps or topics for specific words.
- ✔ Add color to your text for easier communication.
- ✔ Expand or don't expand topics depending on freeze state.
- ✔ Choose and control where to insert topic.
- ✔ Infrared/beam an entire map or send only specific topics.
- ✔ Customize maps by adding colors and codes to topics.
- ✔ Use an intuitive drag and drop interface.
- ✔ Display maps in a straight list or a hierarchical topic view.

Useful Scripts

• •

*I*n this appendix, I assume that you already know something about programming, script editors, and other such things. Therefore, I'll just make a few comments about the key points that each macro demonstrates. If you need more help with programming, check out *VBA For Dummies*, by John Paul Mueller, and the multitude of other *For Dummies* books covering programming.

These examples are for illustrative purposes only and are designed to illustrate the potential of MindManager's macro language. They will work only with MindManager X5 Pro. They are not designed to work impeccably under all conditions, so you should treat them with caution if you use them on anything other than practice maps. They may contain errors, or the MindManager Object Model may have been updated since these macros were published. Be particularly careful to re-test all macros on test maps each time you apply an update from Mindjet.

Neither the authors nor the publisher (or any of their employees, agents, subcontractors, or assigns) has any responsibility for any loss of any kind, including lost profits, arising from your use of any of these code examples.

You don't need to type in any of the comments in these examples (anything following a single quote mark and printed in italic type). Any line ending with "&_" means that what follows on the next line is a continuation of the line. If you don't mind having long program lines in your script, you can drop the "&_" and continue typing what is on the following line. Be careful, however, not to add or delete any spaces. For example, if the last character before the "&_" is a period, there must be no spaces between the period and what follows on the next line.

Closing All Open Maps

You have been working for quite some time with MindManager and have a number of maps open. You are through for the day, but the idea of (perhaps) saving and then closing each open map seems a little burdensome. This is the right macro for you because it automatically detects whether each map has been changed, prompts you to save it if it has, and then closes each map — all with a single mouse-click!

The key ideas in this macro are as follows:

- ✔ Use the Document type declaration.
- ✔ Work with all documents in the document collection.
- ✔ Use the MsgBox command to interact with the user.

```
' "Close All" macro
' This macro looks at each document in the Documents collection and checks to
' see if it has been changed or not. If it has not been changed, the procedure
' closes the document. If it has been changed, the user has the option of saving
' the document before closing, or cancelling the closing of any remaining
' documents.

Option Explicit ' catch any declaration errors

Sub Main
    If Documents.Count = 0 Then Exit Sub  ' no documents open, nothing to do

    Dim docCurrent As Document            ' working document
    Dim iSave As Integer                  ' choose whether to save changes
    Dim strMessage As String              ' Message indicating changed document

    iSave = vbNo                          ' assume there are no changes
    On Error Resume Next
    For Each docCurrent In Documents
        If docCurrent.IsModified Then
            strMessage = docCurrent.Name & " has been modified. Do you want to "
            strMessage = strMessage & "save the changes? " & vbCrLf
            strMessage = strMessage & "(Click Cancel to stop closing documents)"
            iSave = MsgBox(strMessage, vbQuestion + vbYesNoCancel)
            If iSave = vbYes Then docCurrent.Save     ' save it first
        End If
        If iSave = vbCancel Then Exit Sub          ' quit early
        docCurrent.Close
    Next
End Sub
```

Converting Topics to Callouts (And Back)

Callouts are very useful to associate key points or information with a topic when that information is not part of the information tree. When you are creating a map, however, it is not always clear at first whether your information should be a subtopic or a callout. This macro allows you to change one type into the other with one mouse click.

The key ideas in this macro are as follows:

- ✔ Using ElseIf for multiple tests.
- ✔ Using the Insert method to attach subtopics to either a topic or a callout.
- ✔ Using the GetOffset method to detect and then adjust the relative position of two objects on a map.

```
' Swap Topic between Callout and Regular subtopic
Option Explicit
Sub Main
    Dim docCurrent As Document      ' current document
    Dim tpcCurrent As Topic         ' selected Topic
    Dim sxOffset As Single          ' Distance to the right of the selected topic
    Dim syOffset As Single          ' Distance below the selected topic
    Dim lCalloutIndex As Long       ' Pointer to the created callout
    Dim iFail As Boolean            ' Flag set if conditions not satisfied
'-----------------------
' This initial block of code checks to be sure that there is a document open and
' that exactly one topic or one callout has been selected. The output from this
' code is the flag iFail which is set to True if the required conditions
' are not met.
'-----------------------
    iFail = False
    If Documents.Count = 0 Then
        iFail = True                                ' no document open
    Else
        Set docCurrent = ActiveDocument
        If docCurrent.Selection.Count = 0 Then
            iFail = True                            ' nothing selected
        ElseIf docCurrent.Selection.Count > 1 Then
            iFail = True                            ' more than one thing selected
        ElseIf docCurrent.Selection.PrimaryTopic.Type <> &_
                mmDocumentObjectTypeTopic Then
            iFail = True                            ' not a Topic
        ElseIf docCurrent.Selection.PrimaryTopic.IsFloatingTopic Then
            iFail = True                            ' Floating Topic selected
        ElseIf docCurrent.Selection.PrimaryTopic.IsCentralTopic Then
            iFail = True                            ' Central Topic selected
        ElseIf docCurrent.Selection.PrimaryTopic.IsMainTopic Then
            iFail = True                            ' Main Topic selected
        End If
    End If

'---------------------------
'This is the block of code that actually does the switch
'Make sure the created callout has some vertical offset from the topic
'---------------------------
```

```
      If iFail Then
         Exit Sub
      Else
         Set tpcCurrent = docCurrent.Selection.PrimaryTopic
         If tpcCurrent.IsCalloutTopic Then                    ' Convert to subtopic
            tpcCurrent.ParentTopic.SubTopics(False).Insert(tpcCurrent)
         Else                                                 ' Convert to a Callout
            tpcCurrent.ParentTopic.CalloutTopics.Insert(tpcCurrent)
            tpcCurrent.GetOffset(sxOffset,syOffset)
            If syOffset >= 2 Or syOffset <= -2 Then
            Else
               tpcCurrent.SetOffset(5,-2)
            End If
         End If
         tpcCurrent.SelectOnly                     ' select it again after moving
      End If
End Sub
```

Converting Topics to Notes

You have just finished a brainstorming session and you have captured a lot of good ideas at many topic levels. Now you want to consolidate some of the details from level-4 and level-5 subtopics into the topic notes of your more general level-3 topic (just as an example). Cutting and pasting all those topics can be really tedious. This macro does it all for you automatically.

The key ideas in this macro are as follows:

- ✔ Using iterative calls to the same subroutine in order to process an unknown number of subtopic levels.

- ✔ Using collections.

```
' ConsolidateSubtopics
' Removes subtopics and places the text in the notes of the selected topic
' IMPORTANT: this macro is designed to be placed on the Topic Context menu so it
' assumes that the selected object is a topic. If you place this macro on a
' regular menu and then run it when a topic is not selected, you will get
' errors.
' ==>Any subtopics attached to callouts will be discarded
' ==>The macro will not properly format more than seven levels of topics.

Dim strOutput As String                      ' build the output text here
Dim iLevel As Integer
Dim imLevel(7) As Integer

Sub Main
   Dim docCurrent As Document                ' current document
   Dim tpcSelected As Topic                  ' selected Topic
```

```
      If ValidInput(docCurrent) Then
         For iLevel=1 To 7                    ' Initialize numbering matrix
            imLevel(iLevel)=0
         Next iLevel
         iLevel = 1
         Set tpcSelected = docCurrent.Selection.PrimaryTopic ' our selected topic
         strOutput = tpcSelected.Notes.Text              ' Initialize output string
         If Len(strOutput) > 0 Then strOutput = strOutput & vbCrLf
         Call ProcessSubs(tpcSelected)
         tpcSelected.Notes.Text = strOutput              ' write final notes
      End If
End Sub
'-----------------------------------
'This subroutine iterates through all subtopics at a given level,
'deleting them as soon as they have been transferred to the Notes string.
'-----------------------------------
Sub ProcessSubs(ByVal tpcSelected As Topic)
   While tpcSelected.SubTopics.Count > 0
      imLevel(iLevel) = imLevel(iLevel) + 1
      Call TopicToNotes(tpcSelected.SubTopics.Item(1))
      tpcSelected.SubTopics(False).Item(1).Delete
   Wend
   imLevel(iLevel) = 0
   If iLevel > 1 Then iLevel = iLevel - 1
End Sub
'-----------------------------------
'This subroutine actually extracts the topic text (as well as any callouts
'and notes associated with the topic) and adds them to the output string. It
'also checks to see if the topic has any subtopics. If it does, it calls a new
'level of ProcessSubs. This prevents ProcessSubs from deleting a topic until all
'its subtopics have been extracted.
'-----------------------------------
Sub TopicToNotes(ByVal tpcSelected As Topic)
   If Len(tpcSelected.Text) > 0 Then                        ' append topic text
      strOutput = strOutput & TopicID & Replace(tpcSelected.Text, vbLf, " ")
      If Len(tpcSelected.Notes.Text) > 0 Then       ' append topic notes in ASCII
         strOutput = strOutput & "  Notes: " & tpcSelected.Notes.Text
      End If
      If Not(tpcSelected.IsCentralTopic) Then
         While tpcSelected.CalloutTopics.Count > 0
            strOutput = strOutput & "  Callout: "
            strOutput = strOutput & tpcSelected.CalloutTopics.Item(1).Text
            tpcSelected.CalloutTopics.Item(1).Delete
'                                          Discard any callout subtopics
         Wend
      End If
      strOutput = strOutput & vbCrLf
   End If
   If tpcSelected.SubTopics.Count > 0 Then
      If iLevel < 7 Then iLevel = iLevel+1    ' Assume we will never have more
      Call ProcessSubs(tpcSelected)    ' than 7 levels - if we do, it
   End If                              ' will not be properly formatted.
```

```
End Sub
' Check to ensure that there is a document open and that exactly one topic has
' been selected.
Function ValidInput(myDoc As Document) As Boolean
    Dim flgOK As Boolean
    flgOK = False

    If Documents.Count > 0 Then
        Set myDoc = ActiveDocument
        If myDoc.Selection.Count = 1 Then
            flgOK = True
        Else
            MsgBox("Too many topics selected",vbExclamation,"Selection Error")
        End If
    End If
    ValidInput = flgOK
End Function
'--------------------------------
'Build a dotted ID for each topic that shows its original level. Prefix the ID
'with tabs corresponding to its depth level in the tree
'--------------------------------
Function TopicID() As String
    Dim strID As String
    Dim iPtr As Integer

    strID = ""
    For iPtr = 1 To iLevel-1
        strID = strID & vbTab
    Next iPtr
    strID = strID & CStr(imLevel(1))
    For iPtr = 2 To 7
        If imLevel(iPtr)=0 Then Exit For
        strID = strID & "." & CStr(imLevel(iPtr))
    Next iPtr
    TopicID = strID & " "
End Function
```

Creating a Submap from a Topic

You've worked hard on your map, and it has grown so big that you now need to break it up into multimaps. You could select major topics and use File⇨SendTo to create the submap, but then you also have to delete all the subtopics and callouts from the main map and create a hyperlink to the new submap. This macro allows you to do all of this with a single mouse click.

Key ideas in this macro are as follows:

- ✔ Using the Add method to create a new document.

- ✔ Using the XML property to transfer large amounts of map information to the new map.

✔ Creating hyperlinks.

✔ Using an error-processing subroutine.

```
' Export the selected topic with all subtopics and other objects to a separate
' map, delete everything but the selected topic from the source map, and insert
' a hyperlink to the newly created map.
' IMPORTANT: this macro is designed to be placed on the Topic Context menu so it
'            assumes that the selected object is a topic. If you place this
'            macro on a regular menu and then run it when a topic is not
'            selected, you will get errors.
Option Explicit

Sub Main
    Dim SourceDoc As Document        ' Current document
    Dim DestinationDoc As Document   ' New document to be created
    Dim SourceTopic As Topic         ' Selected topic
    Dim iFlg As Boolean              ' Error flag set unless 1 topic selected
    On Error GoTo ErrorRoutine       ' Prepare to process any encountered error
'------------------------
' Check to ensure that there is a document open and that exactly one topic has
' been selected.
'------------------------
    If Documents(False).Count = 0 Then
        iFlg = False
    Else
        Set SourceDoc = ActiveDocument
        If SourceDoc.Selection.Count = 0 Or SourceDoc.Selection.Count > 1 Then
            iFlg = False
        Else
            iFlg = True
        End If
    End If


    '------------------------
' Transfer topic to a new map and attempt to save it. If save is cancelled, warn
' user of consequences and allow a retry. If successful, then delete subtopics
' from main map and replace with a hyperlink.
'------------------------
    If iFlg Then
        Set SourceTopic = SourceDoc.Selection.PrimaryTopic ' The topic to be made
                                                           ' into a separate map
        Set DestinationDoc = Documents.Add                 ' Create a new document
        DestinationDoc.CentralTopic.Xml = SourceTopic.Xml    ' Copy the topic and
                                                           ' all lower level objects
RetrySave:
        DestinationDoc.Save                                ' Prompt for a save location
' Clean all SubTopics off the source Topic
        While SourceTopic.SubTopics.Count > 0
            SourceTopic.SubTopics.Item(1).Delete
        Wend
```

```
' Clean all Callouts off the source Topic
    While SourceTopic.CalloutTopics.Count > 0
        SourceTopic.CalloutTopics.Item(1).Delete
    Wend
' Discard any existing hyperlink and create a new one
    If SourceTopic.HasHyperlink Then SourceTopic.Hyperlink.Delete
    SourceTopic.CreateHyperlink(DestinationDoc.FullName)
    DestinationDoc.Close                        ' Close new document
    SourceDoc.Activate
  End If
ExitMacro:
  Exit Sub

ErrorRoutine:
  If Err.Number = -2147467259 Then              ' User cancelled save
    If MsgBox("Are you sure you want to cancel the export?",vbYesNo+ &_
            vbQuestion,"Please confirm") =vbYes Then
        DestinationDoc.Close
        Resume ExitMacro
    Else
        Resume RetrySave
    End If
  Else
      MsgBox("Unexpected error encountered: " & Err.Number &": "& &_
            Err.Description,vbOkOnly)
      Resume ExitMacro
  End If
End Sub
```

Adding a Submap to a Topic

It is often easier to work with multimaps, but they also have limitations. For example, an extended search for a particular topic is much more difficult if your map is spread over several files. The following macro allows you to import a map as a topic or subtopic in another map.

Key ideas in this macro are as follows:

✔ Using an error-trapping routine.

✔ Using editing function calls.

✔ Working with hyperlinks.

```
' Import the map selected by the user and attach it to the selected topic in the
' current map.
' IMPORTANT: this macro is designed to be placed on the Topic Context menu so it
' assumes that the selected object is a topic. If you place this macro on a
' regular menu and then run it when a topic is not selected, you will get
' errors.
```

```
'==>Floating topics (and relationships between floating topics) that are on the
' map to be imported will not be imported correctly. The floating topics will
' be changed to callouts and the relationships will be orphaned.

Option Explicit
Sub Main

    Dim SourceDoc As Document           ' Document to be imported
    Dim DestDoc As Document             ' Document to receive the import
    Dim DestTopic As Topic              ' Topic to which map is to be attached
    Dim strMap As String                ' Name of the map to be imported
    Dim strMsg As String                ' Error message
    Dim flgIsOk As Boolean          ' Error flag set if missing or invalid input

    On Error GoTo ErrorRoutine          ' Prepare to process any encountered error
    flgIsOk = False                     ' Assume input will fail
    strMsg = "Sorry, you cannot import a map to a topic " & vbCrLf
    strMsg = strMsg & "that already has subtopics or callouts."

'************************
' Validate input. No subtopics or callouts may be attached to the destination
' topic
'************************
    If ValidInput(DestDoc) Then
        Set DestTopic = DestDoc.Selection.PrimaryTopic
        If DestTopic.SubTopics.Count > 0 Or &_
            DestTopic.CalloutTopics.Count > 0 Then
            MsgBox(strMsg,vbExclamation,"Selection Error")
        Else
            If GetMapName(DestTopic,strMap) Then flgIsOk =True
        End If
    End If


'----------------------
' Open destination document invisibly and import it
'----------------------
    If flgIsOk Then
        Set SourceDoc = Documents.Open(strMap, "", False)      ' open it invisibly
        DestTopic.Xml = SourceDoc.CentralTopic.Xml                ' import topics
        SourceDoc.Close                                ' close source document again
    End If
ExitMacro:
    Exit Sub

ErrorRoutine:
    If Err.Number = -2147220992 Then
        strMsg = "Unable to open the hyperlinked map. " & vbCrLf
        strMsg = strMsg & "You may have a specified a relative path."
        MsgBox(strMsg,vbExclamation,"Open Map Error")
    Else
        MsgBox("Unexpected error encountered: " & Err.Number &": " & &_
                Err.Description,vbOkOnly)
    End If
    Resume ExitMacro
```

```
End Sub
'---------------------------------
' If there is a hyperlink present, and it points to a map, use it for the
' import. If there is no hyperlink, request the map name from the user
'---------------------------------
Function GetMapName(myTopic As Topic, strPath As String) As Boolean
    Dim flgHaveName As Boolean
    flgHaveName = False
    If myTopic.HasHyperlink Then
        strPath = myTopic.Hyperlink.Address
        If (UCase(Right(strPath,5))) = ".MMAP" Then flgHaveName = True
    End If
    If Not(flgHaveName) Then
        strPath = GetFilePath$("","MMAP","","Please select map to be imported",0)
        If Len(strPath) > 0 Then flgHaveName = True
    End If
    GetMapName = flgHaveName
End Function
'-------------------------------------------------
' Check to ensure that there is a document open and that exactly one topic has
' been selected.
'-------------------------------------------------
Function ValidInput(myDoc As Document) As Boolean
    Dim flgOK As Boolean
    flgOK = False
    If Documents.Count > 0 Then
        Set myDoc = ActiveDocument
        If myDoc.Selection.Count = 1 Then
            flgOK = True
        Else
            MsgBox("Too many topics selected",vbExclamation,"Selection Error")
        End If
    End If
    ValidInput = flgOK
End Function
```

Adding an Action Item

MindManager allows you to associate a wizard that runs when a template is open, but it does not run wizards associated with map parts. The following macro demonstrates how you can mimic a wizard when you want to add a group of subtopics to your map.

Key ideas in this macro are as follows:

✔ Creating a more user-friendly report on selection errors (if any).

✔ Using the UserDialog type declaration.

✔ Using the Dialog function.

✔ Using the `AddSubTopics` method.

Open this code in the macro editor window, click anywhere in the code between Begin Dialog and End Dialog, and then choose Edit⇔User dialog. . . from the macro window menu bar. The macro editor converts all of the dialog data into a graphical representation of your macro dialog box. You can add new fields, change fields, and modify your dialog box as you like. When you click the Save button (last button on the right-hand side), all your parameters as displayed in your code are updated to reflect your changes.

```
' Create an action item subtopic
' The root topic contains the action item number
' Subtopics are
'    - Action Item description
'    - Responsibility
'    - Due Date
Option Explicit

Sub Main
    Dim myDocument As Document
    Dim myTopic As Topic
    Dim flgOK As Boolean          ' Result of check for valid topic selected

    '------------------------
    'Verify that a document is open and that a single main or subtopic has
    'been selected.
    '------------------------
    If Documents.Count = 0 Then
        flgOK = False
    Else
        Set myDocument = ActiveDocument
        If myDocument.Selection.Count = 1 Then
            If myDocument.Selection.PrimaryTopic.Type = &
                            mmDocumentObjectTypeTopic Then
                Set myTopic = myDocument.Selection.PrimaryTopic
                If myTopic.IsSubTopic Or myTopic.IsMainTopic Then
                    flgOK = True
                Else
                    MsgBox("Please select a main or a subtopic", &_
                            vbOkOnly, "Selection Error")
                    flgOK = False
                End If
            Else
                MsgBox("You haven't selected a topic!",vbOkOnly, "Selection Error")
                flgOK = False
            End If
        Else
            MsgBox("You must select just one topic for the root",vbOkOnly, &_
                    "Selection Error")
            flgOK = False
        End If
    End If
    '---------------------------------
    'Solicit the action item information from the user.
```

```
'If the user clicks cancel, then do nothing
'------------------------------------
    If flgOK Then
        Begin Dialog UserDialog 400,203,"Action Item Definition" ' %GRID:10,7,1,1
            Text 13,7,140,15,"Action Item Number:",.Text1,1
            TextBox 160,7,30,15,.ActionItemNo
            Text 13,28,140,15,"Description:",.Text2,1
            TextBox 160,28,230,56,.Description,1
            Text 13,92,140,15,"Responsible:",.Text3,1
            TextBox 160,92,230,15,.Responsible
            Text 13,115,140,15,"Due Date:",.Text4,1
            TextBox 160,115,230,15, .WhenDue
            OKButton 120,154,50,21,.btnOK
            CancelButton 220,154,60,21,.btnCancel
        End Dialog
        Dim dlg As UserDialog
        If Dialog(dlg,0) Then                       'Set default to cancel
            Set myTopic = myTopic.AddSubTopic(dlg.ActionItemNo)
            myTopic.AddSubTopic(dlg.Description)
            myTopic.AddSubTopic("Who: " & dlg.Responsible)
            myTopic.AddSubTopic("Due: " & dlg .WhenDue  )
        End If
    End If
End Sub
```

Aligning Topics

A large map can be difficult to lay out in a manner that enables you to easily see the relationships between topics. Having a neat and orderly appearance can be a real plus if you are showing your map to a first-time audience in Presentation mode.

The following macro automatically places each main topic so that all of the second-level topics line up vertically.

Key ideas in this macro are as follows:

- ✔ Using function names to make the main subroutine self-documenting.
- ✔ Assessing the topic layout in an entire map.
- ✔ Using the Range property.
- ✔ Using global variables.

```
'------------------------------------
' Position main topics so that all first level subtopics line up.
' If no reference topic is selected, than all topics are aligned with the
' one farthest from the central topic. If a main topic is selected, then
```

```
' align all the other main topics on that side of the map with this as a
' reference.
' May not work with a selected topic if other topics cannot be placed that
' close to central topic.
'-------------------------------


Option Explicit
    Dim docCurrent As Document          ' current document
    Dim tpcReference As Topic           ' Reference point for alignment
    Dim tpcWorking As Topic             ' working Topic
    Dim flgUseReference As Boolean      ' True = main topic selected
    Dim sglTop As Single                ' Size and position
    Dim sglLeft As Single               ' of the
    Dim sglWidth As Single              ' rectangle bounding
    Dim sglHeight As Single             ' the current topic

Sub Main

    Dim sglLeftMax As Single            ' position of left-most topic
    Dim sglRightMax As Single           ' position of right-most topic

    If ValidInput Then
        Call GetReferencePoint(sglLeftMax, sglRightMax)
        ' then adjust all other main topics to have the same settings
        For Each tpcWorking In docCurrent.Range(mmRangeAllTopics, False)
            If tpcWorking.IsMainTopic Then
                tpcWorking.GetBoundingRect(sglTop, sglLeft, sglWidth, sglHeight)
                If tpcWorking.IsOnLeftSide Then
                    If sglLeftMax <> 0 Then tpcWorking.SetOffset(sglLeftMax + &_
                                                sglWidth, sglTop)
                Else
                    If sglRightMax <> 0 Then tpcWorking.SetOffset(sglRightMax - &_
                                                sglWidth, sglTop)
                End If
            End If
        Next
        docCurrent.CentralTopic.SetLevelOfDetail(2)
    End If

End Sub
'-------------------------------
' Check to ensure that there is a document open and that more than two topics
' exist (otherwise nothing to line up). If exactly one topic has been selected
' and it is a main topic, then return that topic handle
'-------------------------------
Function ValidInput As Boolean

    Dim flgOK As Boolean
    flgOK = False

    If Documents.Count > 0 Then
        Set docCurrent = ActiveDocument
```

```
       If docCurrent.Selection.Count = 1 Then
          Set tpcReference = docCurrent.Selection.PrimaryTopic
          If tpcReference.IsMainTopic Then
             flgOK = True
             flgUseReference = True
          Else
             MsgBox("Please select a main topic as the anchor point",&_
                    vbCritical,"Selection error")
          End If
       ElseIf docCurrent.Selection.Count = 0 Then
          flgUseReference = False
          flgOK = True
       Else
          MsgBox("Too many topics selected",vbExclamation,"Selection Error")
       End If
    End If
    ValidInput = flgOK

End Function
Sub GetReferencePoint(sglL As Single, sglR As Single)
    '--------------------------------------------
    'If there is a reference topic, just return the left or right boundaries
    '--------------------------------------------
    If flgUseReference Then
       tpcReference.GetBoundingRect(sglTop,sglLeft,sglWidth,sglHeight)
       If tpcReference.IsOnLeftSide Then
          sglL = sglLeft
          sglR = 0
       Else
          sglL = 0
          sglR = sglLeft + sglWidth
       End If
    Else
       '--------------------------------------------
       'Otherwise start with an arbitrarily small number and find the maximum
       '(minimum) on both sides and return those values. Ignore everything
       'that isn't a main topic. Right boundary has to be calculated as
       'left + width.
       '--------------------------------------------
       sglL = 100
       sglR = -100
       For Each tpcWorking In docCurrent.Range(mmRangeAllTopics, False)
          If tpcWorking.IsMainTopic Then
             tpcWorking.GetBoundingRect(sglTop, sglLeft, sglWidth, sglHeight)
             If tpcWorking.IsOnLeftSide Then
                   If sglLeft < sglL Then sglL = sglLeft
             Else
                   If sglLeft + sglWidth > sglR Then sglR = sglLeft + sglWidth
             End If
          End If
       Next
    End If

End Sub
```

Index

Notes

Notes

Notes

FOR DUMMIES®

A world of resources to help you grow

HOME, GARDEN & HOBBIES

Feng Shui
FOR DUMMIES

0-7645-5295-3

Gardening
FOR DUMMIES
2nd Edition

A Reference for the Rest of Us!

0-7645-5130-2

Play-along audio CD included!

Guitar
FOR DUMMIES

A Reference for the Rest of Us!

0-7645-5106-X

Also available:

Auto Repair For Dummies
(0-7645-5089-6)

Chess For Dummies
(0-7645-5003-9)

Home Maintenance For
Dummies
(0-7645-5215-5)

Organizing For Dummies
(0-7645-5300-3)

Piano For Dummies
(0-7645-5105-1)

Poker For Dummies
(0-7645-5232-5)

Quilting For Dummies
(0-7645-5118-3)

Rock Guitar For Dummies
(0-7645-5356-9)

Roses For Dummies
(0-7645-5202-3)

Sewing For Dummies
(0-7645-5137-X)

FOOD & WINE

Cooking
FOR DUMMIES
2nd Edition

A Reference for the Rest of Us!

0-7645-5250-3

Cookies
FOR DUMMIES

A Reference for the Rest of Us!

0-7645-5390-9

Winner of the Georges Duboeuf Book of the Year Award.

Wine
FOR DUMMIES
2nd Edition

A Reference for the Rest of Us!

0-7645-5114-0

Also available:

Bartending For Dummies
(0-7645-5051-9)

Chinese Cooking For
Dummies
(0-7645-5247-3)

Christmas Cooking For
Dummies
(0-7645-5407-7)

Diabetes Cookbook For
Dummies
(0-7645-5230-9)

Grilling For Dummies
(0-7645-5076-4)

Low-Fat Cooking For
Dummies
(0-7645-5035-7)

Slow Cookers For Dummies
(0-7645-5240-6)

TRAVEL

Italy
FOR DUMMIES
2nd Edition

A Travel Guide for the Rest of Us!

0-7645-5453-0

Hawaii
FOR DUMMIES
2nd Edition

A Travel Guide for the Rest of Us!

0-7645-5438-7

Las Vegas
FOR DUMMIES
2nd Edition

A Travel Guide for the Rest of Us!

0-7645-5448-4

Also available:

America's National Parks For
Dummies
(0-7645-6204-5)

Caribbean For Dummies
(0-7645-5445-X)

Cruise Vacations For
Dummies 2003
(0-7645-5459-X)

Europe For Dummies
(0-7645-5456-5)

Ireland For Dummies
(0-7645-6199-5)

France For Dummies
(0-7645-6292-4)

London For Dummies
(0-7645-5416-6)

Mexico's Beach Resorts For
Dummies
(0-7645-6262-2)

Paris For Dummies
(0-7645-5494-8)

RV Vacations For Dummies
(0-7645-5443-3)

Walt Disney World & Orlando
For Dummies
(0-7645-5444-1)

Available wherever books are sold. Go to www.dummies.com or call 1-877-762-2974 to order direct.

FOR DUMMIES®

Helping you expand your horizons and realize your potential

INTERNET

0-7645-0894-6

The Internet FOR DUMMIES

0-7645-1659-0

The Internet ALL-IN-ONE DESK REFERENCE FOR DUMMIES

0-7645-1642-6

eBay FOR DUMMIES

Also available:

America Online 7.0 For Dummies
(0-7645-1624-8)

Genealogy Online For Dummies
(0-7645-0807-5)

The Internet All-in-One Desk Reference For Dummies
(0-7645-1659-0)

Internet Explorer 6 For Dummies
(0-7645-1344-3)

The Internet For Dummies Quick Reference
(0-7645-1645-0)

Internet Privacy For Dummies
(0-7645-0846-6)

Researching Online For Dummies
(0-7645-0546-7)

Starting an Online Business For Dummies
(0-7645-1655-8)

DIGITAL MEDIA

0-7645-1664-7

Digital Photography FOR DUMMIES

0-7645-1675-2

Photoshop Elements 2 FOR DUMMIES

0-7645-0806-7

Digital Video FOR DUMMIES

Also available:

CD and DVD Recording For Dummies
(0-7645-1627-2)

Digital Photography All-in-One Desk Reference For Dummies
(0-7645-1800-3)

Digital Photography For Dummies Quick Reference
(0-7645-0750-8)

Home Recording for Musicians For Dummies
(0-7645-1634-5)

MP3 For Dummies
(0-7645-0858-X)

Paint Shop Pro "X" For Dummies
(0-7645-2440-2)

Photo Retouching & Restoration For Dummies
(0-7645-1662-0)

Scanners For Dummies
(0-7645-0783-4)

GRAPHICS

0-7645-0817-2

PowerPoint 2002 FOR DUMMIES

0-7645-1651-5

Photoshop 7 FOR DUMMIES

0-7645-0895-4

Macromedia Flash MX FOR DUMMIES

Also available:

Adobe Acrobat 5 PDF For Dummies
(0-7645-1652-3)

Fireworks 4 For Dummies
(0-7645-0804-0)

Illustrator 10 For Dummies
(0-7645-3636-2)

QuarkXPress 5 For Dummies
(0-7645-0643-9)

Visio 2000 For Dummies
(0-7645-0635-8)

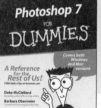

FOR DUMMIES®

The advice and explanations you need to succeed